POPE PIUS XII LIBRARY, ST. JOSEPH COL.
3 2528 07523 1979

DRUG CONTROL POLICY

D1597989

Issues in Policy History
General Editor: Donald T. Critchlow

DRUG CONTROL POLICY

Essays in Historical and Comparative Perspective

Edited by
William O. Walker III

The Pennsylvania State University Press
University Park, Pennsylvania

This work was originally published as a special issue of *Journal of Policy History* (vol. 3, no. 4, 1991). This is its first separate paperback publication.

Library of Congress Cataloging-in-Publication Data

Drug control policy : essays in historical and comparative perspective
/ edited by William O. Walker III.

p. cm.
Includes bibliographical references.
ISBN 0-271-00843-1
1. Narcotics, Control of—United States—History—20th century.
I. Walker, William O., 1946– .
HV5825.D776275 1992
363.4'5'09730904—dc20 91–45160
CIP

Copyright © 1992 The Pennsylvania State University
All rights reserved
Printed in the United States of America

Contents

Editor's Preface

This volume, *Drug Control Policy: Essays in Historical and Comparative Perspective,* edited by historian William O. Walker, provides an in-depth look at drug control policy as it has been shaped historically in the United States and other countries, most notably China and East Asia. In editing this volume, Professor Walker invited leading scholars writing in the field to write essays that offered broad perspectives of the history of drug policy. These essays provide a comparative and historical lens in which to view the current debate over drug policy in the United States.

For those who like their history in didactic doses, these essays appear to offer certain lessons concerning public policy: policies seldom change over time; bureaucracy tends to grow, while becoming more self-protective; and social problems persist, little remedied by policy. To draw only these conclusions from this collection of essays would be misleading.

These essays show a continuity in drug policy as it has emerged in the twentieth century. Drug policy has emphasized suppressing drugs at their source or by curtailing their distribution, but few policymakers have considered legalization of drugs as a remedy. On the other hand, much of drug policy has been a record of bureaucratic infighting and aggrandizement. At the same time, it has reflected nativistic and racial biases.

Much of this story, as Professor Walker observes in his introduction, is well known. These essays suggest, however, that alternative strategies would not necessarily be any more successful. David Courtwright argues that legalization of drugs would create its own problems. Moreover, these authors pose a profound question that confronts those concerned with the history of drug policy in the United States: Given the nature of federal policy, institutional structures, and social mores, could drug policy have been otherwise? In turn, other equally important questions arise. Once the decision was made to pursue a policy of suppression, what went wrong? Why did those involved in drug policy fail to implement a more coherent and effective strategy in pursuing their goals? Why have drug agencies appeared so confused, chaotic, and inefficient in fulfilling their mandates?

The aim of policy history is to provide a context for answering such questions. Policy history seeks to edify and not to specifically instruct. Prescriptions are best left to policymakers actively involved in contemporary problems, and not to historians—those physicians of the buried. Historians of policy history, however, can provide careful dissections of past policies. In this regard, this volume presents a useful pathology to drug policy in recent history.

Donald T. Critchlow
General Editor

WILLIAM O. WALKER III

Introduction

In the last decade, drug usage has become a matter of great concern in American society. Questions abound about who uses drugs and why. Surveys that purport to answer questions such as these remain suspect because of fears that respondents either may be lying or, in fact, may not be the real habitual consumers of drugs. The presumed link between drug usage and violent crimes is an act of faith in a society that perceived itself to be under siege from drugs throughout the 1980s. No prominent public official, whether it was President Ronald Reagan or William J. Bennett, who served as President George Bush's first director of the Office of National Drug Control Policy, could ease the sense of alarm and foreboding evoked by drugs. How could the traffic in drugs be stopped? How would America's streets be made safe again?

From government officials came promises of effective action. Two familiar drug-control strategies, control at the source and interdiction, were called upon, as they had been in the past, to meet the economic and societal threats posed by drugs. By all accounts, including those of the U.S. government, these dual strategies failed appreciably to curtail drug production and trafficking. The Department of State's annual *International Narcotics Control Strategy Report* detailed enormous increases in coca leaf cultivation in Bolivia and Peru and in the processing of cocaine there and especially in Colombia. If some solace could be taken from the determination of Andean governments not to surrender to the so-called kings of cocaine, as the drug bosses in the Colombian cities of Medellín and Cali came to be called, the results were no better than mixed. Indeed, as this introduction is being written in early March 1991, the integrity of governing institutions in Bolivia, Colombia, and Peru faces a serious challenge from the entrepreneurs of the cocaine economy. Compounding that situation is the evidently extensive cultivation of marijuana at home and abroad, notably across the border in Mexico. And finally, the millions of dollars spent to enhance the prospects for interdiction—seen most clearly in the role of the U.S. military in the struggle against drugs—ironically have enabled the American public to learn more than it ever wanted to know about the creativity of major drug traffickers.

With the exception of David T. Courtwright's contribution, it is not necessarily the purpose of the articles prepared for this volume to enter the sometimes acrimonious debate over what ought to be the future direction of drug-control policy in the United States and elsewhere. Admittedly, some readers may see them in that light, but the primary intent of the editor and contributors is altogether different. It is, in the best sense of the word, instructive in nature. Six scholars who devote their careers to investigating and understanding the historically complex role of drugs in several societies have written articles especially for this volume. Although the topics are diverse, it is fair to say that the work of the authors is complementary.

In brief, two broad conclusions follow from the authors' research. First, the drug problems that afflicted the United States over the last decade were scarcely unique. Historically as well as at present, the vexing problems attendant to drugs are manifestly international in scope. Moreover, the various ways in which America and other societies are currently responding to drug problems and related difficulties have historical precedents that may be instructive for contemporary policymaking purposes. And second, drugs have rarely been a self-contained issue. That is, drugs are merely part of, indeed may only be symptomatic of, deeper ills or other concerns within a particular society.

These findings are not exceptional to those involved in the writing of drug history. That this area of study encompasses a growing number of individuals may be one of the few salutary developments of the past decade regarding drugs. For others, the information and interpretations contained in this volume may be something of a revelation. Readers should be forewarned that the essays take a selective look at several aspects of drug policy. And the focus is on policy, narratively and analytically. For the most part, the articles are concerned with the drug policies of the United States, although China and East Asia figure prominently in two of them. One other article addresses drug policy entirely from the perspective of the international effort to control both organically grown and synthetically produced drugs.

In the opening article, John C. McWilliams takes an extensive look at the politics and policies of the five phases of America's war on drugs, a struggle that has been intermittently waged for nearly a century. McWilliams demonstrates that the officials who were charged with controlling drugs in America after the passage of the Harrison Act in 1914 soon realized the impossibility of their task. Rather than reconsider the assumptions underlying their mandate, these officials pursued a policy of containment of drugs that allowed them to construct a bureaucratic empire while they publicly maintained the objective of a drug-free America. No official was more central to this deceptive process than Harry J. Anslinger, commissioner of the Federal Bureau of Narcotics from 1930 to 1962. McWilliams shows that Anslinger's successors learned well from him how to fight the good bureaucratic fight even as the nation's drug problems worsened.

The second article, by David T. Courtwright, examines through a comparative and historical lens the case currently being made for controlled legalization of drugs. Courtwright reaches the conclusion that a policy based upon a coercive, public health approach has the best chance of minimizing the social consequences of drug abuse. (In slight contrast to McWilliams, Courtwright delineates four wars on drugs in the twentieth century, but the difference between the two articles is one of degree rather than kind.) Among the principal objections to controlled legalization for Courtwright are the inevitability of a black market and tax avoidance. He draws on examples from the history of drug control, alcohol prohibition, and the taxation of tobacco to reveal the various limitations of controlled legalization.

The next two articles are international as well as comparative in focus. Kathryn Meyer points out that the recent drug problems in America and the policy responses to them have antecedents in Qing China, specifically at the time of the first Opium War. To Meyer, authorities in Guangzhou (Canton) in the late 1830s and in Miami around 1980 had difficulty eliminating the drug trade for roughly comparable reasons. Building on those specific examples, she argues more generally that the linkage of money, culture, and power with drugs created formidable obstacles in both societies that impeded the effective implementation of antidrug policies. In his revealing article about the close relationship between drug control and security policies in East Asia during and after World War II, Jonathan Marshall contends that U.S. officials sacrificed their longtime objective of opium control in East Asia. Authorities attached greater importance to what were defined as national security considerations, specifically, in this case, access to a strategic commodity, tungsten. To obtain tungsten meant dealing with individuals who also had major roles in the region's illicit narcotics traffic. Such associations had long-term consequences for subsequent political developments in the region.

Whereas the first four articles analyze aspects of the political origins or consequences of American drug policy, the contribution of Douglas Clark Kinder views that policy from yet a different perspective. Complementing nicely McWilliams's essay and suggesting by implication additional reasons for the limits on American policy discussed by Courtwright, Meyer, and Marshall, Kinder describes how nativism has affected narcotics control in the United States. He finds that the historic, basic assumptions that America's drug problems are largely foreign in origin or are exacerbated domestically by ethnic minorities have become controlling ones for policymakers. It is therefore not surprising, he concludes, that drug-control officials have long emphasized law enforcement as the first line of defense against drugs.

At first glance, the final article, by William B. McAllister, who compares the 1961 Single Convention on Narcotic Drugs and the 1971 Convention on Psychotropic Substances, would appear to take the discussion beyond the political fray. But that is not the case. McAllister cogently argues that persistent, substantive differences among the concerned powers are evident in the texts of these two most comprehensive international antidrug treaties. Indeed, it may not be much of an exaggeration to suggest that the political economy of the drug business is never more in evidence than at international deliberations. McAllister's analysis ought to alert us to possible limitations in the recent 1988 United Nations Convention against Illicit Traffic in Narcotic Drugs and Psychotropic Substances.

It is hoped that the articles prepared for this volume will induce other scholars to undertake a revision of the present findings or to analyze other aspects of drug policy in the United States and elsewhere. That such a productive enterprise may already be under way should be evident from a cursory glance at the sources cited in the notes of each article. Finally, in lieu of a formal dedication, a word of thanks is in order. Those readers who are familiar with the history of drugs will recognize the great debt of the editor and contributors to Dr. David F. Musto and Arnold H. Taylor. Without their pioneering books of some twenty years ago about American and international drug control, this volume would not have been possible.

Ohio Wesleyan University

JOHN C. McWILLIAMS

Through the Past Darkly: The Politics and Policies of America's Drug War

Drug wars. Few topics generate more controversy or provoke more debate. Few topics conjure up more futile and dismal images among the American population. Few topics are more synonymous with defeat. Never has our government been mired in a conflict so enduring or fought against an enemy so utterly impossible to conquer. For seventy-five years—nearly four times longer than both World Wars, Korea, and Vietnam combined—the federal government has been waging an endless war against seemingly impossible odds.

Drugs are immensely popular.[1] Millions of Americans use them, including an estimated 500,000 heroin addicts, between 4 million and 15 million cocaine users, and perhaps 25 million people who smoke marijuana at least once a month. Each year we consume 12 tons of heroin, 65 tons of marijuana, and 150 tons of cocaine, or about 60 percent of the world's illegal drugs.[2] Probably half or more of all serious crimes are drug-related. One-third of state prison inmates have committed drug-related offenses. We spend as much as $100 billion a year on drugs—more than we spend for food, or housing, or clothing.[3] Drug use and abuse is directly or indirectly responsible for health problems, shattered lives, widespread corruption, and senseless violence. None of the weapons we have applied in the war against drugs has been effective. Nothing works—or so it seems.

Crop eradication has not been effective and is probably unrealistic. We should not presume that sending Blackhawk helicopters into Peru's Upper Huallaga Valley will succeed in cutting off the supplies of coca leaves in South America and bring an end to the drug scourge in the United States. Despite President George Bush's message to the drug cartels in September

1989, that "the rules have changed," corrupt army officials in several Latin nations have thwarted U.S. efforts to eliminate the coca fields, causing Charles Gutensohn, Chief of the Drug Enforcement Administration's (DEA) Worldwide Cocaine Operations, to conclude that criminal elements in Peru were "out of control there." In December 1990, the House of Representatives Committee on Government Operations characterized the crop eradication program, or the so-called Andean Initiative, as a dismal failure.[4]

Failing to eliminate the problem at its source has not been the only disappointment in the drug war. Military intervention does not appear to be the answer. We should not expect the army to have a significant impact in drug-producing Colombia, a country where 220 judges and court employees have been assassinated and where Medellín, the second largest city, experienced 2,338 murders through just the first six months of 1989.[5]

Zero tolerance sounded like a good idea until a $2.5 million pleasure craft was stopped, searched, and confiscated in early May 1988. The incident became an embarrassment to the DEA and Customs officials when they realized that the owners forfeited their yacht because it carried one-tenth of one ounce of marijuana.[6]

Nor have other tactics proven to be more successful. Interdiction is farcical in two ways: first, the policy affects no more than 10 percent of the drugs coming into the country; and second, federal agents can no more stop drugs from crossing our borders than they can stop illegal aliens.[7] Demand reduction, which conceptually may sound appealing, has not moved beyond the wishful-thinking phase. "Just Say No," while well intended, is ineffective—at least that has been the reaction of Customs and DEA agents and the general public. Current proposed measures, both state and federal, are intended to send a "get-tough" message to casual users, drug addicts, street dealers, and major traffickers.

Scarcely a segment of American society is not directly or indirectly affected by drugs. It is a problem that defies simplistic or one-dimensional solutions. It is a problem that has aroused and agitated the American public like few other issues. It is a problem that will not go away. According to a *Washington Post* and an ABC News survey conducted in the fall of 1989, a huge majority—91 percent of those queried—concurred that the drug problem had escalated to the "crisis" stage.[8]

Increasingly, the public is demonstrating concern about a problem it views as a threat to national security, more foreboding perhaps than even communism. Never before have people felt so alarmed about the pervasiveness of drug abuse. Political scientists Morris J. Blachman and Kenneth E. Sharpe have noted: "Though there is nothing new about a drug problem, the general perception is that America is under siege."[9]

Real or perceived, the drug problem has become a high-priority issue, as evidenced by President Bush's announcement in his 1989 inaugural address that the federal government had declared a war on drugs. Two months later he equated drug abuse with a form of bondage, commenting that it was "America's 20th century version of human slavery." To demonstrate his sincerity and to implement strategies for waging an "unconditional war" against drug abuse, Bush appointed William J. Bennett as director of the newly created Office of National Drug Control Policy. As the new "drug czar," the outspoken Bennett boasted during his confirmation hearings before the Senate Judiciary Committee that he would "likely shake things up" in order to make good the President's pledge that "this [drug] scourge will stop."[10] Finally, it seems, the government is doing something new. Actually, it is more like a sense of déjà vu. Actually, very little is new about the current drug situation in the United States. Certainly the drug problem is not new. Nor is the war on drugs new. Previous wars have targeted opium, cocaine, marijuana, and heroin, and several drug czars have endeavored, in various ways, to alleviate the drug problem.

Politicians, the media, and much of the American public who lack an understanding of history fail to realize that ours never has been a drug-free society, and there is no reason why we should expect to become one anytime soon. Drugs are simply too alluring, and because people take drugs to feel good, they are irresistible to millions of Americans. The dark history of drug use confirms this bleak but realistic assessment.

Although many different strategies have been employed in the ongoing war on drugs that has constituted federal drug policy during this century, a disturbing but recurring pattern can be identified in each. Drug policy always has been highly politicized by opportunistic and self-serving politicians, and too often antidrug legislation has been the by-product of bureaucrats wishing either to justify their existence or legislators who want to advance their careers. On numerous occasions the government has deliberately manipulated addiction-rate figures and seizures of illicit drugs to give a distorted assessment of the drug crisis, usually for the worse, falsely fueling an antidrug frenzy. Frequently, government officials have also escalated statistics to demonstrate a need for increased appropriations, or they have lowered them to prove their effectiveness. They have also exploited communism, organized crime, and law-and-order issues not directly related to drugs to arouse public response to and support of antidrug policies. Drug laws have been enacted as a result of a government-produced hysteria. Punishment rather than treatment has been more preferred, even though it has not been successful. Antidrug policies have been put into effect by legislators who have a surprising lack of knowledge about drugs or drug use.

A "drug mythology" has perpetuated confusion and ignorance about drugs and drug users. Perhaps the earliest manifestation of this mythology was the government-endorsed *Reefer Madness,* a 1937 movie claiming not only that marijuana was more dangerous than heroin but also grossly exaggerating the effects of the drug in an attempt to dissuade school-aged youths from smoking it. Such scare tactics have accomplished nothing but to compromise the credibility of those who rely on them to deter drug use.

Drugs, it is safe to say, are firmly entrenched as a part of American society. Despite this hard reality, Congress included a provision in a 1988 law to "create a drug-free society by 1995."[11] While such an objective is commendable—and many Americans do want a drug-free society—it is also unrealistic and incredibly naive. Regrettably, government officials have been unable or unwilling to look to the past for lessons about how we can avoid committing the same unnecessary errors in formulating drug policies. To appreciate fully the nature of the current drug problem, it is useful to examine the history of drugs in the United States prior to this century as background for an assessment of America's war on drugs, a drama in five phases.

History

When the English founded the colony of Virginia in the early 1600s, in addition to transporting the basic necessities for survival, they brought marijuana plants. Within another two decades, the drug had been introduced to the New England colonies, and it remained an important cash crop in the United States until the Civil War. By the end of the nineteenth century, America had become, according to Edward M. Brecher, "a dope fiend's paradise."[12] Morphine, a common painkiller used during the war, had gained widespread popularity in the latter part of the century as a substitute for alcohol; heroin, a morphinelike compound, was frequently prescribed to reduce the miseries of a cough and as an elixir for chest and lung maladies.

Not only were these drugs widely used, they were easily accessible and could be purchased legally at grocery stores, from physicians who wrote prescriptions indiscriminately, and at drugstores, which sold them without prescriptions to anyone regardless of age. They could even be ordered through the mail.[13] Indicative of the prevalent use of morphine, the 1897 Sears Roebuck catalog sold for $1.50 hypodermic kits containing a syringe, two needles, two vials, and a carrying case.[14] There was so little concern about drug use and addiction that chemist John Styth Pemberton introduced a syrup in 1885 containing cocaine, claiming it was a "delicious, exhilarating, refreshing and invigorating Beverage." Not until 1906, when Congress passed the Pure Food and Drug Act, were Pemberton's successors forced to stop using the drug in Coca-Cola.[15]

At the turn of the century, several factors emerged to cause a pervasive shift in attitudes and values with respect to the social acceptability of drugs. First, the Progressive movement, whose proponents endeavored to create a fairer, more democratic, and more moral society, helped to rejuvenate the temperance crusade, arguing that excessive use of alcohol and other drugs would weaken American society. Second, adverse reactions to cocaine use caused a decline in the drug's popularity. By the early 1900s, cocaine had become the drug of choice for a more unsavory clientele who wanted only to experience euphoria, as opposed to those who relied on cocaine as a source of increased productivity in the workplace.

There was also an element of racism that affected drug legislation. When stories about blacks using cocaine or Asians smoking opium began to circulate, much of the white population became more intolerant of those who used the drugs.[16] After nearly three centuries of virtually no regulation of any drugs, a changing social climate at home and a desire to drive Chinese opium dealers out of the recently acquired Philippines compelled the government finally to act.

Government intervention into the drug problem, however, was no guarantee that such action would bring success. On the contrary, a synopsis of the seventy-five-year history of federal drug legislation reveals an abysmal failure to counter the spread of drugs or to diminish their popularity. Moreover, throughout this century politicians have failed to benefit from past experiences and repeatedly have made the same erroneous assumptions about drug use—as is apparent from an overview and analysis of the five phases of the war on drugs.

The Harrison Act: Phase I

Although several states made attempts, albeit ineffective, to legislate against drug use in the late nineteenth century, there was no effort at the federal level to restrict or control any drugs until Congressman David Foster (R-Vt.) introduced a bill in April 1910 to restrict the nonmedical use of opiates, cocaine, chloral hydrate, and cannabis.[17] Engineered by Dr. Hamilton Wright, a physician and renowned advocate of international control, the Foster Bill was the most comprehensive antidrug measure introduced in Congress. Wright argued that such a law was necessary to combat what he perceived as a major domestic drug problem and that it was not possible for the United States to play a prominent role in an international crusade against drugs without its own regulatory legislation. But the powerful National Drug Trade Conference (NDTC) lobby, objecting to the bill's harsh penalties and lack of exemptions for patent medicines, staunchly opposed it, and the bill never got out of committee.[18]

In the next two years several factors emerged that created more favorable conditions for Dr. Wright's war on drugs. First, as Ronald Hamowy has shown, the composition of the Sixty-second Congress of 1912 was vastly different from its predecessor. Under Democratic control and strongly influenced by Southerners acutely sensitive to race relations, Congress was more receptive to Wright's claims that cocaine was to blame for many of the assaults committed by blacks against whites.[19]

Wright was also able to play on turbulent social conditions surrounding World War I. In this milieu it was not difficult to convince American parents that their children might fall prey to drug-addicted Huns or suspicious Asians who reminded citizens of the "Yellow Peril" fear a decade earlier. As historian H. Wayne Morgan accurately observed, "For the first, though not the last time, drug use appeared un-American and unpatriotic."[20] Ratification of the Eighteenth Amendment in 1919, mandating the prohibition of alcohol "to rid society of all its evils," demonstrated the need for such progressive reform measures intended to uplift the collective American character.

After two more unsuccessful attempts to move the original Foster bill out of committee, Congressman Francis B. Harrison, a New York Tammany Democrat, finally introduced a proposal in June 1913 with the NDTC's approval that made its way to the House floor. For more than a year the bill was subjected to rigorous debate and amendments intended to prevent its passage. By late 1914, though, H.R. 6282 was presented to President Woodrow Wilson, who signed the bill into law to take effect 1 March 1915.[21]

The enactment of the Harrison Narcotic Act, the product of a media campaign stressing the alleged evils of narcotics, did little to achieve a consensus about federal drug policy. Supporters of the act argued it was necessary to head off an expected rise in addicts among servicemen, when in reality only about six percent of them were addicts or alcoholics.[22] Because it contained nebulous language pertaining to enforcement, it was eventually subjected to several legal interpretations that generated widespread controversy over the legal status of drug addicts.

Essentially the Harrison Act was merely a means of regulating the marketing of opium, heroin, and morphine sold over the counter or prescribed by a doctor. Although intended to function as a revenue-raising measure requiring anyone dealing in all major drugs but marijuana to register, and not as a prohibition measure or as an enforcement tool, the Harrison law would be the foundation for subsequent federal antidrug legislation. In fact, according to Ernest R. Abel, those in Congress who supported the law did not intend to make drug addiction a crime, and the Internal Revenue Bureau's (IRB) Narcotics Division was not created to enforce the law as much as it was to audit the collection of stamp revenues.[23] Regardless of its true intent, few contemporary observers could have anticipated in 1914 that this seemingly innocuous act would represent the start of a war on drugs, as its purpose gradually changed from regulation to prohibition and enforcement.

The Narcotics Division interpreted an ambiguous clause in the law—"in the course of his professional practice only"—to mean that a doctor could not prescribe opiates for an addict. Since neither addicts nor addiction was mentioned anywhere in the act, ambulatory or maintenance treatment was deemed illegal. The consequences became manifest almost immediately when IRB agents began to arrest physicians for violating the Harrison Act.[24]

Through a series of decisions between 1916 and 1922, the Supreme Court gradually adopted a strict constructionalist view of the Harrison Act and allowed the government to enforce the law in a way that would prohibit doctors from prescribing any drugs to addicts under any circumstances. As a result, Treasury Department agents put an end to any kind of addiction treatment programs.[25] To justify this policy, the department stated in its 1919 drug report that addicts in the United States numbered between 750,000 and 1.5 million. Obviously, if those estimates were accurate, addiction had reached epidemic proportions and, understandably, drastic measures were necessary to fight such an insidious and pervasive problem. But they were not accurate, as two of the report's authors confirmed years later when they admitted that their findings were based on unsubstantiated research. More recently, historian David Courtwright has concluded that the existing supply of opium in the early 1920s could not have supported more than 300,000 addicts.[26] This would not be the last time the government exaggerated statistics to prove that drugs were a problem and that there was a need for stricter enforcement.

The Harrison Act also created a huge black market. Consuming or selling a drug that always had been legal was suddenly illegal. The government therefore only exacerbated the plight of addicts who were still drug-dependent. A more sweeping consequence of enforcement was altering both the perception and the legal status of the addict. Rather than being regarded as a disease, addiction was considered a criminal act, a vitally important distinction that would be part of the legacy of federal drug enforcement as it took shape in the 1920s and endured over the next seventy years.

With the exception of the 1922 Narcotic Drugs Import and Export Act, also known as the Jones-Miller Act, allowing the government to monitor illicit traffic and legitimate narcotics, Congress adopted no other significant pieces of drug legislation during the Prohibition decade.[27] The Harrison Act remained the keystone of federal narcotics enforcement, despite a heated debate among physicians who objected to closing clinics that not only provided ambulatory treatment but also enabled the government to monitor drug addiction.

An editorial in the *New York Medical Journal* expressed concern that the adoption of the Harrison law would lead to "the commission of crimes which will never be traced to their real cause, and the influx into hospitals for the mentally disordered of many who would otherwise live socially competent lives."[28] Despite concern by members of the medical community who, unlike politicians, were in a position to observe the addiction problem firsthand, the law remained unchanged. Twenty years after the law was enacted, a 1934 editorial writer in the *St. Louis Post-Dispatch* concluded that "the Harrison Anti-Narcotic Act has been a greater failure than was the Eighteenth Amendment." The editorial also noted that the act "made trafficking in narcotics so profitable and led to the establishment of vast underworld rings." Addiction should be treated as a disease: "To withhold drugs is to force the victim to suffer excruciating pain and to stimulate him to whatever action is necessary to obtain a supply." The editorial concluded that the law was a costly failure: "We need to come to grips with the narcotic problem and to treat it, not with a law impossible of enforcement, but realistically."[29]

To ensure more efficient and effective enforcement of the Harrison Act, the Treasury Department had created a special Narcotics Division within the Prohibition Unit in 1920 headed by Colonel Levi G. Nutt, formerly in the Alcohol Tax Division. A registered pharmacist who had been with the Treasury Department since 1901, Nutt was a career bureaucrat in charge of between 170 and 270 agents from 1920 to 1929.[30] Unsympathetic to maintenance clinics for addicts, Nutt and his agents launched a nationwide crusade to shut them down.

The consequences of the anticlinic crusade were felt immediately, as federal prisons filled to more than double their capacity by the end of the decade. By 1 April 1928, penitentiaries, with enough cells to hold 3,738 inmates, were housing 7,598 offenders. Some were traffickers; others, however, were addicts or respected members of the medical profession. On 30 June 1928, according to legal scholar Rufus King, of the 7,738 prisoners incarcerated in the federal system, more than one-third—2,529 or twice the number of the 1,156 prohibition offenders—were serving sentences for violating the Harrison law.[31]

As the person charged with enforcing the nation's most comprehensive drug law, Nutt betrayed an ignorance of the problem he was attempting to solve. In testifying before congressional hearings in January 1921 on the Jones-Miller Bill, Nutt was completely uninformed about the drug situation. He had no idea about how much opium was coming into the United States illegally, nor could he guess whether the number of drug users was declining or increasing. He was confident, however, that the Harrison Act was "enforced better than it ever was" and that "we probably get half" the drugs entering the country, even though he had no idea how much was actually smuggled.[32]

The First Drug Czar and the Federal Bureau of Narcotics: Phase II

In 1929 a grand jury investigating alleged improprieties involving Colonel Nutt concluded that he, as deputy commissioner of the Prohibition Bureau, ordered agents in the New York City regional office to pad arrest reports. On recommendations from the jury, Nutt was demoted and transferred out of the Narcotics Division for misconduct in February 1930.[33] To fill Nutt's position, Secretary of the Treasury Andrew W. Mellon appointed Harry J. Anslinger, formerly assistant commissioner of the Prohibition Bureau, in charge of foreign control.

In the summer of 1930, when President Herbert Hoover signed into law Congressman (R-Pa.) Stephen G. Porter's bill "to create a separate and independent bureau of narcotics in the Treasury Department," Anslinger, the first "drug czar," was named as commissioner of the newly created Federal Bureau of Narcotics (FBN) at a $9,000 annual salary. Having held a minor diplomatic post in the State Department during World War I at The Hague and later assignments in Hamburg, Germany; La Guaira, Venezuela; and the Bahamas, where he chased rumrunners during Prohibition, Anslinger was well qualified to head the FBN. For more than three decades, until he retired in 1962, Anslinger proved to be the consummate bureaucrat.[34]

By cultivating congressional ties and by drawing support from the pharmaceutical lobby and an army of conservative newspapers and civic groups, Anslinger ran a tightly controlled agency that advocated repressive measures to deal with addicts and traffickers.[35] For forty years—he was the U.S. delegate to the United Nations Commission on Narcotic Drugs until 1970—Anslinger was the dominant figure in formulating federal antidrug policies and shaping public opinion.[36]

In the 1930s, Anslinger initiated the second phase of the war on drugs with a force of fewer than 200 field agents to monitor more than 4,000 miles of the American border. In his first few years as commissioner, Anslinger's primary concern was to bolster the bureau's image as an honest and capable agency and to secure sufficient appropriations, a formidable task in the middle of the Depression. He also had to survive at least two reorganizational attempts to merge the FBN with the Secret Service and other law enforcement agencies in the Treasury Department.

To head off these maneuvers and to retain his bureaucratic autonomy, Anslinger quickly learned the importance of being able to demonstrate his bureau's *raison d'être.* In the first years of his tenure, Anslinger successfully capitalized on a horse-doping scandal to thwart reorganization.[37] By the mid-1930s, Anslinger, a shrewd bureaucrat, discovered a more insidious enemy to attack—marijuana.

Prior to the early 1930s, marijuana received little publicity outside the Southwest, where reports linked indolent Mexicans with the drug. But in 1931 the district attorney and a physician in New Orleans published articles dramatizing the alleged violent effects of marijuana and predicted that marijuana smoking would spread beyond the southwestern states.[38] Associating marijuana with blacks in New Orleans and Mexicans in the Southwest—racial groups the mainstream white population perceived as threatening—made it easier for public officials to contend that a "new" drug was suddenly a problem of national scope.

The New Orleans officials made erroneous claims about the effects of marijuana, but they were correct in predicting that the drug would soon spread to other parts of the country. In 1936 some observers said marijuana had become more popular than liquor in Harlem. It seemed to be everywhere. People grew it in urban backyards, vacant lots, along highways, and even in the fields of federal prisons. Narcotics agents found employees in the Civilian Conservation Corps and Works Progress Administration smoking it.[39]

Initially, Anslinger was reluctant to push for a federal law outlawing marijuana, preferring that individual states enact legislation to prohibit its use. Questions regarding the constitutionality of the Harrison Act, the colossal failure of the Volstead Act, economic circumstances, and threats to the existence of the FBN were convincing reasons, he argued, not to adopt a federal antimarijuana statute.[40]

By the mid-1930s, however, succumbing to pressure from the media, particularly the Hearst newspaper chain, which published lurid stories and graphic cartoons detailing how the drug enslaved its users, Anslinger began to reconsider his position on the marijuana issue, and in 1936 the government launched another war on drugs. Rather than hold the states responsible for enforcement, the commissioner felt that federal legislation was necessary to bring the marijuana epidemic under control—stating that the problem was more serious than he originally believed. Testifying at appropriations hearings in December 1936, he claimed that marijuana was "about as hellish as heroin," apparently reversing his conclusion the previous year that it was not even addictive.[41]

Harry Anslinger did not create the marijuana scare. Once he realized, however, that outlawing the drug could be tremendously beneficial in improving his bureau's image, he was not reluctant to magnify the danger it represented to America and to young people in particular. In his article "Marihuana: Assassin of Youth," Anslinger warned that the drug might turn a person into a "philosopher, a joyous reveler in a musical heaven," or that the user might "deteriorate mentally and become insane." Worse, smokers of the drug "may turn to violent forms of crime, to suicide or to murder."[42]

By the late 1930s, such information about marijuana was widely disseminated in various forms of the media, including the Hearst newspapers, *Reefer Madness,* and Anslinger's own sensationalist publications. The commissioner's claims were also confirmed by narcotics agents around the country like William C. Crawford of California's State Bureau of Narcotics, who believed that marijuana "gave men the lust to kill without motive."[43]

Despite the lack of any concrete evidence in the 1930s substantiating the FBN's claims that marijuana possessed the properties to turn otherwise normal and sane users into violent criminals, Robert L. Doughton (D-N.C.) chairman of the House Ways and Means Committee, introduced H.R. 6385 in April 1933 "to impose an occupational excise tax upon certain dealers in marihuana to impose a transfer tax upon certain dealings in marihuana, and to safeguard the revenue therefrom by registry and recording."[44]

On 27 April 1937, Doughton opened five days of hearings that ultimately resulted in legislation that would become a model for future federal antidrug policies. Constructed out of a sense of urgency, the hastily adopted Marihuana Tax Act was based on myth, ignorance, and misinformation. Even members of Congress who supported the legislation betrayed a lack of knowledge about marijuana. Congressman John D. Dingell (D-Mich.) thought marijuana was the same as loco weed.[45] When the bill was presented for debate on the House floor, Congressman Bertrand H. Snell (R-N.Y.) asked, "What is the bill?" Representative Sam Rayburn (D-Tex.) replied, "It has something to do with something that is called marihuana. I believe it is a narcotic of some kind."[46]

The debate on the House floor on the marijuana legislation lasted less than half an hour. Only one witness, Dr. William C. Woodward, legislative counsel for the American Medical Association, opposed the bill during the hearings. The committee's reaction was hostile. Not only did members ignore Woodward's objections, but several questioned his credentials and challenged virtually every statement he made against the legislation.[47]

The most influential proponent of the bill was Anslinger, and the reaction to his testimony sharply contrasted with that of Woodward. Anslinger repeatedly recounted marijuana cases culled from a file that graphically described gruesome details of users' behavior. Although to an enlightened observer some of the incidents provided comic relief, most were intended to elicit an emotional response to the horrible effects of the drug. Perhaps antcipating his appearance before Congress, Anslinger maintained a file of reports submitted by FBN agents linking marijuana with violence. Typically they described offenders who raped, violently attacked police officers, or committed brutal murders, all of whom, the investigators noted, were smoking marijuana prior to or while they committed their crimes.

Anslinger's favorite case was that of twenty-one-year-old Victor Licata, a young Mexican in Florida who, "under the influence of marijuana," axed his mother, father, two brothers, and sister to death.[48] Committee members were horrified. Licata did smoke marijuana, he did have an ax, and he did murder his family. Anslinger's testimony was factual, but it was not complete. He did not mention that eleven days after the murder a psychiatric examination report appeared in the *Tampa Times* confirming that Licata was criminally insane and subject to "hallucinations accompanied by homicidal impulses." Authorities also concluded that his insanity was most likely inherited and was not marijuana-induced.[49]

With the Licata case, Anslinger, as the recognized authority on the drug problem, established the government's marijuana-insanity link in 1937 and perpetuated it for the next quarter century. That he disclosed only selected facts about the emotionally and mentally unstable Licata created a problem of credibility. That no one during either the House or

Senate hearings was curious enough to press for more details about marijuana's effects demonstrated an unwillingness to demand more conclusive evidence that the drug really was an "assassin of youth."

As drug czar, Anslinger ensured that his assessments about marijuana were widely publicized. He contributed numerous articles to periodicals, testified before congressional hearings, and, shortly after the Tax Act became law, declared that marijuana should be outlawed. He believed that a person under the drug's influence could be provoked by "the slightest opposition arousing him to a state of menacing fury or homicidal attack. During this frenzied period, addicts have perpetuated some of the most bizarre and fantastic offenses and sex crimes known to police annals."[50] In the absence of scientific evidence, Anslinger made marijuana a "killer weed."

Initial reaction to the Marihuana Tax Act, like that of the Harrison Act, was minimal. *Newsweek*'s brief coverage reiterated Anslinger's claims that "users were capable of violence," like in the case of a "California man who decapitated his best friend while under the violent spell of the smoke, and a Florida youngster [who] put the ax to his mother and father." Surprisingly, the article contradicted Anslinger's claim that it was destroying America's youth, noting that "sensational press stories about its use in grade and high schools generally prove unfounded." The *New York Times* commented only that "President Roosevelt signed today a bill to curb traffic in the narcotic, marihuana, through heavy taxes on transactions."[51]

There were a number of similarities between the Harrison Act and the Marihuana Tax Act. The primary intent was for each to function as a revenue measure, but they were ultimately modified to facilitate enforcement. Both Dr. Wright and Commissioner Anslinger were able to capitalize on social and cultural conditions to gain passage of their respective bills. Each law created a new class of criminals. The responsibility for the enforcement of each piece of legislation was assigned to individuals who emphasized tough enforcement rather than treatment or education: Levi Nutt led a crusade to shut down the clinics; Anslinger urged judges to "jail offenders, then throw away the key." For the next three decades Anslinger would be the architect, implementor, and staunchest advocate of the government's punitive approach.

Getting Tough(er): Phase III

Because World War II dominated global affairs and disrupted drug-trafficking routes, Narcotics Bureau enforcement activities were limited mostly to the domestic scene through the 1940s. With the recent enactment of the Marihuana Tax Act, few politicians were likely to question the need for such legislation or for a federal drug agency.[52] In 1950, as he began his third decade as the nation's drug czar, Anslinger's position was more secure than ever. He was so confident of his congressional support in fact that in 1951 he renewed the war on drugs.

Once again the existing social climate created conditions favorable for Anslinger to push for and get the toughest federal antidrug laws ever passed. In the Cold War era a combination of an FBN-promoted scare about a dramatic rise in addiction rates among returning GIs, a pervasive fear of a Communist invasion at the height of McCarthyism, congressional hearings investigating the mysterious Mafia organization, and Anslinger's enhanced reputation as a no-nonsense bureaucrat with twenty years' experience observing the drug situation enabled the commissioner to persuade Congress that it was necessary to get tough with drug offenders.[53]

Convinced that the use of marijuana would lead to experimentation with harder drugs, Anslinger asserted that existing penalties were inadequate and could not deter potential users. What was needed, he argued, were more severe measures, preferably in the form of mandatory sentences and longer prison terms. The legislation providing for the escalation of penalties came in two stages and was introduced, at Anslinger's behest, by politicians quite willing to play on the drug hysteria to win reelection.

The major reason for the increase in drug violations, according to Anslinger, was a soft judicial system that was reluctant to assess sufficient prison terms. If the government was going to prevent the Mafia from flooding the country with drugs, save the youth of America from addiction, or stop a Communist take-over, existing penalties needed to be increased to keep traffickers out of circulation.[54] Anslinger's reasoning made sense, at least to those in Congress who introduced more than two dozen bills in 1951 related to drug enforcement.[55] Just as he had fired the public's ire about the emergence of a "killer weed" in the 1930s, which led to outlawing marijuana and the introduction of penalties to crack down on a new criminal class, Anslinger shaped and redefined the public consensus about drug policy in the 1950s by linking drugs with other unpopular issues like communism and the Mafia.[56]

Anslinger's solution to the drug problem was tougher law enforcement, and Congressman Hale Boggs (D-La.) accommodated him in early April 1951, when he introduced H.R. 3490 "to amend the penalty provisions applicable to persons convicted of violating certain narcotics laws."[57] With only Representative Emmanuel Cellar (D-N.Y.) voicing opposition to the provision for mandatory minimum sentences, the bill sailed through both houses, which passed it with overwhelming margins in November 1951.[58] By including uniform penalties for violations of the Narcotic Drugs Import and Export Act and the Marihuana Tax Act, the Boggs legislation was the most sweeping and most punitive federal law to date.

For a first conviction of possession, an offender would receive a sentence of up to five years, with a mandatory minimum of two years. A second offense was punishable with a mandatory five to ten years, with no probation or suspension of the sentence permitted. A third-time violator faced a mandatory ten to twenty years, with no probation or the possibility of a suspended sentence. All offenses also included a $2,000 fine, a relatively modest amount, because the legislators did not think fines would deter traffickers.[59]

The enactment of the Boggs Act, with its unprecedented harsh sanctions, stimulated debate among many professional groups over federal drug-control strategies. In particular, the American Bar Association (ABA) and the American Medical Association (AMA), which felt that such penalties were inappropriate, requested Congress to reevaluate the efficacy of the Harrison Act, the Marihuana Tax Act, and the Boggs legislation. Responding to ABA–AMA pressure, the Senate Judiciary Committee initiated a comprehensive study of antidrug laws in March 1955.

Over the next eighteen months a subcommittee chaired by Senator Price Daniel (D-Tex.) conducted hearings in thirteen cities throughout the country. To the dismay of the medical and legal community, but to the delight of Commissioner Anslinger, the Daniel Committee proposed that the penalties for drug-related offenses be stiffened again, apparently reasoning that if tough, long sentences were good, then tougher, longer sentences were even better. The committee also recommended against further discussion of opiate clinics and favored the highly idealistic objective of eliminating drug addicts so they would not spread "this contagious problem."[60]

Testifying during the Daniel Committee hearings, Anslinger relied on the same tired but effective tactic of linking marijuana smoking to violent crimes, confirming for Senator Herman Welker (R-Idaho) that in many cases "the most sadistic, terrible crimes, solved or unsolved, we can trace directly to the marijuana user."[61] Whether or not Anslinger really believed the wild pronouncements he made about marijuana's effects, he had to be pleased with how easily he could influence committee members, who possessed little or no knowledge about marijuana or any other illicit drug.

Essentially the legislation resulting from the Daniel Committee investigation, the Narcotic Control Act of 1956, doubled the penalties stipulated in the Boggs Act. The first-possession offense carried a penalty of two to ten years' imprisonment, the second offense a mandatory five to twenty years with no probation or parole, and the third offense a mandatory ten to forty years with no probation or parole.[62] Discretion of judges to suspend sentences or permit probation was virtually eliminated. The most extreme provision allowed the imposition of the death penalty for anyone selling heroin to a person under eighteen years of age. The only progressive resolution, to provide hospital and treatment facilities for addicts, offered by Senator Herbert H. Lehman (D-N.Y.), received no consideration. In the third phase of America's war on drugs, Anslinger ensured that punishment rather than treatment would be the primary strategy.

The Nixon Years: Phase IV

In the turbulent 1960s the United States experienced a dramatic increase in the use of drugs. Marijuana and heroin had been widely recognized for decades as the drugs of choice among blacks, Mexicans, jazz musicians, Asians, and rebellious youths—deviant or marginal social groups who challenged or rejected traditional values.[63] Marijuana was especially popular among the latter group, and as drug historian David F. Musto has noted, state-level arrests for marijuana violations increased tenfold between 1965 and 1970. Of greater concern than marijuana, however, was the rapid popularity of amphetamines and LSD, a newer and more powerful hallucinogen accidentally discovered in the 1940s.[64] In the middle of this drug scare, President Richard Nixon emerged after a six-year absence from politics to orchestrate a successful 1968 presidential campaign around a law-and-order theme.

Shortly after his inauguration in January 1969, however, Nixon realized that translating his campaign rhetoric into reality would be extremely difficult because the federal government had no jurisdiction over burglaries, assaults, or muggings. These street crimes, or offenses commonly associated with drug addicts, were not violations of federal law. But the White House quickly discovered that narcotics trafficking was a violation, and the administration had a new weapon in yet another drug war.[65]

Never before or since has the executive branch waged the kind of war on drugs that occurred in the early 1970s during the Nixon administration. In an unprecedented move, the White House played a direct and active role, first in generating widespread hysteria and then in using that hysteria to justify creating investigative agencies that abrogated the basic constitutional rights of American citizens.

Once the hysteria factor took effect, the next logical step, à la Harry Anslinger, was to convince the public that there was a drug problem of epidemic proportions. The emergence of such a problem would demonstrate the administration's need for additional funds and, more important, the need to create appropriate enforcement agencies to assist the newly reorganized Bureau of Narcotics and Dangerous Drugs (BNDD), which replaced the Federal Bureau of Narcotics in 1968.[66] To create the drug scare in the early 1970s, Nixon's advisers exaggerated the estimates of heroin addicts and conducted a propaganda blitz through the media, capitalizing especially on television. Congress responded to public alarm by passing—82–0 in the Senate—a bill with tough penalties for drug dealers selling to minors or trafficking for profit and a controversial provision authorizing "no-knock" raids, allowing federal agents to enter suspected premises without a search warrant.[67] John E. Ingersoll, Director of the BNDD, reinforced the hysteria in an interview with *U.S. News & World Report* in 1970, when he stated that the drug problem "has exploded into frightening proportions."[68]

Calling it "America's Public Enemy Number One," President Nixon announced the fourth phase of the nation's war on drugs in June 1971.[69] Although the attack on the drug problem included methadone treatment for heroin addicts, most attention was given to law enforcement, international as well as domestic.[70] To end the flow of heroin into the United States, Nixon decided to stop it at its source before it entered the country and struck an agreement with Turkey, where an estimated 80 percent of the drug originated. The effort in international diplomacy seemed effective when the Turkish government gave assurances that it was "totally committed to stopping all growing of the opium poppy and also totally committed to stopping smuggling through Turkey." The U.S. government encouraged Turkish farmers not to grow poppies by compensating them for the losses they incurred by growing other crops. The United States also paid the Turkish government $35 million. It was not long, however, before production in Mexico and especially the "Golden Triangle" countries in Southeast Asia more than compensated for Turkey's withdrawal from the heroin trade.[71]

Once the White House succeeded in convincing the public that narcotics addiction threatened American lives, it could then portray federal law enforcement agencies as the most effective weapon against the spread of addiction. Nixon's advisers correctly anticipated little resistance, public or political, to the creation of such agencies. In January 1972 the administration created the Office of Drug Abuse and Law Enforcement (ODALE) to wage the drug war on the domestic front, a title that belied its real nature. Established by executive order, ODALE operated out of the Justice Department but was directed by Myles Ambrose, who was in Nixon's Executive Office of the President. To put pressure on the street-level or the lower-echelon dealer and pusher, ODALE had the authority to transfer agents from the BNDD, Customs, the Internal Revenue Service, and the Bureau of Alcohol, Tobacco, and Firearms. The office was also permitted to conduct court-authorized wiretaps, no-knock search warrants, and warrantless raids. If legal means were not effective in the drug war, the White House was willing to resort to extralegal ways to control a problem that President Nixon warned "will surely in time destroy us."[72]

But what was the rationale for an agency like ODALE in the administration's assault on drugs? According to Henrik Kruger, "Nixon's heroin war was no more than window dressing," and fighting drugs was a guise for establishing a White House-controlled intelligence and enforcement unit that, on the surface, seemed consistent with the law-and-order theme that was central to his 1968 campaign. Ultimately, Kruger asserts, Nixon's war on drugs was "converged in a conspiratorial and political-criminal network of hitherto unimagined dimensions."[73]

To implement these activities the White House set up a Special Action Office for Drug Abuse Prevention to work in conjunction with a Special Investigative Unit, otherwise known as the Plumbers. This unit included Egil Krogh, deputy assistant to the president for law enforcement; John Caulfield; G. Gordon Liddy; E. Howard Hunt, a former Central Intelligence Agency (CIA) agent once employed as a special adviser on narcotics problems in Southeast Asia; and Lucien Conein, CIA agent and expert on the Corsican Mafia stationed in Vietnam from the end of World War II until 1968.[74]

In reality ODALE had little to do with fighting drugs. It was a private police force conceived by Liddy that reported directly to the President, circumventing congressional control. Functioning as a domestic strike force, ODALE was notorious for illegal raids and the physical harassment of innocent people.[75] To monitor drug traffickers on the international level, Krogh suggested creating an intelligence unit as part of the White House drug war, since the CIA seemed reluctant to get involved in a law enforcement problem. That responsibility ultimately fell to Hunt, who proposed that drug intelligence reports be directed to the Office of National Narcotics Intelligence (ONNI).[76] With the creation of ODALE and ONNI, Nixon's plumbers acquired broad, discretionary powers that allowed them to pursue a hidden agenda under the auspices of fighting a presumed surging increase in the number of heroin addicts in the United States.

When President Nixon agreed in 1970 to use "forceful action in [stopping] international trafficking of heroin at the host country," Krogh proposed a $100 million fund over a three-year period to disrupt narcotics traffic, if necessary through assassinations. According to Dr. J. Thomas Ungerleider, a member of the National Commission on Marijuana and Drug Abuse in 1972, some BNDD officials talked of "establishing hit squads," and a BNDD memorandum stated that "with 150 key assassinations, the entire heroin refining operation can be thrown into chaos."[77]

Nixon's narcotics bureaucracy was again reorganized in July 1973. According to Reorganization Plan Number Two, the BNDD was abolished after only five years of operation. To fill the void, former BNDD agents, approximately five-hundred Customs agents, and fifty agents from the CIA were merged into the Drug Enforcement Administration (DEA).[78] To implement the assassinations discussed in the BNDD, Hunt suggested using Conein, also known as "Black Luigi," who had been involved in the overthrow of South Vietnam's President Ngo Dinh Diem.

Conein allegedly was charged with carrying out the assassination program within a DEA Special Operations Group (SOG). Twelve experienced agents were transferred from the CIA to conduct the operation. In an interview with journalist George Crile, Conein denied allegations that he or his SOG, or "Dirty Dozen," was established as a hit team. Crile quoted a DEA official, however, who claimed that "Conein was organizing an assassination program." DEA sources also told Crile that "meetings were held to decide whom to target and what method of assassination to employ."[79]

Unlike previous antidrug crusades, the Nixon war on drugs was not waged to justify a *raison d'être* or to secure greater appropriations. In the 1970s the drug war was more comprehensive, meshing clandestine operations to affect international diplomacy and national security. Nixon's advisers fabricated a drug hysteria to enable the Executive Branch to seize the power of domestic law enforcement agencies, move them inside the White House, and manipulate them for self-serving purposes. Peter Dale Scott commented in 1973: "It is no coincidence that key figures in Watergate—Liddy, Hunt, Sturgis, Krogh, Caulfield—had been drawn from the conspiratorial world of government narcotics enforcement, a shady realm in which operations of organized crime, counter-revolution and government intelligence have traditionally overlapped."[80] The Nixon administration demonstrated in its antidrug campaign that a war on drugs could be useful for a variety of purposes. It is frightening even to consider how agencies like ODALE and ONNI might have further subverted constitutional protections had not the Nixon administration been compromised as a result of a "third-rate burglary" in June 1972.

The Enlightened(?) Eighties: Phase V

Through the remainder of the 1970s, Watergate, Nixon's resignation, and a feeble economy demanded greater priority than drugs. Nixon's successor, President Gerald Ford, did not ignore the problem. However, he did not share Nixon's intense determination to emphasize law enforcement, opting for more flexible policies. In 1975 the Domestic Council Drug Abuse Task Force recommended a change in strategy, concluding that the "total elimination of drug abuse is unlikely but governmental actions can contain the problem and limit its adverse effects." The report also recognized that all drugs are not equally dangerous and that all drug use is not equally destructive.[81]

Jimmy Carter's administration took an even bolder position. More than recognizing that drugs were a part of American culture, the administration favored decriminalizing the possession of small amounts of marijuana, and, as Musto has observed, in March 1977, forty years after the Marijuana Tax hearings, officials from the DEA, Customs, and the Departments of State and Justice supported decriminalization before the House Select Committee on Narcotics Abuse and Control.[82] Commissioner Anslinger surely would have been flabbergasted at such a radical proposal.[83]

The government's more enlightened and tolerant approach to the drug problem was shortlived. The 1981 inauguration of President Ronald Reagan, who launched the most recent phase of the war on drugs, represented an ideological retreat into the dark past of failed drug policies. Law enforcement was again given a higher priority than education and treatment programs, which experienced cuts throughout the 1980s, resulting in waiting lines for treatment in many major American cities.

The situation had not improved by the end of the decade. In November 1989 Dr. Charles P. O'Brien, psychiatrist and director of a program for drug addicts, informed President Bush: "It's ridiculous for us to talk about a war on drugs because there's actually less treatment available today than there was 15 years ago." In early 1990 it was estimated that, if states maintained their current rate of funding for treatment, between 400,000 and 600,000 places would exist to assist approximately 1.7 million patients annually.[84]

Three times during the Reagan years, in 1984, 1986, and 1988, Congress passed antidrug legislation to curb the abuse of illicit substances, each law more severe than the previous one.[85] Announcing on 30 July 1986 that "the time has come to give notice that individual drug use is threatening the health and safety of all our citizens," the president made his position clear in his war on drugs. As they had so often in the past, legislators on Capitol Hill competed with one another, introducing more than eighty drug-related bills.[86] Six weeks later, in an overwhelming 392–16 vote, the House of Representatives voted to spend more than $2 billion over three years as part of the Omnibus Drug Enforcement, Education, and Control Act of 1986.[87]

Reflecting a sense of urgency to take decisive action, the House also approved the deployment of the military, allowed a mandatory life sentence for an adult who sold drugs to a juvenile for the second time, and weakened the exclusionary rule by permitting the use of illegally seized evidence in drug trials. Representative George W. Gekas (R-Pa.) later tacked on the death penalty for drug-related murders, the bill's most controversial amendment.[88]

In an attempt to outdo one another, legislators ignored deficit restrictions and potential constitutional challenges, preferring to allow the courts to wrestle with legal questions as they arose. Drugs were simply too important. Acknowledging that the drug bill was "out of control," Congressman Dave McCurdy (D-Okla.) also reflected the general mood in Congress by adding, "But of course I'm for it." So was virtually every other legislator.[89] Yet even in an election year not all lawmakers were ready to support a measure as drastic as the death penalty. To ensure the House's chances of writing a bill that would get through the Senate and that would allow an opportunity for the maximum number of supporters, the House passed two bills, one with the death penalty and one without it.[90] The Senate would have to choose.

By mid-October members of both parties in both houses who regarded the enactment of antidrug legislation as crucial to their campaigns agreed to a compromise measure without the death penalty that required less than an hour of perfunctory debate. The $1.7 billion Omnibus Antidrug Act of 1986 allocated $1.1 billion for local, state, and federal law enforcement. Only $200 million, or 12 percent of the total appropriation, was set aside for education.[91] Legislators, more interested in appeasing frustrated voters than they were in putting together a more carefully developed policy in 1986, adopted the most punitive and far-reaching drug law since Congress passed the Narcotic Control Act thirty years earlier.

On 27 October, President Reagan signed the bill into law, claiming that because "the American people want their government to get tough and go on the offensive," he would attack the problem "with more ferocity than ever before." But while Reagan called for a stronger and more vigorous effort in the war against drugs during the first six years of his presidency, local funding for drug enforcement was cut 6 percent and funds for treatment programs were cut 40 percent. While the President talked tough, First Lady Nancy Reagan admonished young people to "Just Say No" to drugs. The President also noted: "Our goal in the crusade is nothing less than a drug-free generation."[92] Drugs still made for good, if unethical, politics. The government reacted to public opinion by eschewing increased funding for treatment facilities or educational programs, preferring to implement laws that were not likely to be effective. President Reagan also ignored the history of drugs in the United States when he expressed his desire for a "drug-free generation." Both Congress and the president rediscovered the value of politicizing drugs, and, in the middle of a drug epidemic, logic and history gave way to an irrational but politically expedient government reaction.

In reality, though, there was no epidemic in 1986. Both the *New York Times* and *U.S. News & World Report* noted that available statistics showed no sudden rise in drug use. Although several polls indicated that drugs were the public's primary concern, no evidence supported the kind of frenzy that would justify the politicians' panicky response. The drug problem was serious in the mid-1980s, but it had been serious for twenty years. Moreover, data showed that contrary to the general perception, some forms of drug abuse were actually on the decline in the first half of the decade.[93] Nevertheless, no proposals, it seemed, were too drastic, too outlandish, or too expensive.

With the emphasis on action rather than analysis, Congress revitalized the drug war two years later when it passed another antidrug bill. The Omnibus Drug Initiative Act was intended to send a message to drug users—and constituents—that legislators were serious about drug abuse.[94] Embarking on what the American Medical Association called the "adversarial approach," lawmakers were again quick to endorse draconian measures that could easily have been identified with the 1950s drug hysteria.[95] In the milieu of election-year politics, the House approved amendments that included penalties for mere possession of an illegal substance with a $10,000 fine and declared violators ineligible for student loans, public housing, and a driver's license. This time the death penalty was first introduced in the Senate by Alfonse D'Amato (R-N.Y.) to prevent "drug dealers from embarking on killing sprees." Congressman Gekas again introduced it in the House, claiming such drastic action was necessary as a "swift and certain" deterrent against drug-related killings. By a vote of 375–30 the House also authorized more than $2 billion in the toughest and most sweeping antidrug legislation yet.[96]

Still, Congress had not produced a coherent strategy in the war on drugs. Again employing a punitive approach, the 1988 legislation would punish anyone for possession of even small amounts of marijuana by making offenders ineligible for college loans or public housing. The government was simultaneously extending one hand to help, the other to punish. As a *New Republic* editorial observed, "Uncle Sam is more willing than ever to help a drug user back on his feet, provided that getting back on his feet doesn't involve college education or having a place to live."[97]

Two months after his inauguration President George Bush indicated that he would continue his predecessor's war on drugs, giving warning that "I have some bad news for the bad guys: Hunting season is over."[98] Despite the severity of the antidrug laws of 1986 and 1988, however, and the billions of dollars Congress approved for fighting drug abuse, it was clear that the government was losing the drug war. Mandatory sentences caused prisons to overflow with drug-related offenders when such facilities were needed for child abusers, rapists, and murderers; treatment centers were hopelessly understaffed and overcrowded; and even the death penalty was a minimal deterrent to dealers who stood to realize fantastic profits in the seemingly insatiable black market in drugs.

To help stop the drug scourge, and to satisfy a requirement in the 1988 antidrug legislation, President Bush nominated William J. Bennett to be Director of the Office of National Drug Policy. Even though, as a member of President Reagan's Drug Enforcement Policy Board, he had no law enforcement experience, Bennett was easily confirmed as the new drug czar in March.[99] Aggressive and fiercely determined to be a leader in the war against drugs, Bennett urged citizens to patrol their neighborhoods and admonished them to fight back. He once responded to a suggestion that drug dealers be executed with a sword to the neck as in Saudi Arabia, by commenting: "Morally, I don't have a problem with it."[100]

Shortly after his confirmation, Bennett outlined his antidrug strategies. He fulminated against liberal policies and attributed the drug problem to crises of political, social, and moral authority.[101] The only viable solution to such a problem, he argued, was a policy of consequences and confrontation. Bennett targeted not only drug traffickers but also casual users, advocating that drug violations, even minor ones, would no longer go unpunished. His policies would guarantee that punishment was certain, that it would be more than a possible consequence. To realize his goal of decreasing drug use by 10 percent within two years and by 50 percent in ten years, Bennett encouraged schools to suspend or expel students dealing drugs and recommended that states revoke the driver's licenses of anyone convicted of a drug violation. To deter people from experimenting with drugs, he advocated scare tactics. For those who ignored these admonitions, the czar called for more law enforcement personnel to apprehend offenders, more prosecutors to convict them, and more prisons to hold them.[102]

In favoring tougher sanctions against drug users, Bennett's recommended strategies essentially continued the policies implemented by the Reagan administration. They were, in fact, not unlike those advanced by Anslinger when he testified at the Marihuana Tax Act hearings in 1937 or when he endorsed the draconian Boggs law and the Narcotic Control Act that Congress enthusiastically passed in the 1950s. In the fifty years after Anslinger's unsuccessful crusade to outlaw marijuana, federal antidrug legislation had come full circle. The cycle that began in the 1930s, with a punitive approach that regarded drug addiction as a crime and not a disease, continued through the 1960s, gave way to more benevolent policies in the 1970s, including treatment and decriminalization, and got tougher in the 1980s as politicians responded to public anxieties and disdain over drugs and the perceived epidemic.

The similarities between Commissioner Anslinger and Director Bennett were remarkable. Both mandated stricter law enforcement as the cornerstone of any antidrug strategy, both eschewed treatment and education, both were intolerant of illegal drug use, and both were convinced that the solution to the drug problem was to build more prisons to hold offenders serving longer sentences. It is disconcerting that so long after Anslinger's reign of repressive, inflexible, and irrational drug policies that failed to arrest the drug problem, Bennett would apply essentially the same approach. Anslinger, were he alive, no doubt would share Bennett's views about fighting drugs and delight in his strategy for transforming the drug scene in America. Neither czar seemed to realize, however, that getting tough does not work. Since mandatory sentences, life imprisonment without parole, and the death penalty failed to eliminate drug use in the 1950s, it did not make sense that the same penalties would be more effective in the 1980s.

In September 1990, one year after President Bush declared a continuation of the Reagan war on drugs and eighteen months after Bennett took over as federal drug czar, no general consensus existed to support the administration's claims that the cocaine epidemic was peaking. Even Bennett conceded there had been little improvement in many major cities. Cocaine and heroin were widely available in Philadelphia, for example, where drug-related murders were projected to reach a record high. The situation was so desperate that the city's prisons were 41 percent over capacity, and nonviolent inmates were released before the end of their sentences to alleviate overcrowding.[103]

After twenty months as the Bush administration's general in the drug war, Bennett resigned.[104] In his final report he emphasized law enforcement rather than treatment or education and reiterated, in Anslinger style, his call for more prisons. Also consistent with Anslinger, Bennett praised several states for their antidrug efforts and was critical of New York and California for not doing enough, claiming that their "sentences were notoriously weak."[105] The Bennett approach to the war on drugs differed little from the Reagan approach, which was in some ways the same as the Nixon approach and owed much to the Anslinger approach. The last fifty years of federal drug policy saw the wheel reinvented several times.

Final Thoughts

The philosopher George Santayana once observed that those who do not remember the past are condemned to repeat it. Politicians and bureaucrats concerned with drug control have proven this exhortation by ignoring lessons from the past. Rather than considering alternative and innovative strategies or placing greater emphasis on treatment and education, they continue to politicize and exploit the drug issue, thus preventing any real progress in the ongoing drug war.

In the 1980s the federal government increased funds for the current war on drugs by nearly 200 percent. In that time the government expenditures exceeded $20 billion in an effort to stop drug abuse.[106] Numerous law enforcement agencies, at the state and federal levels, received substantial increases in their budgets to fight drugs. Virtually every congressional committee deals with drug-related legislation. Yet the drug scourge has scarcely abated. Despite the almost incomprehensible sums of money expended, the involvement of various agencies and committees, and the appointment of a drug czar to coordinate federal policy, drug abuse is as prevalent in 1990 as it has been at anytime since the war on drugs began in 1914. Illegal drugs are still consumed by members of every occupation, every educational level, and every economic strata.

Unfortunately, government policies in this latter-day (almost) Hundred Years' War have failed to produce measurable results in combating illicit trafficking, much less achieve the utopian goal of a drug-free society. The tragedy is that, despite numerous attempts during this century to stem the flow of drugs, politicians have demonstrated an incredible inability and/or unwillingness to learn from the past. With a seeming disregard for history, they have continued to commit the same errors as their predecessors. After reviewing the dark past of federal drug legislation, it is possible to draw several conclusions.

First, while policymakers may have been well intentioned, they have betrayed a lack of knowledge and an inadequate understanding of drugs and drug use in enacting legislation. Not only have drug laws been ill-conceived, but politicians and the public have demonstrated little concern about the consequences of such policies. A repressive approach stressing mandatory sentences, lengthy prison terms, or the death penalty will no doubt attract support from a frustrated and exasperated public that wants the government to do something. The immediate ramification of repressive policies—excluding the death penalty—is that our prison system rapidly has become hopelessly overcrowded.[107] Imprisonment under such conditions is hardly conducive to rehabilitative efforts. It is not realistic to presume that a period of incarceration will reduce drug offenders' rate of recidivism. Noting the problem of prison overcrowding, Anthony Travisono, the executive director of the American Correctional Association, pessimistically concluded: "We have spent $20 billion on correctional building since 1978 and the crime rate hasn't been affected."[108]

Second, the drug war always has been—and currently is—as much a political and ideological issue as it is an effort to eradicate a social menace. Since the enactment of the Harrison Act, drugs have been propagandized to mesh with racism, xenophobia, and anticommunism. They have been exploited for the benefit of individual politicians and bureaucrats. They have been used as a cover to organize a private White House intelligence agency. They have frequently influenced foreign policy, most recently in U.S. support of Panamanian dictator Manuel Noriega. Until drugs are depoliticized, there is little hope for an end to the drug scourge.[109]

Third, tough law enforcement is not effective. Both the Boggs Act and the Narcotic Control Act proved that getting tough is not enough. It defies logic to assume that if long, mandatory sentences did not work in the 1950s they should be effective in the 1990s, when more Americans are using illegal drugs and generating fantastic profits for traffickers. The risk of a lengthy prison sentence is offset by the possibility of amassing huge sums of money.[110] Drug dealers know that crime does pay.

Fourth, we have made no real progress in the war on drugs in the past seventy-five years. Federal policies have contributed more to developing a prosperous criminal class than they have to lowering addiction rates. Antidrug campaigns largely reflect a presidential administration's desire to placate constituents by declaring war against drugs rather than to formulate specific and realistic policies that are more people- or user-oriented. More recently, Congress and the Reagan and Bush administrations have been too willing to embrace simple solutions inappropriate for a complex problem, preferring to heed the old adage, "If the cure doesn't work, give more of the same medicine."[111]

No presidents have spoken out more against drugs than Reagan and Bush. Between them they participated in an unprecedented number of international drug actions—including a $2 billion commitment to Colombia, Bolivia, and Peru over a four-year period—and signed three major pieces of antidrug legislation.[112] No presidents have spent more money, talked tougher, or enjoyed more popular support for their antidrug policies than Reagan or Bush.

Despite the treaties, the money, and the rhetoric, recent polls indicate that drugs remain the nation's most serious domestic problem. Though the number of casual consumers of cocaine and marijuana decreased in 1990, there was little reason for optimism, contrary to Bush's assessment that "we're on the road to victory." In the first half of 1990, the nation's violent crime rate increased by 10 percent, armed robbery by 9 percent, and murders by 8 percent. The nation's capital, Washington, D.C., experienced a third straight year of record-breaking homicides, 483, and had the highest murder rate in the country. Philadelphia, New York, Boston, and Dallas were among the major cities that also had all-time high murder rates. According to FBI estimates, 40 percent—down from 60 percent—of these tragedies were drug-related.[113]

It is difficult to determine how much progress has been realized in the current phase of the war on drugs. The Bush administration's National Institute on Drug Abuse (NIDA) estimated the number of once-a-week cocaine users at 662,000, allowing the President to claim that "Americans have taken a 'startling turn' away from drugs." The Senate Judiciary Committee released a study in December, however, that sharply refuted NIDA's figures. According to the Senate report, the number of cocaine users was considerably larger and had actually increased from 2.2 million to 2.4 million. In response to President Bush's assertion that "our hard work is paying off," Tom Deloe of the Pennsylvania Office of Drug and Alcohol Programs questioned the government's optimism, noting that cocaine admissions into drug programs in his state had doubled from 1985 through 1990.[114]

If they are serious about curbing drug abuse, politicians need to realize that the only way to achieve any success is to reduce demand and come to grips with certain realities.[115] Punitive measures do not work. Crop eradication and interdiction are little more than superficial attempts that do not get to the heart of the problem. If the United States is going to win its long war on drugs, it will have to achieve victory at home, not in some South American coca field.

We must, through rehabilitation and, in particular, comprehensive educational programs, convince users and potential users that using drugs—including alcohol and tobacco—is a health risk and socially unacceptable. Any policy intended to reduce drug abuse must effect a change in attitude. Education does work. Fewer young people now smoke cigarettes because of intensive educational efforts to eliminate smoking.[116] The disadvantage of stressing education from a political vantage point is that the results are not immediate. Education must be viewed as a long-term investment requiring several years, perhaps a generation or more, before it will produce results. Unfortunately, most federal legislators, who are elected every two years, have been too myopic, feeling compelled to promise quick-fix solutions.

In a December 1990 issue of *Time* magazine, the cover story about the drug war had the subtitle: "Why We're Losing."[117] Santayana was right. The war continues.

The Pennsylvania State University—DuBois Campus

Acknowledgments

The author wishes to thank William O. Walker III and Polly D. K. McWilliams for their constructive criticisms of the manuscript, and Mary-Ann Himes, a tireless research assistant. This project was funded in part by the DuBois Educational Foundation and a Penn State University Research Development Grant.

Notes

1. The term "drugs" includes not only the illicit drugs marijuana, cocaine, and heroin but also alcohol and tobacco, legal drugs that are even more abused and are responsible for forty times the number of cocaine and heroin deaths combined. Political cartoonist Tony Auth illustrated how alcohol causes approximately 90,000 deaths per year; tobacco 390,000, cocaine 8,000, and heroin 6,000. There are few reports of marijuana-related fatalities. About 57 tobacco-related deaths occur every 79 minutes each year, more than the number of American lives lost during World War II. Auth cartoon, 4 May 1990; Marsha Rosenbaum, "Just Say What? An Alternative View on Solving America's Drug Problem," National Council on Crime and Delinquency, June 1990, 5–6; Matthew Purdy, "The Other Drug-Use Problem," *Philadelphia Inquirer,* 17 December 1989; and Barbara Ehrenreich, "Drug Frenzy," *Ms.*, November 1988, 20.

Not only do alcohol and tobacco cause more deaths than cocaine, heroin, or marijuana, they are also the most highly addictive. In a survey ranking addiction on a scale of 1 to 100, with the latter being the most addictive, a panel of medical experts rated nicotine at 100 and alcohol at 80. Heroin was rated at 79, cocaine 70, and marijuana 20. Deborah Franklin, "Hooked: Why Isn't Everyone an Addict?" *In Health,* November–December 1990, 39–52.

2. Jeffrey A. Eisenach, "How to Win the War on Drugs: Forget the User," *USA Today,* January 1989, 46–48; and John S. Lang, "America on Drugs," *U.S. News & World Report,* 28 July 1986, 48.

3. Thomas Reese, "Drugs and Crime," *America,* 11 June 1983, 458; and James Mills interview, *U.S. News & World Report,* 25 August 1986, 19. For statistics on drug-related crimes, see "Profile of State Prison Inmates, 1986"; and "Drug Law Violators, 1980–86," in *Bureau of Justice Statistics Special Report* (Washington, D.C., 1988); and Ethan Nadelmann, "U.S. Drug Policy: A Bad Export," *Foreign Policy,* no. 70 (Spring 1988): 99.

4. Mark Fazlollah, "2 Latin Nations Stymie Drug War," *Philadelphia Inquirer,* 19 December 1990; Editorial, *Philadelphia Inquirer,* 28 December 1990; and Edmundo Morales, *Cocaine: White Gold Rush* (Tucson, 1989).

5. Joseph Contreras, "Anarchy in Colombia," *Time,* 11 September 1989, 30–32.

6. William F. Buckley, "Enlisting Military to Fight Drugs," syndicated column, 19 May 1988.

7. Even in North Dakota, border patrol agents have reported the increased smuggling of illegal drugs arms and European immigrants who pay from $1,500 to $5,000 to get into the United States by way of Montreal and Winnipeg, Canada. John McCormick, "We Can't Catch What's Coming," *Newsweek,* 20 August 1990, 45.

8. Cited in Morris J. Blachman and Kenneth E. Sharpe, "The War on Drugs: American Democracy Under Assault," *World Policy Journal* 7 (Spring 1990): 138.

9. Ibid.

10. "Bennett to 'Shake Things Up' If Confirmed," *Centre Daily Times,* State College, Pa., 2 March 1989; and Merrill Hartson, "Bush Starts Anti-Drug Drive," Associated Press, *Centre Daily Times,* 3 March 1989.

11. *National Drug Control Strategy,* September 1989 (Washington, D.C., 1989), 9. See Omnibus Drug Initiative Act of 1988, H.R. 5210, 21 October 1988, *Congressional Record,* 100th Cong., 2d sess., 134:11108–271.

12. Edward M. Brecher, *Licit and Illicit Drugs* (Boston, 1972), 3, 403; and David F. Musto, *The American Disease: Origins of Narcotic Control* (New York, 1973), 1–8. For a more comprehensive account of drug use in the nineteenth century, see H. Wayne Morgan, *Drugs in America: A Social History, 1800–1980* (Syracuse, 1981), 1–87.

13. Brecher, *Licit and Illicit Drugs,* 3. Probably the most abused drug in nineteenth-century America was not an opiate like morphine or cocaine but alcohol. See, for example,

William J. Rorabaugh, *The Alcoholic Republic: An American Tradition* (New York, 1979); and Ian R. Tyrell, *Sobering Up: From Temperance to Prohibition in Antebellum America, 1800–1860* (Westport, Conn., 1979).

14. James A. Inciardi, *The War on Drugs: Heroin Cocaine, Crime, and Public Policy* (Palo Alto, Calif., 1986), 6. Additional needles could be purchased for 25¢ each or $2.75 for a dozen.

15. Brecher, *Licit and Illicit Drugs,* 270; Inciardi, *The War on Drugs,* 7–8; and Musto, *The American Disease,* 3.

16. Morgan, *Drugs in America,* 88–93; and Inciardi, *The War on Drugs,* 16.

17. Morgan, *Drugs in America,* 106; David T. Courtwright, *Dark Paradise: Opiate Addiction in America Before 1940* (Cambridge, Mass., 1982), 103–4; and David F. Musto, "The History of Legislative Control Over Opium, Cocaine, and Their Derivatives," in Ronald Hamowy, ed., *Dealing With Drugs: Consequences of Government Control* (San Francisco, 1987), 54.

18. Daniel Kagan, "How America Lost Its First Drug War," *Insight,* 20 November 1989, 13; Courtwright, *Dark Paradise,* 103–4; and Musto, *The American Disease,* 54–56.

19. Musto, "American Legislative Control," 55.

20. Rufus King, " 'The American System': Legal Sanctions to Repress Drug Abuse," 21–22, in James A. Inciardi, *Drugs and the Criminal Justice System* (Beverly Hills, 1974); and Morgan, *Drugs in America,* 109.

21. "Message from the President of the United States," *Congressional Record,* 13 January 1914, 63d Cong., 2d sess., 50:1559. Unfortunately, because he antagonized Secretary of State William Jennings Bryan, Dr. Wright's influence began to wane. It was an incredible irony that Wright was dismissed from the State Department when, at Bryan's insistence, Wright refused to take a pledge of abstinence when the secretary smelled liquor on his breath during the Third Hague Conference. Musto, *The American Disease,* 61.

22. Morgan, *Drugs in America,* 108; and Ernest Abel, *Marihuana: The First Twelve Thousand Years* (New York, 1980), 196.

23. Officially, the Harrison Act was "to provide for the registration of, with collectors of internal revenue, and to impose a special tax upon all persons who produce, import, manufacture, compound, deal in, dispense, sell, distribute, or give away opium or coca leaves, their salts, derivatives, or preparations, and for other purposes." Brecher, *Licit and Illicit Drugs,* 49; and Representative Francis B. Harrison introducing H.R. 6282, 23 June 1913, *Congressional Record,* 63d Cong., 1st sess., 50:2143–44. Abel also points out that the Harrison Act was not intended to eradicate narcotics but was "merely a save-face piece of legislation . . . passed to honor American pledges given at The Hague convention," and that "it was never meant to stand in the way of any addict who wanted to continue using drugs." *Marihuana: The First Twelve Thousand Years* (New York, 1980), 196–99.

24. Courtwright, *Dark Paradise,* 106; King, *The Drug Hang-Up,* Brecher, *Licit and Illicit Drugs,* 49–55; Inciardi, *War on Drugs,* 21; and King, "The Narcotics Bureau and the Harrison Act: Jailing the Healers and the Sick," *Yale Law Journal* 62 (April 1953): 736–49.

25. In the first case involving a Harrison violation, *United States v. Jin Fuey Moy,* 241 U.S. 394 (1916), the Supreme Court wrote in a 7–2 decision that the defendant, who prescribed morphine for an addict, could not be criminally prosecuted under a revenue act. In three subsequent cases, *United States v. Doremus,* 249 U.S. 86 (1919), *Webb v. United States,* 249 U.S. 96 (1919), and *United States v. Behrman,* 258 U.S. 280 (1920), the Court reversed the *Jin Fuey Moy* ruling and permitted stricter enforcement. See Morgan, *Drugs in America,* 110–11; Courtwright, *Dark Paradise,* 106–7; Musto, *The American Disease,* 121–35; and King, "The Narcotics Bureau and the Harrison Act," 113–31.

For a physician's firsthand recollections of the impact the Harrison Act had on ambulatory treatment and maintenance programs, see an interview with Dr. Willis Butler of Shreveport, Louisiana, who operated an addiction treatment from 1919 until he was forced to close in 1925, in David Courtwright, Herman Joseph, and Don Des Jarlais, *Addicts Who*

Survived: An Oral History of Narcotic Use in America, 1923–1965 (Knoxville, Tenn., 1989), 279–89.

26. Both the Treasury Department report and Courtwright's assessment of the addict population are discussed in Kagan's "How America Lost Its First Drug War," 14.

27. This legislation is also known as the Jones-Miller Act. See James A. Inciardi, *The War on Drugs,* 17. The Jones-Miller Act also established the Federal Narcotics Board, composed of the Secretaries of State, Treasury, and Commerce. Musto, *The American Disease,* 197.

28. Cited in Brecher, *Licit and Illicit Drugs,* 50.

29. Editorial, *St. Louis Post-Dispatch,* 17 December 1934, in the Harry J. Anslinger Papers, Box 5, Scrapbook 4-B, 1934–39. The Anslinger collection is held by the Labor Archives and Historical Collections Department of Pattee Library at The Pennsylvania State University, University Park. Hereafter referred to as HJAP.

30. Musto, *The American Disease,* 183–84.

31. Musto, *The American Disease,* 189; U.S. Congress, House, *Establishment of Two Federal Narcotics Farms, Hearings before the Committee on the Judiciary on H.R. 12781,* 70th Cong., 1st sess, 26–28 April 1928, 12; King, "The Narcotics Bureau and the Harrison Act," 736; and John C. McWilliams, *The Protectors: Harry J. Anslinger and the Federal Bureau of Narcotics* (Newark, Del., 1990), 35.

32. Cited in Musto, *The American Disease,* 195–96.

33. A Grand Jury investigation revealed that Nutt's son-in-law was doing some accounting work for Arnold Rothstein, a powerful gangster who was involved in narcotics, prostitution, and bootlegging in the 1920s. Musto, *The American Disease,* 208–9; McWilliams, *The Protectors,* 39–42; and Richard J. Bonnie and Charles H. Whitebread II, *The Marihuana Conviction: A History of Marihuana Prohibition in the United States* (Charlottesville, Va., 1974), 66.

34. McWilliams, *The Protectors,* 28–33.

35. Morgan, *Drugs in America,* 119–22.

36. Several scholars and journalists have evaluated Anslinger's role as Commissioner of the Federal Bureau of Narcotics. See Morgan, *Drugs in America,* 118–48; Musto, *The American Disease,* 206–28; King, *The Drug Hang-up,* 78–228; Bonnie and Whitebread, *The Marihuana Conviction,* 53–221; and Larry Sloman, *Reefer Madness: Marijuana in America* (New York, 1979).

37. McWilliams, *The Protectors,* 87–88.

38. A. E. Fossier, "The Marihuana Menace," *New Orleans Medical and Surgical Journal* 84 (May 1931): 247–52; and Eugene Stanley, "Marihuana as a Developer of Criminals," *American Journal of Police Science* 2 (May–June 1931): 256. The government's response to the marijuana situation in the early 1930s is discussed in Bonnie and Whitebread, *The Marihuana Conviction,* 55–77; Himmelstein, *The Strange Career of Marihuana,* 49–71; Morgan, *Drugs in America,* 118–32. For the connection between Mexicans and marijuana, see John Helmer, *Drugs and Minority Oppression* (New York, 1975), 54–79.

39. McWilliams, *The Protectors,* 49.

40. Himmelstein, *The Strange Career of Marihuana,* 54–57; Bonnie and Whitebread, *The Marihuana Conviction,* 79–91.

41. U.S. Congress, House, Committee on Appropriations, *Treasury Department Appropriations Bill for 1938. Hearings before a subcommittee of the House Committee on Appropriations,* 75th Cong., 1st sess., 19 December 1936, 184.

42. Harry J. Anslinger and Courtney Riley Cooper, "Marihuana: Assassin of Youth," *American Magazine,* July 1937, 18–19, 150–53.

43. Wooster Taylor, "Economy Cut Ties Hands of 'Dope' Agents," *Washington Herald,* 7 November 1933, Box 1, File, "Articles on Narcotics 1930–1937," HJAP.

44. Representative Robert L. Doughton introducing H.R. 6385, 14 April 1937, *Congressional Record,* 75th Cong., 1st sess., 81:6.

45. U.S. Congress, House, Committee on Ways and Means, *Taxation of Marihuana, Hearings,* on H.R. 6385, 75th Cong., 1st sess., 27–30 April and 4 May 1937, 20.

46. For the floor discussion in the House of Representatives on the Marihuana Tax Act, see Occupational Excise Tax on Marihuana, H.R. 6906, 10 June 1937, *Congressional Record,* 75th Cong., 1st sess., 81:5575.

47. William O. Walker III, *Drug Control in the Americas* (Albuquerque, 1981), 106; Sloman, *Reefer Madness,* 75–79; and Bonnie and Whitebread, *The Marihuana Conviction,* 164–72.

48. Sloman, *Reefer Madness,* 61–63. Anslinger's gore stories are in Box 9, File, "Marihuana and Crime (1930–1937)," HJAP.

49. Licata suffered from dementia praecox for at least a year prior to murdering his family. Institutionalized at the Florida State Mental Hospital, he hanged himself on 4 December 1950. See John Kaplan, *Marijuana: The New Prohibition* (New York, 1970), 94–97.

50. "Federal Control," 21, statement, Box 3, File 9, HJAP.

51. "Marihuana: New Federal Tax Hits Dealings in Potent Weed," *Newsweek,* 14 August 1937, 22–23; and "Signs Bill to Curb Marijuana," *New York Times,* 3 August 1937. For an interpretative study of the marihuana legislation, see John F. Galliher and Allyn Walker, "The Puzzle of the Social Origins of the Marihuana Act of 1937," *Journal of Social Problems* 24 (February 1977): 367–76.

52. There was at least one notable exception. Congressman John M. Coffee (D-WA) was highly critical of enforcement of the Harrison Act and of the Federal Bureau of Narcotics, calling it "the costliest bureau or government department in the world." In April 1938 Coffee introduced an unsuccessful House Joint Resolution 642 to investigate the FBN. McWilliams, *The Protectors,* 92–95; and King, *The Drug Hang-up,* 59–68.

53. Musto, *The American Disease,* 231. In the 1950s Anslinger was nearly as fervent an anticommunist as his counterpart, FBI Director J. Edgar Hoover. The commissioner made repeated charges privately and publicly that the Communists were planning to invade the United States with a "Fifth Column" of heroin addiction. See "Soviet Retorts on Heroin," 3 May 1952, and "Anslinger Replies to Zakusov Charges," 6 May 1952, both in the *New York Times;* Anslinger's testimony in U.S. Congress, Senate, Committee on the Judiciary, *Communist China and Illicit Narcotic Traffic, Hearings,* before the Subcommittee to Investigate the Administration of the Internal Security Act and Other Internal Security Laws, 84th Cong., 1st sess., 8 March–13 May 1955, 14–17; and Letter from H. J. Anslinger to William T. McCarthy, 6 December 1956, Box 3, File "Correspondence William T. McCarthy, 1937–1963," HJAP.

Anslinger was also the only federal law enforcement official at the time who supported the theory of a Mafia. During the Kefauver Committee hearings in 1950–51, several FBN agents throughout the country testified about Mafia organization and activities. Two FBN senior agents, Charles Siragusa and George H. White, were committee investigators. See Estes Kefauver, *Crime in America* (Garden City, N.Y., 1951), 1–34; and McWilliams, *The Protectors,* 140–41.

54. Bonnie and Whitebread, *The Marihuana Conviction,* 209.

55. Sloman, *Reefer Madness,* 187–88; and the *Congressional Record,* 1951–56.

56. For studies of Anslinger mixing drug enforcement with communism, the Mafia, and foreign policy in general, see Douglas Clark Kinder, "Bureaucratic Cold Warrior: Harry J. Anslinger and Illicit Narcotics Traffic," *Pacific Historical Review* 50 (May 1981): 169–91; Kinder and William O. Walker III, "Stable Force in a Storm: Harry J. Anslinger and the United States Narcotic Foreign Policy, 1930–1962," *Journal of American History* 72 (March 1986): 908–27; Jonathan Marshall, "Drugs and United States Foreign Policy," 137–79, in Hamowy, *Dealing With Drugs;* William Howard Moore, *The Kefauver Committee and the Politics of Crime* (Columbia, Mo., 1974); and Alan A. Block and John C. McWilliams, "On the Origins of Counterintelligence: Building a Clandestine Network," *Journal of Policy*

History 1, no. 4 (1989): 353–72; and Stephen Fox, *Blood and Power: Organized Crime in Twentieth-Century America* (New York, 1989), 139–46.

57. Congressman Hale Boggs introducing H.R. 3490, 3 April 1951, *Congressional Record,* 82d Cong., 1st sess., 97:3306.

58. Bonnie and Whitebread, *The Marihuana Conviction,* 210.

59. Ibid., 210–11.

60. Ibid., 217.

61. U.S. Congress, Senate, Committee on the Judiciary, *Illicit Narcotics Traffic, Hearings,* before the Subcommittee on Improvements in the Federal Criminal Code of the Committee of the Judiciary, on S. Res. 67, 84th Cong., 1st sess., Part I, 2 June–15 December 1955, 18.

62. Bonnie and Whitebread, *The Marihuana Conviction,* 217–19; and King, *The Drug Hang-up,* 142–50.

63. For a discussion of how drug policy relates to drug users and culture, see Joseph R. Gusfield, "The (F)Utility of Knowledge?: The Relation of Social Science to Public Policy toward Drugs," *American Academy of Political and Social Science* 417 (January 1975): 1–15.

64. Musto, *The American Disease,* 254. The number of arrests for marijuana possession increased from 18,000 in 1965 to 188,000 in 1970. LSD, or d-lysergic acid diethylamide, was accidentally discovered in April 1943 by Dr. Albert Hofmann in Basel, Switzerland. John Marks, *The CIA and Mind Control: The Search for the "Manchurian Candidate"* (New York, 1980), 3–5. For a more comprehensive account of the discovery and experimentation of LSD, see Brecher, *Licit and Illicit Drugs,* 346–93.

65. Edward Jay Epstein, "The Incredible War Against the Poppies," *Esquire,* December 1974, 148.

66. In 1968 the Federal Bureau of Narcotics was reorganized as the Bureau of Narcotics and Other Dangerous Drugs and transferred from the Treasury Department to the Department of Justice.

67. "The No-Knock Drug Bill," *Time,* 9 February 1970, 11; "Moving Forward: Drug Abuse Bill," *U.S. News & World Report,* 9 February 1970, 4; "Narcotics: New Look," *Newsweek,* 9 February 1970, 24; and William F. Buckley, Jr., "No Knock?" *National Review,* 24 February 1970, 220. Though the bill contained tough enforcement measures, it also reduced the penalty for marijuana possession from a felony to a misdemeanor.

68. Inverview with John E. Ingersoll, *U.S. News & World Report,* 25 May 1970, 38; and Edward Jay Epstein, *Agency of Fear: Opiates and Political Power in America* (New York, 1977), 165–72.

69. King, *The Drug Hang-up,* 331.

70. Musto, *The American Disease,* 255–56.

71. "Drive to Curb Hard Drugs Gets A No. 1 Priority," *U.S. News & World Report,* 3 April 1972, 36; Epstein, "The Incredible War Against the Poppies," 148; Nelson Gross, "The Collective International Effort Against Drug Abuse, *Department of State Bulletin,* 9 October 1972, 407–8; King, *The Drug Hang-up,* 338–39; and Musto, *The American Disease,* 256–57. The best account of drug production and exportation in the Golden Triangle is Alfred W. McCoy, *The Politics of Heroin: CIA Complicity in the Global Drug Trade* (Brooklyn, NY, 1991)

72. Epstein, *Agency of Fear,* 173. The Special Action Office for Drug Abuse Prevention, created by Executive Order on 17 June 1971, consolidated thirteen government agencies and was to operate only for a period of three years, to be extended for two years at presidential discretion. "President Calls for Comprehensive Drug Control Program," *Department of State Bulletin,* 12 July 1971, 59–60; "Drive to Curb Hard Drugs Gets A No. 1 Priority," *U.S. News & World Report,* 3 April 1972, 36; and Myles Ambrose, "The War Against Drugs: Can It Be Won?" *Vital Speeches of the Day,* 1 October 1972, 738–40.

73. Henrik Kruger, *The Great Heroin Coup: Drugs, Intelligence, and International Fascism* (Boston, 1980), 159, 171.

74. Ibid., 159–60; and McCoy, *The Politics of Heroin* 249–51. Colorful and outspoken,

Lucien Conein began his career in intelligence with the Office of Strategic Services during World War II and continued with the Central Intelligence Agency until he retired in 1968. Most of that time he was stationed in Indochina, where he worked closely with General Edward Lansdale and was acquainted with all the Vietnamese generals. In the early 1970s Conein was doing intelligence work for the BNDD and its successor agency, the Drug Enforcement Administration, when E. Howard Hunt brought him into the White House. Although it is difficult to know exactly what Conein's role was in the Nixon war on drugs, some of his activities required the approval of Henry Kissinger's 40 Committee. Author's interview with Lucien Conein, 10 May 1990; George Crile, "The Colonel's Secret Drug War," *Washington Post,* 13 June 1976; and Taylor Branch, "Raising a Glass to 'Beau Geste,' " *Esquire,* August 1976, 30–34.

75. Epstein, *Agency of Fear,* 18–20, 208–15; Kruger, *The Great Heroin Coup,* 162–63.

76. Kruger, *The Great Heroin Coup,* 161; and Epstein, *Agency of Fear,* 218–19.

77. Epstein, *Agency of Fear,* 143–44.

78. Reorganization Plan Number Two dismantled the five-year-old BNDD in 1973 and restructured it as the Drug Enforcement Administration as it still exists in 1990. Ibid., 230.

79. The DEA's Special Operations Group also had connections with Mitch WerBell, a soldier of fortune and specialist in assassinations. WerBell was an old war buddy of Hunt and Conein from OSS days. Two of WerBell's associates included Frank Sturgis, one of the Watergate Plumbers, and Robert Vesco, financier and drug trafficker. Interview with Lucien Conein, Kruger, *The Great Heroin Coup,* 164; Crile, "The Colonel's Secret Drug War." For a more detailed account of Conein's intricate DEA/SOG plot, see Jim Hougan, *Spooks: The Haunting of America—The Private Use of Secret Agents* (New York, 1978), 138–51.

80. Peter Dale Scott, cited in Kruger, *The Great Heroin Coup,* 163.

81. Cited in Musto, *The American Disease,* 263–64.

82. Musto, *The American Disease,* 266.

83. Anslinger died in November 1975, in Hollidaysburg, Pennsylvania.

84. "Can Crack Addicts Be Treated? Yes, but . . . ," *Philadelphia Inquirer,* 19 November 1989; and Herbert K. Kleber, "No Quick Fixes for Drug Addicts," *New York Times,* 26 January 1990.

85. Antidrug legislation was included in the Comprehensive Control Act of 1984.

86. Brian Duffy, "Drugs Now Prime Time," *U.S. News & World Report,* 11 August 1986, 16.

87. "Omnibus Drug Legislation," *Congressional Digest,* November 1986, 259, 263, 288. The Senate passed its version of the Omnibus Drug bill, 97–92, but removed the death-penalty provision, preferring a mandatory life sentence without parole for drug-related murder cases.

88. Linda Greenhouse, "Compromise Plan for Anti-Drug Bill," 17 October 1986; Greenhouse, "Congress Approves Anti-Drug Bill as Senate Bars a Death Provision, 18 October 1986; Joel Brinkley, "Anti-Drug Law: Words, Deeds, Political Expediency, 27 October 1986; and Gerald M. Boyd, "Reagan Signs Anti-Drug Measure: Hopes for 'Drug-Free Generation,' " 28 October 1986, all in *New York Times.*

89. Tom Morgenthau, "Drug Fever in Washington," *Newsweek,* 22 September 1986, 39. "High on Hot Air," 6 October 1986, 7; "Lining Up to Join the War Against Drugs," 22 September 1986, 6; and Brian Duffy, "War on Drugs: More Than a 'Short-term High,' " 29 September 1986, 28–29, all in *U.S. News & World Report.*

90. Greenhouse, "Congress Approves Anti-Drug Bill as Senate Bars a Death Provision."

91. Greenhouse, "Compromise Plan for Anti-Drug Bill"; and Brinkley, "Anti-Drug Law."

92. Paul Ruffin, "Critics Say No to Reagan's Policy," *Black Enterprise,* August 1988, 29; and Charles Mohr, "Drug Bill Passes, Finishing Business of 100th Congress," *New York Times,* 23 October 1988. For a complete account of the House and Senate votes and the major provisions, see "In Its Last Act, Congress Clears Anti-Drug Bill," *Congressional Quarterly,* 29 October 1988, 3145–51.

93. Not only was there a lack of evidence to support a drug frenzy, but "reliable data

show[ed] some forms of drug use declining." Duffy, "War on Drugs," 28; and Peter Kerr, "Anatomy of the Drug Issue: How, After Years, It Erupted," *New York Times,* 17 November 1986.

94. Other drug-related bills introduced in 1988 included the War on Drug Smuggling Act, the Drug-Free America Act, the National Narcotic Leadership Act, the Serious Drug Offender Death Penalty Act, and the Anti-Toy Gun Threat Act, which would increase penalties for using a toy gun in a drug-related crime. Republican Congressman Richard F. Schulze of Pennsylvania also sponsored the Bounty Hunter Act, which would offer incentives to anyone informing on a drug user. Another provision of the act was to call in all $100 bills in circulation since that was thought to be the denomination drug dealers used for making buys. See Viveca Novak, "The War on Drugs Gets Serious," *Common Cause,* July–August, 1988, 34.

95. John Hargan, "Ignorance in Action," *Scientific American,* November 1988, 17.

96. Anti-Drug or Anti-People?" *Time,* 19 September 1988, 20; Alan Fram, "Drug Bill Adds Death Penalties, *Centre Daily Times,* 11 June 1988; and "House OK's Tough Bill on Drugs," Associated Press, *Philadelphia Inquirer,* 26 September 1988.

97. "The Quack Epidemic," *New Republic,* 14 November 1988, 8.

98. Merrill Hartson, "Bush Starts Anti-Drug Drive," Associated Press, *Centre Daily Times,* 10 March 1989.

99. Although as drug czar, Bennett would receive a salary of $99,500 a year, the same as a cabinet member, President Bush never supported his position at that level. Bennett had the authority to temporarily reassign personnel from approximately thirty federal agencies, but he could not dictate agency budgets. Essentially, his most important function was to formulate a national drug strategy. Charles Mohr, "Experts Question Drug Bill's Impact," 30 October 1988, and Julie Johnson, "Reagan Signs Bill to Curb Drug Use," 19 November 1988, both in *New York Times.*

100. "Cowboy in the Capitol: Drug Czar Bill Bennett, *Rolling Stone,* 2 November 1989, 41–42. Bennett once commented to a reporter that "I don't have any objection to beheading drug dealers. Kingpins who sell to pregnant women, people who kill children—its morally deserved." He was not opposed to allowing the military to shoot down planes transporting drugs into the United States. See Jane Sims Podesta, "William Bennett," *People's Weekly,* 11 June 1990, 97; and "The Top Drug Warrior Talks Tough," *Fortune,* 12 March 1990, 74.

101. William J. Bennett, "Moralism, and Realism in the Drug War," *New Perspectives Quarterly* 6 (Summer 1989): 4–7.

102. R. A. Zaldivar, "Drug Czar Calls for Scare Tactics," *Philadelphia Inquirer,* 4 May 1989; Fred Barnes, "General Bennett, *The National Review,* 18, 25 September 1989, 14; and "Mr. Bennett's War," *New Republic,* 15 September 1989, 13.

103. Editorial, "5,300 and Counting," 4 September 1990; David Zucchino, "Bennett: No Gains in City's Drug War," 8 September 1990; and Zucchino, "Mixed Success Noted in Drug War," 9 September 1990, all in *Philadelphia Inquirer.* Philadelphia was not atypical. All of Pennsylvania's prisons and most state prisons throughout the country experienced serious overcrowding. The Rockview State Correctional Institution in Pennsylvania, for example, has a capacity of 1,250 inmates. On 28 November 1990 its population was nearly double that number, at 2,034. Editorial, *Centre Daily Times,* 28 November 1990.

104. Shortly after Bennett resigned, President Bush appointed former Republican Florida Governor Bob Martinez as the new drug czar. In November 1990, Martinez's unsuccessful campaign for reelection was headed by Jeb Bush, the President's son. Martinez, like Bennett, emphasized tough law enforcement. While governor, he vigorously supported a death-penalty law for drug kingpins and doubled the number of beds in Florida's state prisons. He has demonstrated relatively little concern for the treatment of drug addicts. "The Man for the Job," *Time,* 3 December 1990, 48; and Carolyn Skorneck, "Martinez Likely to Be Drug Czar," *Philadelphia Inquirer,* 19 November 1990.

105. Shrona Freeman, "Retiring Drug Czar Bennett Calls for Tougher State Laws," *Philadelphia Inquirer,* 10 November 1990; "The Czar's Resignation," editorial, *Washington Post,* 12 November 1990; and "Remember the Drug War?" editorial, *Philadelphia Inquirer,* 14 November 1990.

106. Eisenach, "How to Win the War on Drugs," 46.

107. Such hard-line policies can actually make a mockery of the criminal justice system when cities like Philadelphia, for example, are periodically compelled by a court order to alleviate overcrowding by releasing nonviolent offenders before they complete their sentences. For a broader discussion of drug politics and policy, see Peter Andreas and Coletta Youngers, "U.S. Drug Policy and the Andean Cocaine Industry, *World Policy Journal* 6 (Summer 1989): 529–62.

108. Matthew Purdy, "No Place to Hold Drug War's Prisoners," *Philadelphia Inquirer,* 9 October 1989.

109. On the connection between Noriega, drug traffickers, and American intelligence agencies, see Jonathan Marshall, "The White House Death Squad," *Inquiry,* 5 March 1979, 15–21; Guy Gugliotta and Jeff Leen, *Kings of Cocaine: Inside the Medellín Cartel—An Astonishing True Story of Murder, Money, and International Corruption* (New York, 1989), 171–77; and John Dinges, *Our Man in Panama: How General Noriega Used the U.S.—and Made Millions in Drugs and Arms* (New York, 1990).

110. For an evaluation of the tough-sentences approach, see Gerry Fitzgerald, "Dispatches from the Drug War," *Common Cause,* January–February 1990, 13–19.

111. Alexander Cockburn, "The War on Drugs," *The Nation,* 27 October 1984, 406–7; "The Crackdown," editorial, *The Nation,* 30 August 1986, 131–32; "The Lost Drug War," editorial, *National Review,* 27 May 1988, 18–19; Eliot Marshall, "Flying Blind in the War on Drugs," *News & Comment,* 17 June 1988, 1605–7; Jefferson Morley, "The Great American High: Contradictions of Cocaine Capitalism," *The Nation,* 2 October 1989, 341–47; and Arnold Trebach, *The Great Drug War: And Radical Proposals That Could Make America Safe Again* (New York, 1987).

112. "Bush Takes 'Drug War' Too Literally," Editorial, *Centre Daily Times,* 12 January 1990.

113. Elaine Shannon, "A Losing Battle," *Time,* 3 December 1990, 44–48; and Matthew Purdy, "In '91 Washington Again U.S.'s Drug-Murder Capital," *Centre Daily Times,* 2 January 1991.

114. David S. Martin, "U.S. Drug Report Draws Criticism," *Harrisburg News-Patriot,* 20 December 1990; and Charles Green, "U.S. Reports Sharp Drop in Casual Drug Use," *Philadelphia Inquirer,* 20 December 1990. The reason for such a discrepancy between the NIDA 1990 Household Survey numbers and the Senate Judiciary Committee figures is that the NIDA only surveyed people living at home and did not include those in rehabilitation centers, treatment programs, prisons, or who live on the streets. The survey also assumed that respondents were honest in admitting or denying they use cocaine.

President Bush's "wonderful and welcome news" about the National Household Survey was not shared by personnel at the Philadelphia Diagnostic and Rehabilitation Center, where Irving Shander, the center's president, stated: "We still have a waiting list. We still have beds filled. We still have indications of a crisis." Matthew Purdy, "Cocaine Still is a Crisis Experts Say," *Philadelphia Inquirer,* 30 December 1990.

115. Like some who claimed that the government was not really interested in winning in Vietnam, there are critics who argue that the government is not sufficiently committed to winning a war against drugs. Former DEA agent Michael Levine, who spent twenty-five years working undercover, has commented that "[his] career was meaningless and had had absolutely no effect whatsoever in the so-called war on drugs. The war itself is a fraud." Michael Levine, *Deep Cover: The Inside Story of How DEA Infighting, Incompetence, and Subterfuge Lost Us the Biggest Battle of the Drug War* (New York, 1990), 9–10.

Other observers, though, not questioning the government's level of commitment, do dispute President Bush's and Drug Czar Bennett's assertions that the government has been effective in interdiction and law enforcement, and warn against the politicization of drugs. Editorial, *Harrisburg News-Patriot,* 9 November 1990.

116. The number of female high school students who smoked cigarettes daily dropped from 26 percent in 1975 to 19 percent in the period 1987–89; the number of male students who smoked dropped from 27 percent to 18 percent in the same period. Melissa Dribben, "Teens and Smoking: They Know It's Bad for Them, But . . . ," *Philadelphia Inquirer,* 15 November 1990.

117. Elaine Shannon, "Why We're Losing."

DAVID T. COURTWRIGHT

Drug Legalization, the Drug War, and Drug Treatment in Historical Perspective

One thing that all parties in the American drug-policy debate agree upon is the desirability of eliminating the traffic in illicit drugs and the esurient criminal syndicates that control it. There are two divergent strategies for achieving this end. The first is the war on drugs. The second, which emerged in the late 1980s as a highly controversial alternative to the drug war, is controlled legalization. What follows is a historically informed critique of both approaches.

History and policy can be conjoined in two ways: through a conventional narrative of the evolution of policy, based on primary sources and told from the historical actors' point of view, and through a critical assessment of current policy and its alternatives, using evidence of past experience and historically derived insights.[1] Properly done, both are valuable and informative. It is essential, however, to say at the outset exactly what one is about. This article is very much a critical assessment, although I have tried to weigh the evidence on both sides and to avoid anything like a polemical tone. My principal conclusion is that neither the drug war as presently configured nor controlled legalization is likely to effect the greatest reduction of misery and death. Public health efforts backed by coercion are a better and more rational way of minimizing the long-term consequences of drug abuse.

The Drug War

The drug war is the name conventionally given to the efforts of the Reagan and Bush administrations against the widespread availability and use of illicit drugs in the United States. It is actually the fourth of four such wars, there having been sustained legislative and governmental efforts against drug abuse in 1909–23, 1951–56, and again in 1971–73. Journalists have nevertheless referred to *the* Reagan-Bush drug war in the singular, and the name has stuck. To avoid confusion I will use the same nomenclature.

The drug war has included treatment of addicts and educational programs designed to discourage new users, but the emphasis has been on law enforcement. Control at the source, interdiction, arrest, prosecution, imprisonment, and seizure of assets have been at the heart of the campaign. This was made apparent in the 1986 and 1988 omnibus antidrug laws and again in the 1989 *National Drug Control Strategy*, a document unapologetically martial in tone. The *Strategy*'s introduction, written by the director of the National Drug Control Office, William Bennett, called for execution as "an appropriate sentence of honest justice" for "the worst and most brutal drug gangsters."[2] This was war indeed.

News from the front has been mixed. Price and purity levels, treatment and emergency-room admissions, urinalyses, and most other indices of drug availability showed a worsening of the problem during the 1980s, with some improvement in late 1989 and 1990. The number of casual cocaine users has recently declined, but addiction to the drug remains widespread, with anywhere from 662,000 to 2.4 million compulsive users, depending on whose estimates one chooses to believe.[3] There has been some success in stopping marijuana imports—shipments of the drug are relatively bulky and therefore easier to detect—but this has been offset by the increased domestic cultivation of high-quality marijuana, which has more than doubled since 1985. Heroin likewise has become more available and potent than it was in the late 1970s, so much so that politicians and government officials have begun openly discussing the likelihood of another major heroin epidemic.[4]

Cocaine has been the drug of greatest concern. Just how severe the crisis has become may be gauged by federal cocaine seizures. Fifty years ago the annual haul for the entire nation amounted to a pound or two, an amount that would easily fit in the glove compartment of a car. As late as 1970 the total was under 500 pounds, an amount that could be contained within the trunk of a car. In fiscal year 1988 it was 198,000 pounds, not counting seizures in foreign jurisdictions—an amount that weighed as much as fifty medium-size cars. This represented a fraction, no more than 10 percent, of what went into the nostrils and lungs and veins of the roughly eight million Americans who used cocaine during 1988. Worse may be in store. Worldwide production of coca surged during 1989 to a level of 225,000 metric tons, despite U.S. efforts to eradicate cultivation. Global production of opium, marijuana, and hashish has likewise increased since President Ronald Reagan formally declared war on drugs in 1986.[5]

The single most important reason for the ineffectiveness of the law enforcement strategy in reducing supply has been the enormous amount of money generated by the illicit traffic. Drug profits have been used to buy off foreign and domestic officials and to secure protection for the most vulnerable stages of the drug cultivation, manufacturing, and distribution process. The profits have been used to hire various specialists, from assassins to money launderers to drug lawyers, needed to cope with criminal and police interlopers. Profits have purchased technological devices such as cellular phones, radar detectors, racing boats, and jet planes to minimize the risk of successful eavesdropping, arrest, and interdiction. Profits have also ensured that, should a trafficker die or land in jail, there will be no shortage of replacements. The money is enormously attractive to those born to poverty and inured to violence. Dealing represents their best chance to realize, however briefly, a life of wealth, status, and luxury.[6]

Controlled Legalization

These stubborn economic realities, together with the uneven and often disappointing results of the drug war, have led several commentators to question the wisdom of what they call the prohibition policy. What is unprecedented is that several of these disenchanted critics are establishment figures, including mayors, prominent lawyers, federal judges, nationally syndicated columnists, a congressman, and a Nobel laureate in economics.[7]

Perhaps the best known and most trenchant of these critics is Professor Ethan Nadelmann, who published in the journal *Science* a widely discussed analysis of the prospects for controlled legalization. Controlled legalization means permitting the sale of substances like marijuana, heroin, and cocaine under conditions that are designed to restrict and limit consumption, such as no sales to minors, no advertising, and substantial taxation. The advantages of this approach, which Nadelmann thinks should be applied to alcohol and tobacco as well as illicit drugs, are numerous. A net benefit of at least $10 billion per year would be realized from tax revenues and savings on law enforcement. These monies could be redirected to drug treatment and prevention programs. Crime would be reduced because there would be fewer arrests for possession. Addicts would not have to hustle to keep themselves supplied with drugs. Perhaps most important, the murders associated with big-city drug trafficking would abate as the traffickers were driven out of business by the availability of lower-cost, legal drugs. Because these drugs would be of known quality and potency, and because they would not have to be injected with shared, possibly contaminated needles, the risk of overdose and infection would be lowered among users. The issue of foreign complicity in the drug traffic, which has complicated American diplomatic relations with many countries, would disappear. Under a policy of controlled legalization, it would be no more criminal or controversial to import coca from Colombia than it would be to import coffee.

Nadelmann is candid in admitting that these and other advantages would be purchased at the cost of increased drug abuse. Widespread availability, lower prices, and the elimination of the criminal sanction would result in more drug users, a percentage of whom would become abusers and addicts. But how many more? Nadelmann doubts that there would be nearly as many as there are smokers and heavy drinkers. Ultimately, legalization might succeed in making drug use less glamorous and hence less appealing, as has apparently happened with marijuana smoking among teenagers in the Netherlands.[8]

The most common rebuttal is that legalization would result in an unconscionably large epidemic of drug abuse. Herbert Kleber, the Yale addiction treatment specialist who in 1989 became deputy director of the Office of National Drug Control Policy, has argued that cocaine and heroin are more addicting than alcohol, and that there would be between 12 million and 55 million addicted users if these substances were legally available. In countries such as Thailand, where narcotics are cheap, potent, and readily available, the prevalence of addiction is much greater. Professions like medicine, in which drugs are easily obtained, historically have had high addiction rates. Kleber has also attacked the crime-reduction rationale by pointing out that addicts will generally use much more of an illicit substance if the cost is low. They would therefore spend most of their time using drugs and little of it in gainful employment, thus continuing to resort to crime to acquire money. If the total number of addicts rose sharply as availability increased, total crime would also increase. There would be less crime committed by any single addict but more crime in the aggregate because of the larger number of addicts.[9] The widespread use of drug testing to screen employees lends force to this argument. Addicts who sought work would have trouble finding it and thus would have few alternatives to crime to pay for drugs and other expenses.

The debate over decriminalization is, in essence, an argument about a high-stakes gamble. Proponents like Nadelmann have listed the many social, economic, and health advantages that might be gained from controlled legalization; opponents like Kleber have argued that the losses stemming from increased addiction would sooner or later outweigh these advantages. The opponents represent the majority view. As of November 1989 four out of five Americans were against the legalization of marijuana, let alone drugs like PCP or cocaine. If the drug war produces another decade of mixed or indifferent results at great expense, it is possible that public opinion will change. The same sort of disillusionment and war-weariness that were occasioned by the Vietnam conflict could conceivably wind down the war on drugs and prompt experiments in controlled legalization.[10]

Sales to Minors and Other Excluded Groups

The assumption upon which the controlled-legalization argument rests is that legal sales would largely eliminate the illicit traffic and its attendant evils. The history of drug use, regulation, and taxation in the United States suggests otherwise. The concept of controlled legalization implies not making drugs available to certain groups. Minors are the most obvious exception. Nadelmann has stressed that the sale of drugs to children should remain illegal.[11] Presumably selling drugs to anyone under twenty-one would remain a criminal offense, since that is the cutoff point for sales of beverage alcohol, and drugs like heroin and cocaine are at least comparable to alcohol in their potential for overdose, addiction, and other forms of abuse.

Forbidding the sale of powerful psychoactive drugs to young people makes social, moral, and political sense. Unfortunately, illicit drug abuse in this century has become concentrated among the young, that is, among those who are most likely to be made exceptions to the rule of legal sales. Until about 1900 the most common pattern of nonalcoholic drug dependence in the United States was addiction to opium or morphine, brought about by the treatment or self-treatment of chronic diseases and painful symptoms. Persons so addicted were mainly female, middle-class, and middle-aged or older. Eugene O'Neill's mother, fictionalized as Mary Tyrone in *Long Day's Journey into Night,* was an instance of this type. Habitual users of morphine, laudanum, and other medicinal opiates under the age of twenty were extremely rare, even in large cities like Chicago.[12]

There was another and originally less widespread pattern of drug use that was nonmedical in character and had its roots in marginal, deviant, and criminal subcultures. The "pleasure users," as they were sometimes called, smoked opium, sniffed cocaine, injected morphine and cocaine in combination, or, after 1910, sniffed or injected heroin. Nonmedical addicts began at a much earlier age than their medical counterparts. The average age of addiction (not first use, which would have been lower still) for urban heroin addicts studied in the 1910s was only nineteen or twenty years.[13] These addicts were also more likely to be male and to have been involved in delinquent or criminal activities than those whose addiction was of medical origin.

During the first two decades of the twentieth century—the same period when the police approach to national drug control was formulated—the number of older, docile medical addicts steadily diminished relative to nonmedical addicts. There were several reasons for the shrinkage of medical addiction. Doctors became better educated and more conservative in their use of narcotics; the population became healthier; patent-medicine manufacturers were forced to reveal the contents of their products; and the numerous morphine addicts who had been created in the nineteenth century began to age and die off. As a result, drug use and addiction were increasingly concentrated among young men in their teens and twenties. This is still true, not only for the opiates and cocaine, but for substances like marijuana or PCP or LSD that emerged during the twentieth century as major illicit drugs.

The age distribution of arrests for drug law violations provides a rough estimate of the extent of youthful involvement with drugs.[14] This involvement has diminished somewhat during the last decade but remains significant. In 1980, 44 percent of drug arrests nationwide were of persons under the age of twenty-one. More arrests occurred among teenagers than among the entire population over the age of twenty-five; eighteen-year-olds had the highest arrest rate of any age group. By 1987 the proportion under age twenty-one among those arrested for drug law violations had declined to 25 percent.[15] This decline was partly due to the aging of the population and, to an unknown degree, to the effects of drug education on students. But when large numbers of "echo boomers," or children of the baby boomers, become adolescents during the 1990s, the percentage of under-twenty-one drug arrests may very well increase.

This age pattern has important implications for a controlled-legalization system predicated on the denial of sales to those under twenty-one. Depending on timing and demographic circumstances, a quarter, a third, or more of all customers would be underage, and there would be a great deal of money to be made by selling drugs to them. The primary source of supply would likely be diversion. Adults who had legally purchased drugs would sell all or part of their supply to those who were below the legal age. The sellers (or middlemen who collected and then resold the legal purchases) would realize a profit through marking-up or adulterating the drugs sold to minors. There might well be turf disputes and hence violence among those who resold drugs. Some of the dealers and their underage purchasers would be caught, prosecuted, and imprisoned, with the result that the criminal justice system would still be involved with and burdened by drug arrests. The black market would be altered and diminished but would not disappear.[16]

The potential for illegal sales and use goes beyond minors, because they would not be the only group excluded under controlled legalization. Pilots, policemen, firemen, bus, train, taxi, and ambulance drivers, surgeons, active-duty military personnel, and others whose drug use would jeopardize public safety and security would be denied access to at least some drugs. Yet those among them who began or persisted in drug use would be liable to criminal and in some instances civil actions, as would their suppliers. Pregnant and possibly nursing women would also pose a problem. Drugs transmitted to fetuses can cause irreversible and enormously costly harm. Federal and local governments may soon be spending $15 billion a year just to prepare the impaired children of addicts for kindergarten.[17] Society has the right and the obligation to stop this developmental and neurological carnage both because drug abuse handicaps innocent children and because it harms everyone else through higher taxes and health insurance premiums. Paradoxically, the arguments for controlled legalization might lead to denying alcohol and tobacco as well as narcotics and stimulants to pregnant women. Alcohol and tobacco are potentially teratogenic, or harmful to fetal development. Nadelmann and other critics have observed that it is both inconsistent and unwise to treat them as if they were not dangerous because they are legal.[18] If cocaine is denied to pregnant women, why not alcohol too? The point to be made here is simply that every time an exception is made for good and compelling reasons—every time the accent is placed on "controlled" as opposed to "legalization"—the likelihood of continued illicit sales and use increases.

The supposition that this illegal market would be fueled by diversion is well founded historically. There has always been an undercurrent of diversion, especially in the late 1910s and 1920s, when black-market operators like "Legs" Diamond got their supplies, not necessarily by smuggling, but by purchases from legitimate drug companies. One possible way to deal with this problem is to require of all legal purchasers that which is required of newly enrolled methadone patients: consumption of the drug on the premises. Unfortunately, this would not work well with heroin and cocaine because these drugs, unlike methadone, are short-acting and compulsive users must administer them every few hours or less. The dayrooms of drug treatment clinics set up in Britain after 1968 to provide heroin maintenance (theretofore the province of individual doctors, some of whom proved excessively liberal in their prescriptions) were often clogged with whining addicts. In other instances the addicts loitered outside, waiting impatiently for their next fix. Frustrated and angry, the clinic staffs largely abandoned heroin during the 1970s, switching instead to methadone maintenance.[19] Methadone has the advantage of oral administration and twenty-four-hour duration; it is also much easier to stabilize an addict on a maintenance dosage. These properties make it much more suitable for clinic-based distribution. The same cannot be said of heroin or cocaine or other street drugs. Confining their use to clinics would be a logistical nightmare, considering the number of users involved. But the alternative, take-home supplies and consumption off the premises, invites illegal sales to excluded groups.[20]

Another historical pattern of black-market activity has been the smuggling of drugs to prisoners. Contraband was in fact one of the reasons why the government built specialized narcotic hospitals in Lexington, Kentucky, and Fort Worth, Texas, in the 1930s. Federal wardens wanted to get addicts out of their prisons because they were constantly conniving to obtain smuggled drugs.[21] When drug-related arrests multiplied after 1965 and the Lexington and Fort Worth facilities were closed, prisons and jails were again filled with prisoners who sought to obtain drugs.[22] The result was a good deal of smuggling and in-prison trafficking involving the active or passive cooperation of corrupt prison officials. Birch Bayh, who chaired a 1975 Senate investigation of the matter, observed that in some institutions young offenders had a more plentiful supply of drugs than they did on the outside.[23]

What has happened since 1975 is that more jails and prisons have been crammed with more prisoners—850,000 at the end of 1987—and that these prisoners are more likely than ever to have had a history of drug use.[24] In 1989, depending on the city in question, 60 percent to 80 percent of male arrestees tested positive for drugs shortly after they were apprehended.[25] It is hard to imagine a controlled-legalization system that would permit sales to prisoners, either because drug use would be considered inappropriate for those who were being punished, or because some prisoners would be participating in abstinence-oriented treatment programs, or because of the fear that drugs (particularly cocaine) would trigger violence and other retrograde behaviors. Alcohol, although a legal drug, is not sold licitly in prisons, and for good reason, as more than 40 percent of prisoners were under its influence when they committed their crimes.[26] If drugs are similarly denied to inmates, then the contraband problem will persist. If, moreover, we insist that our 2.6 million parolees and probationers remain clean on the theory that drug use aggravates recidivism and impairs rehabilitation, then the market for illegal sales would be so much the larger.[27]

The problem should by now be clear. If drugs are legalized, but not for those under twenty-one, or for public safety officers, or transport workers, or military personnel, or pregnant women, or prisoners, or probationers, or parolees, or psychotics, or any of several other special groups one could plausibly name, then just exactly who is going to buy them? Noncriminal adults, whose drug use is comparatively low to begin with? Controlled legalization entails a dilemma. To the extent that its controls are enforced, some form of black-market activity will persist. If, on the other hand, its controls are not enforced, and drugs are easily diverted to the aforementioned groups, then it is a disguised form of wholesale legalization, and as such is morally and politically unacceptable.

Tax-Avoidance Smuggling

One of the selling points of controlled legalization, which was also one of the decisive arguments for the repeal of Prohibition, is taxation. The government, which spends billions attempting to suppress the illicit traffic, could reap billions if it imposed duties on legitimate imports or taxes on domestically grown or manufactured drugs. These revenues could be earmarked for drug treatment and education programs. They would also increase the price paid by the consumer, which would discourage consumption, especially by adolescents.

The U.S. government has had extensive historical experience with the taxation of legal narcotics. In the nineteenth and early twentieth centuries opium, which was not cultivated domestically, was imported and subject to customs duties. The imports were assigned to one of three categories. The first was crude opium, which was used mainly for medicinal purposes and for the domestic manufacture of morphine. The second was foreign-manufactured morphine, codeine, and, after 1898, heroin. The third was opium prepared for smoking, most of which was manufactured in Hong Kong and shipped to San Francisco.

The imposts on these imported drugs fluctuated but were generally quite stiff. For fiscal years 1866–1914 the average ad valorem duty on crude opium was 33 percent; for morphine or its salts, 48 percent. For fiscal years 1866–1908 the average ad valorem duty on smoking opium was an extraordinarily high 97 percent. The latter was in the nature of a sin tax, since congressmen identified opium smoking with Chinese coolies, gamblers, pimps, and prostitutes and therefore wished to discourage its importation and use.

These customs duties produced revenue, but they also produced widespread smuggling, much of it organized by violent criminal societies like the Chinese tongs. The smugglers, who used everything from hollowed-out lumber to snake cages to secrete their shipments, could save as much as three dollars a pound on crude opium, three dollars an ounce on morphine, and twelve dollars a pound on smoking opium by avoiding the customs collectors. Twelve dollars may seem like a trifling sum by modern standards, hardly worth the risk of arrest. But in the nineteenth century it represented a great deal of money, more than most workers earned in a week. Someone who smuggled in fifty pounds of smoking opium in 1895 had gained the equivalent of a year's wages. One knowledgeable authority estimated that, when the duty on smoking opium was near its peak, the amount smuggled into the United States was nearly twice that legally imported and taxed. This was true of crude opium and morphine as well. The higher the tax, the lower the level of legal imports and the greater the incentive to smuggle. Something similar happened with eighteenth-century tobacco imports to the British Isles. More than a third of the tobacco consumed in England and Scotland circa 1750 had been clandestinely or fraudulently imported in order to avoid paying a duty of over five pence per pound.[28] The principle is the same for domestically produced drugs: if excise and other taxes are sufficiently onerous, then an illegal manufacturing and distribution system will spring up. Moonshining existed before and after, as well as during, Prohibition.

The obvious solution is to set taxes at a sufficiently low level to discourage smuggling and illegal manufacturing. But again there is a dilemma. The most important illicit drugs are processed agricultural products that can be grown in several parts of the world by peasant labor. They are not, in other words, intrinsically expensive. Unless the products are heavily taxed, legal consumers will be able to acquire them at little cost—ten dollars or less for a gram of cocaine.[29] If drugs are that cheap, to say nothing of being 100 percent pure, the likelihood of a postlegalization epidemic of addiction will be substantially increased. But if taxes are given a stiff boost to enhance revenues and discourage consumption, black marketeers will reenter the picture in numbers proportionate to the severity of the tax. There would also be more addict crime, since the purchase of either highly taxed or black-market drugs would force compulsive users, many of whom would be unemployed, to raise larger sums than if they could buy legal, minimally taxed drugs.

Another potential problem with drug taxation is that tax revenues, like drugs themselves, can be addictive. In the twelve years after the repeal of Prohibition, federal liquor tax revenues ballooned from $259 million to $2.3 billion. The government's dependence on this money was one important reason why antiliquor forces made so little progress in their attempts to restrict alcohol consumption during World War II.[30] Controlled drug legalization would also bring about a windfall in tax dollars, which would surely be welcomed and quickly spent in an age of chronic deficits. But should legalization fail, should addiction rates become too high, a conflict between public health and revenue concerns would ensue. To abandon legalization would be to abandon the tax dollars it generated. Taxation creates an automatic temptation to retain what may or may not be a successful drug policy.

Nadelmann has asserted that legalization would evolve gradually, with ample opportunity to halt, reevaluate, and redirect drug policies that begin to go awry.[31] This seems an optimistic assessment, given the fiscal temptation. Once legalization reached the point where significant tax revenues and other vested economic interests were involved, it would be difficult to return to a more restrictive policy. Certainly taxes and corporate revenues are formidable political impediments to adopting more stringent alcohol and tobacco policies. The same can be said of gambling. The spectacle of states proliferating legal games of chance despite their patently regressive nature does not inspire confidence that drug sales would be taxed or regulated in the most socially responsible manner.

When proponents and opponents of controlled legalization make claims about drug taxes, they generally assume a single level of taxation. This assumption is incorrect. The nature of the federal system permits state and local governments to levy their own taxes on drugs, apart from and in addition to uniform federal customs and excise taxes. This means that aggregate drug taxes, and hence prices paid by consumers, will vary from place to place. Variation invites interstate smuggling. If the variation is large enough, the smuggling can be extensive and involve elements of organized crime.

The history of cigarette taxation serves to illustrate this principle. In 1960 state taxes on cigarettes were low, between zero and eight cents per pack. After 1965 a growing number of states sharply increased cigarette taxes in response to health concerns and as a politically painless way of increasing revenue. Some states, mainly in the Northeast, were considerably more aggressive than others in raising taxes. By 1975 the difference in state taxation ranged from two cents to twenty-one cents per pack, creating marked price differentials. North Carolina purchasers were paying thirty-six cents per pack in 1975, compared to fifty-four cents in New York State. The price was higher still in New York City, due to a local levy that reached eight cents per pack (as much as the entire federal tax!) at the beginning of 1976.

Thus was born an opportunity to buy cheap and sell dear. Those who bought in volume at North Carolina prices and sold at New York (or Connecticut or Massachusetts) prices realized a substantial profit, pocketing most of the difference between the small state tax and the large one. Net revenue losses had reached well over $300 million a year by the mid-1970s. Much of this went to organized crime, which was at one point bootlegging 25 percent of the cigarettes sold in New York State and half of those sold in New York City. The pioneer of the illegal traffic, Anthony Granata, established a trucking company with thirty employees operating vehicles on a six-days-a-week basis. The methods employed by Granata and other big-time cigarette smugglers, including concealed cargoes, dummy corporations, forged documents, fortresslike warehouses, bribery, hijacking, assault, and homicide, were strikingly similar to those used by illicit drug traffickers and Prohibition bootleggers.[32]

Although high-tax states like Florida or Illinois still lose millions annually to cigarette bootleggers, the 1978 federal Contraband Cigarette Act and stricter law enforcement and accounting procedures had some success in reducing over-the-road smuggling during the 1980s.[33] But it is relatively easy to detect illegal shipments of cigarettes, which must be smuggled by the truckload to make a substantial amount of money, or at any rate the amount of money that would make the enterprise attractive to organized crime. Drugs like cocaine and heroin are more compact, more profitable, and very easy to conceal. Smuggling these drugs to take advantage of state tax differentials would consequently be much more difficult to detect and deter. If, for example, taxed cocaine retailed in Vermont for ten dollars a gram and in New York for twelve dollars a gram, anyone who bought just five kilograms at Vermont prices, transported them, and sold them (illegally) at New York prices would realize a profit of $10,000. Five kilograms is an amount that could be concealed in an attaché case.

Should all states legalize drugs and tax them at the same rate, this sort of illegal activity would not exist. The difficulty is that it is constitutionally and politically infeasible to ensure uniform rates of state taxation. There is also reason to suppose that, under controlled legalization, states would impose different tax rates. The extent of drug abuse and addiction vary markedly. States with older, more rural populations typically have fewer drug problems and hence would have less incentive to impose heavy taxes to finance treatment programs or discourage consumption. The opposite would be true of states with younger, more urban populations.

Federalism poses other challenges. Laws against drug use and trafficking have been enacted at the local, state, and federal levels. It is probable that if Congress repeals or modifies the national drug laws some states will go along with controlled legalization, but others will not.[34] Nevada, long in the legalizing habit, might jettison its drug laws, but conservative, Mormon-populated Utah might not. Alternatively, governments could experiment with varying degrees of legalization. Congress might decide that anything was better than the current mayhem in the capital and legislate a broad legalization program for the District of Columbia. At the same time, Virginia and Maryland might experiment with the decriminalization of marijuana, the least risky legalization option, but retain prohibition of the nonmedical use of other drugs. The result would again be smuggling, whether from Nevada to Utah or, save for marijuana, from the District of Columbia to the surrounding states. Given that the internal political boundaries of the United States are guarded by nothing more than highway signs bearing governors' messages of welcome, it is hard to see how any state that chose to retain laws against some or all drugs could possibly stanch the influx of prohibited drugs from adjacent states that opted for their legalization.

New York City's efforts to control guns illustrate the near impossibility of locally restricting the sale of commodities that are freely available elsewhere. To circumvent the city's strict gun-control laws, black marketeers have traveled to Virginia, Texas, Ohio, Florida, and Georgia, where it is possible to purchase several handguns in different stores in a single day. Loaded up with Tec-9s and Mac-11s, they return to New York and sell their wares for as much as double the original price. A popular weapon retailing for $500 can fetch $1,000 on the black market.[35] Officials concede that they can seize no more than a fraction of the illegal weapons. The reasons for their failure are obvious. The guns are compact and valuable, and their smuggling is no more difficult than driving home on Interstate 95.

Controlled Medicalization as a Middle Course

I referred earlier to the legalization debate as an argument about a colossal gamble, viz., whether society should risk an unknown increase in drug abuse and addiction to eliminate the harms of drug prohibition, most of which stem from illicit trafficking. "Take the crime out of it" is the rallying cry of the legalization advocates. After reviewing the larger history of narcotic, alcohol, and tobacco use and regulation, it appears that this debate should be recast. It would be more accurate to ask whether society should risk an unknown increase in drug abuse and addiction in order to bring about an unknown *reduction* in illicit trafficking and other costs of drug prohibition. Controlled legalization would take some, but by no means all, of the crime out of it. Just how much and what sort of crime would be eliminated would depend upon which groups were to be denied which drugs; the overall level of taxation; and differences in state tax and legalization policies. If the excluded groups were few *and* all states legalized all drugs *and* all governments taxed at uniformly low levels, then the black market would be largely eliminated. But these are precisely the conditions that would be most likely to bring about an unacceptably high level of drug abuse. The same variables that would determine how successful the controlled-legalization policy would be in eliminating the black market would also largely determine how unsuccessful it was in containing drug addiction.

The dilemmas and dangers of controlled legalization do not mean that the drug war is the only alternative. A case also can be made for the reallocation of resources and for selective legal changes that stop short of making drugs legally available. In order to understand this it is helpful to visualize drug policy as a continuum ranging from laissez-faire to controlled legalization to medical and public health approaches to criminalization. Historically, American drug policy has moved from left to right across this continuum, from no laws to tax laws to prescription laws to laws that denied and punished addicts and nonmedical users. By the mid-1950s the United States had evolved one of the most rigid, punishment-oriented systems of drug control in the world. There was a reaction against this extreme criminalization in legal, medical, social scientific, and public policy circles. New treatment modalities were introduced during the 1960s and 1970s, and a more even balance between medical and criminal approaches to the problem was temporarily achieved. In the 1980s the balance tipped again toward law enforcement efforts, which received substantially increased appropriations while, in constant dollars, funding for public treatment programs declined. Whether the decade-long tilt to enforcement was the wisest course is questionable. By 1990 the jails were full, but the traffic was still flourishing and illicit drug use remained widespread.

Prosecutorial efforts should not be abandoned. The mere fact that some potentially harmful drugs are illegal, and that their possession and sale are occasionally detected and punished, is sufficient to deter the majority of the population from using them. The essential point about law enforcement and interdiction efforts is not that they fail, but that large investments in them produce diminishing returns. Additional appropriations for the drug war would be better spent on educational and therapeutic efforts. In both budgetary and strategic terms it is possible to move closer to the center-right of the spectrum—that is, toward a more balanced medical–police approach—without embracing legalization, controlled or otherwise.[36]

Shifting resources into treatment would be pointless if treatment were no more cost-effective than police crackdowns and interdiction campaigns. Treatment does work, although not by producing instant cures. Of those seeking drug treatment, 75 percent to 90 percent are addicted, sometimes to more than one substance. Addiction is a chronic, relapsing disorder. Seldom does one treatment episode produce permanent abstinence. What treatment can accomplish is detoxification followed by a period of abstinence, reduced criminality, lessened exposure to AIDS and other infections, improved work performance and employability, and the inculcation of socially responsible values—all for less than it costs to park a prisoner in a cell. Although there are variations across treatment types, programs in which a patient is enrolled for a sustained period of time, six months or more, have the best chance of producing favorable results. Relapse may occur, but treatment can reestablish abstinence. The situation is somewhat like treating strep throat in children, a disease for which there is an antibiotic "cure" but no guarantee of nonrecurrence. If the infection returns, it is treated again to eliminate the health risks to the child and to others, with the expectation that the child will one day outgrow the condition. For drug treatment the ultimate goal is abstinence from illicit drugs and the normalization of life, but with a similar expectation of relapses along the way.

Drug treatment, like American medicine as a whole, is a two-tiered system of public and private providers. The public tier stagnated between 1975 and 1988, while the private tier grew explosively, due to the expansion and redefinition of health insurance plans. Coverage of alcohol and drug treatment, together with the fact that many younger patients had combined alcohol-drug problems, has led to the creation of hybrid chemical-dependency units. These units are often hospital-based and provide relatively expensive, shorter-term care to middle- and upper-income patients. Most of these patients are workers referred through employee assistance programs or their adolescent children.

Roughly 140 million Americans have specifically defined coverage for drug treatment. Another 61 million have private health insurance or

Medicaid but lack specified coverage; they can be reimbursed for emergency services, such as treating drug overdoses, but they may or may not qualify for extended care under the general or psychiatric provisions of their insurance plans. Then there are 37 million Americans who are continuously without any kind of health insurance. Some of them can afford to pay for drug treatment out-of-pocket, but this percentage is not large. The total number of people who, for reasons of insufficient income or insurance, cannot afford outpatient drug treatment is approximately 40 million. The total number who cannot afford residential drug treatment is probably closer to 60 million. It is from this same 60 million that the most socially disruptive drug abusers are drawn. In a word, the most serious drug problems are to be found among those least likely to have access to private care. Beds in chemical-dependency units are unoccupied while many addicts roam the streets.

The mismatch between private capacity and uninsured need would not be so troubling if public programs could absorb all the indigent addicts who seek treatment. They cannot. In September 1989 there were 66,000 individuals in forty-three states on waiting lists, a figure equal to more than one-fourth of the total daily enrollment in public treatment programs. There are between two and three million other drug-dependent individuals not currently on waiting lists who need and who could benefit from public treatment programs, but for whom no places are currently available. Making treatment readily available to all who wish to enter it would require increased federal operating support of at least a billion dollars a year, plus a minimum one-time expenditure of $500 million for training staff, construction, and the renovation of substandard facilities. In addition to eliminating waiting lists, increased funding can improve quality by retaining the services of the most capable and experienced therapists (who are often hired away by private programs) and by decreasing their oppressively heavy caseloads. What is true of the school system is true of drug treatment: patients who are treated in a dump by harried, underpaid therapists teetering on the brink of burnout are less likely to do well, other things being equal. There is also a critical need to develop more, and more appropriate, facilities for treating pregnant women. At present only 30,000 expectant women receive drug treatment annually, although an estimated 105,000 women are simultaneously pregnant and drug-dependent during the course of the year. One obvious defect is the lack of on-site child care for pregnant addicts who already have children. Despite the widely publicized stories about crack babies silting up urban hospitals, most pregnant addicts are not maternal sociopaths, nor are they willing to stay for long in treatment if it means separation from their children.[37]

More controversial than upgrading public treatment, but a step short of legalizing drugs, is making available sterile injection equipment. State drug laws typically prohibit both the nonmedical use of certain substances and the means to administer them. Forty-four states and the District of Columbia bar the possession, distribution, and sale of hypodermic needles and syringes by unauthorized persons, including intravenous drug addicts and users. Fear of detection and arrest has for many years encouraged addicts to share or rent illegal needles and syringes, with the result that syphilis, hepatitis, tetanus, malaria, AIDS, and other infections have spread among them and thence to third parties. Programs designed to ameliorate this public health catastrophe by educating users about the dangers of infection and permitting them to exchange old, potentially contaminated needles and syringes for sterile new ones have been established in Great Britain, the Netherlands, Australia, Sweden, Switzerland, Germany, Canada, and on a very limited basis in the United States. Needle exchange is a prime example of a medically oriented strategy to reduce the harmful consequences of drug abuse that is neither punitive nor likely to produce the higher levels of addiction that the legalization of drugs would entail.[38]

The same may be said of methadone maintenance. The most thoroughly evaluated of the drug treatments to have emerged in the last quarter century, methadone works because it eliminates both the cravings of narcotic addicts and the most serious logistical problems of providing a controlled supply. By taking a daily oral dose of this inexpensive agonist, or substitute drug, it is possible for methadone patients to escape the grind of hustling, scoring, and injecting drugs that dominated their lives as intravenous narcotic addicts. The principal limitation of methadone's effectiveness is that it is pharmacologically irrelevant to the abuse of stimulants, hallucinogens, and other nonopiate drugs—except in the narrow sense that addicts in high-dose methadone programs are less likely to "cheat" and use other drugs than those enrolled in low-dose programs. There is as yet no equivalent to methadone maintenance for the hardcore cocaine addict. The modest but very real success of methadone maintenance suggests that if comparable agonists are developed for other addictive drugs, they should be made available under therapeutic auspices, particularly to compulsive users who have repeatedly tried drug-free treatments but who have failed to remain abstinent.

Controlled medicalization is a better alternative than either controlled legalization or intensified criminalization. Federal, state, and local governments should shore up the public treatment sector; experiment with and carefully evaluate needle-exchange programs, expanding them if they prove successful; and pursue pharmacotherapeutic research while maintaining school- and community-based education and prevention efforts. Public health approaches are far more promising than radar balloons, Caribbean task forces, Andean coca eradication subsidies, and various other supply-reduction schemes whose results are bound to be less admirable than their intentions.[39] That we have in the past poured disproportionate sums into law enforcement and interdiction projects has more to do with the political appeal of the drug war—its moral drama, technological glamor, and abundant video opportunities—than to its objective effectiveness. The drug war is the best way to get on the evening news. It is not necessarily the best way to save lives and conserve resources.

Drug abuse is an intractable social problem. The misuse of psychoactive substances is almost as old as civilization, but it has been greatly aggravated during the last four centuries, owing to discoveries and technological advances that no one could have foreseen or controlled. The voyages to the New World, which brought tobacco and coca to Europeans and alcohol to Native Americans; the growth of global commerce, which facilitated the shipment of drugs from continent to continent; innovations such as the isolation of morphine or the flue-curing of tobacco or the hypodermic syringe, which made drug use more potent and pleasurable—these and other developments ensured a worsening of drug abuse and dependency. Addiction is preeminently a modern disease, causally entangled with and impossible to understand apart from the technological, social, and economic foundations of industrial civilization itself. But it is also a disease that can be fought and to some extent controlled. The rational goal is to minimize simultaneously the undesirable consequences of the control effort. This end has not yet been achieved.

University of North Florida

Acknowledgments

I am grateful to Avram Goldstein, Ethan Nadelmann, Peter Reuter, Herman Joseph, Don Des Jarlais, Dean Gerstein, G. Bruce Douglas, and William O. Walker III for making comments on this article, which began life as a paper circulated at a conference on addiction at the Banbury Center, Cold Spring Harbor, New York, 25–27 January 1990.

Notes

1. Examples of the two types are David F. Musto, *The American Disease: Origins of Narcotic Control,* expanded ed. (New York, 1987), a sequential account grounded in legislative, medical, and diplomatic sources, and Edward M. Brecher et al., *Licit and Illicit Drugs* (Boston, 1972), a lively assessment of drugs and drug laws that draws heavily (and at times selectively) from American and British historical experience.

The seminal work in the field of drug history and policy was Charles C. Terry and Mildred Pellens, *The Opium Problem* (New York, 1928). The origins and influence of this book are described in David T. Courtwright, "Charles Terry, *The Opium Problem,* and American Narcotic Policy," *Journal of Drug Issues* 16 (1984): 421–34.

2. The White House, *National Drug Control Strategy* (Washington, D.C., 1989), 7. Bennett's confrontational approach is discussed in Michael Massing, "The Two William Bennetts," *New York Review of Books* 37 (1 March 1990): 29–33.

3. The low figure comes from the 1990 National Household Survey on Drug Abuse, the high figure from a Senate Judiciary Committee staff report. See Mike Snider, "Gains Don't Mean Drug War's Won," and Jack Kelley, "Senator: Survey 'Wildly Off the Mark,' " *USA Today,* 20 December 1990.

4. Charles B. Rangel, "The Killer Drug We Ignore," *New York Times,* national edition, 15 August 1990.

5. *National Drug Control Strategy,* 64, 75; David Courtwright, Herman Joseph, and Don Des Jarlais, *Addicts Who Survived: An Oral History of Narcotic Use in America, 1923–1965* (Nashville, 1989), 344–61, 365 n. 28; U.S. Department of Health and Human Services, Public Health Service, Alcohol, Drug, and Mental Health Administration, National Institute on Drug Abuse, *National Household Survey on Drug Abuse: Population Estimates 1988* (Washington, D.C., 1989), 29; U.S. Department of State, Bureau of International Narcotics Matters, *International Narcotics Control Strategy Report* (Washington, D.C.: State Department Publication 9749, March 1990), 19–20.

6. The same was true of Prohibition-era bootlegging, which provided, in the words of crime historian Mark Haller, "a path of upward mobility for those who were among the most marginal of America's urban dwellers." "Bootlegging: The History of an Illegal Enterprise," paper presented at the 1980 meeting of the Organization of American Historians, p. 1.

7. This trend is also in evidence in other countries, such as Australia, where controlled legalization has reportedly been endorsed by some prominent citizens. Alex Wodak, "Australia," The International Working Group on AIDS and IV Drug Use *Newsletter* 4 (September 1989): 4. In Germany the illegality of methadone maintenance has recently been challenged. Ingo Michaels, "Federal Republic of Germany," ibid., 5, and Robert G. Newman, "Is There a Role for Methadone in Germany?" and "Law Enforcement and Treatment: Complementary Responses to the Problem of Addiction," conference papers presented, respectively, at Frankfurt, 14 November 1987, and for the Gewerkschaft der Polizei, Munich, 3 March 1989.

8. Ethan A. Nadelmann, "Drug Prohibition in the United States: Costs, Consequences, and Alternatives," *Science* 245 (1 September 1989): 939–47. Arnold S. Trebach, *The Great Drug War and Radical Proposals That Could Make America Safe Again* (New York, 1987), made many of the same arguments and charged further than prohibition blocks legitimate therapeutic applications, e.g., marijuana for overcoming nausea experienced by cancer patients. Other arguments, pro and con, are summarized in U.S. Congress, House, Select Committee on Narcotics Abuse and Control, *Legalization of Illicit Drugs: Impact and Feasibility: (A Review of Recent Hearings),* 100th Cong., 1st sess. Connoisseurs of irony are directed to Mayor Marion Barry's comments on p. 12. Two recent or forthcoming anthologies are James A. Inciardi, ed., *The Drug Legalization Debate* (Newbury Park, 1991) and Rod L. Evans, and Irwin M. Berent, *Drug Legalization: For and Against* (Peru, Ill., 1991). Also

recent is Richard Lawrence Miller, *The Case For Legalizing Drugs* (New York, 1991). Miller's analysis is exactly what his title promises: one sided.

9. Remarks delivered 10 October 1988; photocopy made available by Dr. Kleber to the author.

10. National Opinion Research Center poll data cited in David Corcoran, "Legalizing Drugs: Failures Spur Debate," *New York Times,* national edition, 27 November 1989.

11. Nadelmann, "Drug Prohibition," 941.

12. Charles Warrington Earle, "The Opium Habit: A Statistical and Clinical Lecture," *Chicago Medical Review* 2 (1880): 443.

13. David T. Courtwright, *Dark Paradise: Opiate Addiction in America before 1940* (Cambridge, Mass., 1982), 88.

14. Though by no means a perfect estimate. Under-twenty-one drug arrests do not exactly match under-twenty-one drug use because some of the arrests are of young persons recruited to sell drugs precisely because they are young, and thus not liable to the severe penalties that can be meted out to adult dealers. The bias is not large, however, since the vast majority of these teenage dealers are or very quickly become users themselves. (Terry Williams, *The Cocaine Kids: The Inside Story of a Teenage Drug Ring* [Reading, Mass., 1989], 8, 39, 47, 58, 85.) It is also possible that arrest data *understate* youthful prevalence because police are more likely to notice and apprehend older users, more of whom are addicted and consume more drugs, thus committing more crimes. Other things being equal, a twenty-four-year-old addict is more apt to be arrested than a seventeen-year-old experimenting with drugs on the weekend.

15. These statistics are derived from three Department of Justice publications: *Age-Specific Arrest Rates and Race-Specific Arrest Rates for Selected Offenses* (Washington, D.C., 1986), 120; *Sourcebook of Criminal Justice Statistics—1982* (Washington, D.C., 1983), 394–95; and *Sourcebook of Criminal Justice Statistics—1988* (Washington, D.C., 1989), 490–91.

16. The late John Kaplan made a similar argument in "Taking Drugs Seriously," *The Public Interest* 92 (Summer 1988): 39.

17. Stephen Labaton, "The Cost of Drug Abuse: $60 Billion a Year," *New York Times,* national edition, 5 December 1989.

18. E.g., Rufus King, "A Worthless Crusade," *Newsweek,* 1 January 1990, 4–5. Among the current group of legalization proponents, King can almost certainly claim seniority; he has been an ardent critic of the drug prohibition policy since the Anslinger era. His major work is *The Drug Hang-Up: America's Fifty-Year Folly* (Springfield, Ill., 1972).

19. Arnold S. Trebach, *The Heroin Solution* (New Haven, 1982), chap. 7; Jara Krivanek, *Heroin: Myth and Reality* (Sydney, 1988), 222–32; Susanne MacGregor and Betsy Ettorre, "From Treatment to Rehabilitation—Aspects of British Policy on the Care of Drug-takers," and Nicholas Dorn and Nigel South, "Reconciling Policy and Practice," both in Nicholas Dorn and Nigel South, eds., *A Land Fit for Heroin? Drug Policies, Prevention and Practice* (New York, 1987), 125–45 and 146–69, respectively.

20. Courtwright, Joseph, and Des Jarlais, *Addicts Who Survived,* 181–84, 289–90, for historical examples of diversion. The drawbacks and difficulties of controlled legal narcotic sales are discussed in the Vincent Dole narrative in ibid., 335, and in John Kaplan, *The Hardest Drug: Heroin and Public Policy* (Chicago, 1983), esp. chaps. 3 and 4. What Dole and Kaplan have to say about the difficulties of managing legal heroin supplies would certainly apply to cocaine, which is an even shorter-acting drug.

21. U.S. Congress, House of Representatives, Committee on the Judiciary, *Hearings on the Establishment of Two Federal Narcotic Farms,* 70th Cong., 1st sess., 26–28 April 1928, 10, 22–23.

22. U.S. Department of Justice, Federal Bureau of Investigation, Uniform Crime Reporting Program, *Age-Specific Arrest Rates and Race-Specific Arrest Rates for Selected Offenses, 1965–1985* (Washington, D.C., 1986), 115–21.

23. U.S. Congress, Senate, Committee on the Judiciary, Subcommittee to Investigate Juvenile Delinquency, *Hearings on Drugs in Institutions,* 94th Cong., 1st sess., 18 August 1975, 3 vols., III: 3 (quotation), 447–454, 463–544.

24. *National Drug Control Strategy,* 18. *Sourcebook of Criminal Justice Statistics—1988,* 605, 612, gives 295,873 as the average daily population for jails in 1987 and 556,748 as the number of sentenced state and federal prisoners at the end of the same year.

25. *National Drug Control Strategy,* 18.

26. *Hearings on Drugs in Institutions,* 454.

27. *Sourcebook of Criminal Justice Statistics—1988,* 591, 652.

28. Robert C. Nash, "The English and Scottish Tobacco Trades in the Seventeenth and Eighteenth Centuries: Legal and Illegal Trade," *Economic History Review* 35 (August 1982): 354–72. Evidence for duty-avoidance smuggling of opium is in Courtwright, *Dark Paradise,* 16–28.

29. Ten dollars: Kleber, "Drug Legalization," 3–4. Or less: Kaplan, "Taking Drugs Seriously," 41.

30. Jay L. Rubin, "The Wet War: American Liquor Control, 1941–1945," in Jack S. Blocker, Jr., *Alcohol, Reform and Society: The Liquor Issue in Social Context* (Westport, Conn., 1979), 250–51. Tobacco tax revenues also rose steeply during and after World War II. See Tobacco Institute, *The Tax Burden on Tobacco: Historical Compilation,* vol. 23 (Washington, D.C., 1989), 1–5.

31. Nadelmann, "Drug Prohibition," 945.

32. Advisory Commission on Intergovernmental Relations, *Cigarette Bootlegging: A State AND [sic] Federal Responsibility* (Washington, D.C., 1977), 1–36, 69–74, 105–7, 111–14; Paul R. Johnson, *The Economics of the Tobacco Industry* (New York, 1984), 127–132. Something similar has happened with alcohol along the U.S.-Canadian border. Federal and provincial taxes have made liquor much more expensive in Canada, with the result that two million and possibly as many as four million cases are smuggled annually. Marialista Calta, "Liquor Smuggling to Canada Is Brisk," *New York Times,* 22 November 1987.

33. Advisory Commission on Intergovernmental Relations, *Cigarette Tax Evasion: A Second Look* (Washington, D.C., 1985), 5–6, estimated that cigarette tax evasion dropped 45 percent between the mid-1970s and the mid-1980s. For the persistence of large revenue losses in high-tax states, see Tobacco Tax Section of the National Association of Tax Administrators, *Presentations at the 1987 Annual Meeting* (Washington, D.C., 1987), 7; Michael J. Berry, "Tobacco Tax Enforcement," in Federation of Tax Administrators, Tobacco Tax Section, *Proceedings of the 1988 Annual Meeting* (Washington, D.C., 1988), 12–13; and Florida, House of Representatives, "Cigarette Industry and Tax Study Commission Report" (Tallahassee: typescript document, 1988), 13, 27–29. I am grateful to Walker Merryman for calling certain of these documents to my attention.

34. Nadelmann himself raises this possibility. "The federal government need not play the leading role in devising alternatives; it need only clear the way to allow state and local governments the legal power to implement their own drug legalization policies" ("Drug Prohibition," 945). This is not a formula for consistency.

35. Craig Wolff, "In New York, the Brazenness of Illegal Gun Dealers Grows," *New York Times,* national edition, 6 November 1990.

36. Among those who have suggested a readjustment of strategy and expenditures are Kaplan, "Taking Drugs Seriously," 49–50; Peter Reuter, *Can the Borders Be Sealed? A RAND Note* (Santa Monica, Calif., 1988), 15; Massing, "The Two William Bennetts," 33; and Avram Goldstein and Harold Kalant, "Drug Policy: Striking the Right Balance," *Science* 249 (28 September 1990): 1513–21. "[A] massive shift of available funds is called for, from supply reduction to demand reduction (prevention education, treatment, and research)," write Goldstein and Kalant. "The federal drug war budget would be more cost-effective if the presently proposed ratio of supply reduction to demand reduction—71% to 29%—were reversed" (1517).

37. The treatment system and its defects are assessed in Dean R. Gerstein and Henrick J. Harwood, eds., *Treating Drug Problems: A Study of the Evolution, Effectiveness, and Financing of Public and Private Drug Treatment Systems,* vol. 1 (Washington, D.C., 1990).

38. U.S. Congress, House, Committee on Energy and Commerce, Subcommittee on Health and the Environment, *Hearings on AIDS Issues,* 100th Cong., 1st sess., 29 September 1987; and 100th Cong., 2d sess., 19 February and 15 March 1988, part 1, 281–554. The Bush administration has evinced no enthusiasm for needle-exchange programs because they are inconsistent with its zero-tolerance agenda and because they could be viewed as sanctioning intravenous drug abuse. Despite these fears, there is as yet no evidence from any country that needle-exchange programs encourage intravenous drug abuse.

39. Those who wonder why the drug war has made but fitful progress in choking off the cocaine shipments from the Andean nations should consult the excellent study by Rensselaer W. Lee III, *The White Labyrinth: Cocaine and Political Power* (New Brunswick, 1989).

KATHRYN MEYER

Fast Crabs and Cigarette Boats: A Speculative Essay

Imagine, if you will, that you live in the richest, most influential nation on earth. This is a country whose political system has been consciously adopted by neighboring heads of state seeking to duplicate the same stability and prosperity in their own societies. It is a country that has certainly experienced unprecedented growth and cultural achievement in its past two hundred years and thus contains some of the most magnificent and intellectually exciting urban centers in the world. You would be justifiably proud to live in such a place.

Yet you would be aware of certain social ills darkening the tranquillity of the nation. Farmers are losing their land and a growing army of unemployed are becoming increasingly difficult to ignore. Seditious religious cults and rebellious minority groups have required strong policing actions over the past fifteen or twenty years. There has been a noticeable increase in organized crime. The economy also shows signs of trouble. Prices are not stable, taxes are a great burden, and the country suffers an unfavorable balance of trade that defies attempts to bring it under control.

If you lived isolated from the cares of the world and had therefore managed to remain unaware of these problems, you still could not avoid hearing talk of the mounting evil of drug abuse. You would hear of well-organized men from foreign shores showing complete contempt for the laws of your nation, smuggling narcotic drugs along the southern coast. Official estimates would claim that one in a hundred of your compatriots had at least tried drugs, adding to the decline in productivity and increasing official corruption and social lawlessness.

Now examine for a moment your most cherished images of China. Perhaps you will think of glittering Hong Kong or up-and-coming Taiwan. But these places seem especially successful in contrast to the rest of China, the mainland, where this century has seen a drab uniformity of sparse consumption replace earlier poverty and political instability. We think of China as poor. Our twentieth-century images are not ones of abundance. Yet the country just described is the Chinese empire of the early 1800s. Ruled by the Manchurian-born Qing emperors since 1644 using Confucian political systems, the subsequent years of domestic calm brought Chinese culture to its height. It was a nation controlled by a bureaucracy of the best and brightest the country could produce. It was not industrial, but it had a flourishing interregional trade. The wealth generated by participating in the bureaucracy or in commerce supported an urban culture marked by luxury and consumption. Yet over the reigns of three Emperors—Qianlong (1736–96), Jiaqing (1796–1820), and Daoguang (1820–50)—China reached its peak and then began to experience the problems mentioned above.[1]

Traditional China, to most Americans, seems an alien, exotic land, with a mystique about it that is rendered as romantic or sinister to fit the occasion. Until recently it would have been difficult, even impossible, to make any comparison between imperial China and the United States of the present day. The two political systems—authoritarian Confucianism and constitutional democracy—are fundamentally dissimilar. Only in their respective claims to be the model for the civilized world and in their mutual provision for social mobility through merit can they be compared. Yet now that America's systematic success has produced the wealth, the leisure, and the frustrations that attract the supply and create the demand for illegal, recreational drugs, we must look anew at the imperial Chinese experience.

This article will examine the similarities between two periods of crisis: Guangzhou (Canton), China, in the 1830s and Miami, Florida, in the 1980s. It will consider not the vast differences between the two, but some of the similar problems that they experienced in facing a multinational business that, although illegal, has proved over the past hundred and fifty years to be vital and adaptable.

Don't Trust Anyone Over Thirty

Americans like to think of drug use, or abuse, as being a contemporary problem. Yet narcotic drugs in one form or another have been available in the United States since this nation's inception. Patent medicines routinely contained opiates and doctors generously prescribed them until the Pure Food and Drug Act of 1906 took them off the shelf and the Harrison

Narcotic Act of 1914 restricted opiates nationwide. Cocaine and marijuana followed opiates onto the proscribed lists through the first half of the twentieth century. While certain drugs remained attractive to particular subcultures—marijuana, for instance, had generally been associated with Mexicans and musicians—in the early twentieth century mainstream Americans turned to aspirin to cure their aches and to liquor to relieve ennui. World War II saw drugs almost entirely eliminated from the United States.[2]

Then came the 1960s. Early in that decade recreational drugs began to reappear in polite circles. No longer used to cure pain, they became a modern tool to capture the religious ecstasies of a preindustrial age. The drug of the day was LSD. Created by a major pharmaceutical company, lysergic acid diethylamide was used in the 1950s by psychologists to recreate madness and by American intelligence as a possible weapon in the battle of nerves accompanying the Cold War. But LSD created euphoria too intense to contain in the lab. It leaked into artistic circles and soon became a cornerstone of the counterculture created by middle-class children in response to an unpopular war perceived to have been made by their parents. Vietnam became the organic symbol of an industrial society gone wrong. At the same time acid flowed into the streets. It was the perfect drug. Produced by the military-industrial complex the protesters opposed, acid provided the children of an affluent generation with an easy spiritual experience while at the same time signaling their rejection of the commercial society from which they came. Marijuana accompanied LSD in the rounds of the protesters, while some soldiers returning from tours of duty in Vietnam brought back with them a taste for high-quality heroin.[3]

In the 1960s drugs were associated with the young, the rebellious, the unkempt. Drug use defined the generation gap between those over thirty, who created the war and compliantly knuckled under to the drudgery of the daily routine, and the youthful protesters, who flaunted the system. Some challenged the material comforts of the consumer society either by withdrawing into one of the many religious sects that followed in the wake of rebellion, such as the Hari Krishna, or by forming cults of violence, as did Charles Manson or the Hell's Angels. Yet the size of the youth movement as a whole, demonstrated by summers in Haight-Ashbury or the Woodstock concert of August 1969, pushed the aesthetics and some of the values of the young into the mainstream.

The so-called flower children were, after all, a market. And so men like Peter Max appeared, bringing psychedelic art to advertising. By 1969, Max's mind-expanding designs backed the sales of forty products. War protest coincided with the rediscovery of drugs, but when the war ended the protesting generation demonstrated a propensity to consume that pushed the margins beyond anything before imagined. Former protestors entered the work force; many brought their grass with them. As they made the transition from blue jeans to blue suits, many found that after a hard day at the office a joint tasted better than a martini.[4]

In the 1970s, marijuana, at least, became a semihidden vice, although not without its critics, and it opened the way for more sophisticated experiences. Once considered a drug of poor blacks, cocaine became the elite high of the late 1970s and the 1980s. Cocaine was not a drug of protest; it was a drug of success. It was expensive. It reputedly left the user able to function in the dazzling career paths of Ronald Reagan's America. Usage took on a certain respectability. It reached all levels of society. In 1978, when Jimmy Carter's presidential aide, Hamilton Jordan, was allegedly seen in a New York discotheque snorting cocaine, the incident raised a brief flurry of criticism, but Jordan kept his job.[5]

If cocaine was the drug of the age, then Miami was its capital. The city that hosted the Republican convention and launched Ronald Reagan's victorious presidential campaign became the major port of entry for coke. Coca leaves grow only in the Andean regions of South America and unlike marijuana cannot be cultivated closer to the market. Cocaine's immense popularity in the United States gave enterprising individuals south of the border an opportunity for remarkable profits. Miami became the major point of entry for cocaine. Located geographically close to the Latin American source, with ample coastline and the convenience of the many Caribbean islands to provide safe haven, Miami also had a large Hispanic population among which traffickers could hide and recruit. At first it was the Cuban community that dominated the traffic, but soon Colombians, who out-competed all contenders through superior organization, eclipsed the Cubans.

The early 1980s witnessed the emergence of the Medellín cartel. Created primarily to maximize profits and to control the risks in a dangerous business, the organization thrived in Colombia because it fit so neatly into the political conflicts of that troubled nation. The cartel thrived in a region where widespread poverty and astronomical debt made the organizers seem like a heaven-sent alternative. The kingpins managed, through bribes, intimidation, or persuasion, to compromise a good portion of the standing Colombian government. Thus Carlos Lehder, a major smuggler for the cartel, talked about his enterprise in anti-American political terms, even as he grew rich.[6]

As the Colombians entered the American market, their methods seemed so disturbingly violent that they captured the public imagination as well. Incidents such as the Dadeland Shopping Center shoot-out, which set the tone for the television show *Miami Vice,* and the publicity given to *Palo Maombe,* a Cuban form of voodoo including human sacrifice, made cocaine seem at once exotic, foreign, and dangerous. The appearance of a cheaper, stronger derivative of cocaine, crack, emphasized coke's dangers as crack spread like dye into poorer communities and into America's ghettoes. Wherever crack went it seemed to enrich street gangs in the cities across America where unemployment figures ran high. Cocaine became a national scourge.

Thus the course of the 1980s has seen the clamor for control drown out the panache that drugs had acquired in the 1970s. Ronald Reagan announced his war on drugs in 1982, commissioning then Vice President George Bush to head a special task force on drug control for South Florida. George Bush, an American aristocrat from Ivy League schools, a member of the right clubs, whose political career moved unfaltering to the centers of power, went south, bringing money and the latest in military technology to guard the southern coast. Drug traffickers became the object of growing media coverage and the target of political rhetoric as well as foreign-policy strategies. In Illinois, a candidate for governor advocated the death penalty for drug dealers. In Columbus, Ohio, as in many urban centers, the mayor announced a tough drug enforcement program calling for stiff penalties for users and life sentences for kingpins.[7]

Strict enforcement and mandatory sentencing have created seriously overcrowded prisons, and the prospects for the future offer little relief. This situation in turn has brought some strangely retrogressive proposals in response. In the state of Delaware, for instance, some legislators have recommended a return to flogging minor drug-law violators. Most recently, the House Armed Services Committee proposed turning the Pacific possessions of Wake and Midway into prison islands.[8]

It has only been since 1988 that the antidrug campaign seems to have had some noticeable effect. President Bush, deprived of the traditional American enemy by Soviet President Mikhail Gorbachev's initiatives, outlined new programs for drug control, including more active law enforcement, aid to Latin American nations fighting the drug industry within their borders, and an increased military presence in the Caribbean, including AWACs and radar balloons. As the Cold War justification for a large military budget disappeared, members of the armed forces turned their attention to contributing to the interdiction effort in order to dodge budget cuts. The 1989 Christmas invasion of Panama brought national coverage of the drug war as combat to the nation's living rooms, providing relief to a country haunted by the embarrassing defeat in Vietnam.

The debate over the control of narcotics trafficking has become entwined with many of the larger issues America faces in the last decade of the twentieth century. Efforts to stop the smuggling and distribution of cocaine create dilemmas in a society that prides itself on individual freedoms and the rights of the accused before the law. How far is a nervous public willing to tolerate official monitoring of private activities? To the point of sanctioning mandatory, random drug testing? Beyond that? There remains the question of due process, a cornerstone in the U.S. Constitution. What happens to the rights of society at large when an accused drug dealer can afford legal fees far in excess of the ordinary district attorney's budget? How many rules of police procedure can safely be set aside to assure capture of cocaine smugglers? And there is the question of budget allocations: technology versus human resources. Should limited resources be channeled toward the purchase of more and better hardware to guard the nation's extensive borders or toward rehabilitation clinics and education programs?

Because drug smuggling implies borders, there is a foreign policy element involved as well. Is it the Colombians, people stereotypically considered to be passionate rather than rational, with a government teetering on the edge of anarchy or worse, who are poisoning America's children and who must be brought under control? Or must the war on drugs be won on the home front? The drug traffic underscores persistent problems of a staggering imbalance of payments. With such an imbalance in legitimate foreign trade, can the nation afford the illicit money slipping out of the country in money-laundering operations? Will legalization offer a solution by eliminating the border?

Each of the above concerns is immediate and contemporary. Yet the business of narcotics has a long history that parallels, in a shadowy way, the course of Western expansion and modernization. Colombians and Bolivians were not the first to profit from the habits of a large and wealthy nation—Portuguese and Dutch traders hold that distinction. The first drug kingpins were Scots, not Latinos; the first cartel was located in Calcutta, not Medellín.

The Barbarian Nature Is Crafty and Stubborn

Westerners associate opium smoking as a Chinese vice, and so it was a century ago. Yet is was only with the coming of the Europeans to Asia that the Chinese took up the habit. Although long known as a medicine in China, opium was not smoked for pleasure until the seventeenth century, when the introduction of tobacco taught Chinese how to draw the smoldering substance into their lungs. It was, after all, only with the introduction of tobacco that Chinese learned how to smoke. Tobacco first reached the China coast in the late sixteenth century with the first European merchant explorers. By the middle of the seventeenth century, some Chinese were smoking *madak,* tobacco dipped into a treacly opium solution. By the late eighteenth century pure opium had supplanted this comparatively mild mixture. Pure opium produced a greater euphoria and required the sophisticated equipment of the opium pipe and lamp, some of which could be ornately fashioned.[9]

Opium was illegal, yet it was a product of consumption that grew in popularity in a prosperous age. At first it came legally into China, being listed as a medicine on the tariff schedule. But it found a different market. By 1729, an imperial edict banned opium smoking; the ban was largely ignored. By 1813, the number of opium smokers had risen dramatically. New edicts appeared, sentencing officials who profited in the trade or enjoyed its product to various penalties: loss of post, two months wearing the wooden collar, and one hundred blows with the bamboo. These rules, too, proved to be ineffective. The number of Chinese smokers continued to increase.[10]

Although aware of growing opium use, the Jiaqing emperor and his government had more urgent problems. Jiaqing began his reign with the need to clean his political house. The nineteenth century opened with scandals close to the throne. Heshen, an imperial bodyguard and close friend of the previous emperor, had used his influence to advance his own career and those of his friends. Heshen became incredible wealthy over the forty years before his fall. His influence left the taste of corruption throughout the Chinese government even after his demise.

The Jiaqing years also saw problems in the Chinese countryside. Prosperity in the eighteenth century led to a doubling of the Chinese population and put great pressure on available agricultural land. The tax burdens of the population increased as well. Tax rates, set in ounces of silver, had to be paid in copper coins. The nineteenth century saw the copper price of silver rise, disturbing the ability of the average peasant to pay taxes and increasing the price of anything valued in silver. The standard value of 1,000 copper coins to an ounce of silver went as high as 1,800 per ounce in some areas. At the same time, farm prices fell. Farmers losing their land added to a growing restlessness in the countryside.

Some people retreated from a confusing and decadent world into groups of social refuge. We can see the same phenomenon in America today where some seek acceptance in antisocial groups, such as street gangs or organized crime, while other find meaning for their lives in religious sects or fundamentalism. The Jiaqing and Daoguang eras saw the rise of both. Triads, those Chinese secret societies depicted romantically in *Kung Fu* films, grew in number during both reigns. In 1830, a memorialist reported to the throne describing a gang called the Hook Sword Society, which controlled an area near the city of Shaoxing. It boasted a complex organization that the select entered by taking an oath, while its richest members ensured the group influence and protection by buying government positions for themselves.

Heterodox religious movements are not phenomena limited to the modern age. China had its share of such groups and in times of social stress they attracted a large membership. For the first seven years of his reign, Jiaqing faced an open rebellion by the White Lotus sect in the central provinces of the empire. The White Lotus sect claimed to be Buddhist; it was millenarian and populist in its appeal. It attracted the down and out of Chinese society, bringing them together for prayer, meditation, and martial arts, by promising them the end of the present, decadent cosmic era and by foretelling salvation in the next. Harassed by official proscriptions, the White Lotus rose in rebellion. The difficulties the imperial army had in quelling this popular revolt diminished the stature of the dynasty as much as did Heshen's corruption.[11]

Accompanying the trouble of the times was a growing alienation among the intellectuals of the emprie. China's government was a meritocracy, awarding the highest offices to those demonstrating their literary skills in competitive examination. Yet the culture produced more bright scholars than the government could employ, especially so after Heshen's influence increased the practice of selling official rank to those who would not have succeeded in the competitive exams. Intellectuals complained of corruption in office. Many criticized the examination system because it produced men of spectacular mediocrity. Thus in the 1820s, when opium use emerged as the empire's major concern, it played against a background of social tension and structural problems that were more complicated than mere illegal traffic.

It was during the early years of the Daoguang emperor's reign that opium increasingly occupied the attention of the authorities. There was not any one incident of lawbreaking that made the problem jump to the foreground. Well-place persons had periodically been caught in possession of opium, bringing bursts of antiopium edicts soon to be lost in the press of official life. It was the impact that the opium traffic made when viewed through the eyes of officials concerned with economic woes that brought opium to a state of crisis. In the 1820s opium memorialists showed increasing concern about the drain of silver into foreign lands. In a complicated economic situation, which scholars still do not entirely understand, opium became a simple answer. It explained the rising price of silver—silver was leaking into the sea. It explained corruption and crime and put the source of Chinese problems on the heads of foreign scoundrels.

Opium had come along with the European trade, an activity that the Chinese dynasty frowned upon at the same time that it enjoyed a certain income from tariffs and fees. More control-minded than mercantile, the Chinese government considered foreign merchants potential troublemakers. In the seventeenth century, China limited the scope of international commerce to one city, Guangzhou, and to one season, spring. All trade had to be conducted through specially designated merchant houses, known as the *hongs.* But Guangzhou, the city, and the surrounding Fanyu county, like the city of Miami and Dade county, was also a perfect place for smuggling. Located on the southern coast, it was accessible to the sea and laced with inland waterways. The area, like Florida, had a large minority population, in this case the *Danjia,* people who lived on the waterways in boats, people whose customs and dress were markedly different from the Han Chinese. The *Danjia* were poor. When they did earn enough money to move ashore, they were not welcome as neighbors or marriage partners by the majority society. These people knew the sea and were ready to connive with foreign merchants.[12]

The first traders were the Portuguese, the Spaniards, and the Dutch, who came to China seeking silk, rhubarb, and tea. They paid for these goods in silver, which at first they brought with them from distant places. As the Chinese market for opium expanded, foreigners found it more expedient to obtain the necessary silver illegally along the coast. During the course of the eighteenth century, it was the British merchants who came to dominate this trade; like the Colombian cartels of today, the British did so by superior organization and by controlling the entire supply from production to sales. They were not called a cartel, but rather the British East India Company. The company grew opium by license in India and sold it at auction in Calcutta. The British government kept itself free of risk or blame by allowing free traders to run the chests of monopoly-produced opium to the China coast in clipper ships and to make the final arrangments to get it across the border.

These opium traders came from the British Isles and brought with them to the China coast the European social and political attitudes of the day. They were independent traders, yet they advanced the interests of a

British government monopoly. Men like William Jardine, James Matheson, and Lancelot Dent represented, or at least sided with, a progressive faction in political circles at home that wished to see the end of all trade restrictions. On the domestic front, they were rewarded with the demise of the East India Company in 1833. (The opium monopoly remained, entering the British Colonial office budget.) In China they wanted to break official barriers to trade as well, arguing that if they had a freer access to the market, then Chinese could be persuaded to purchase British products other than opium. Like the Colombians long after them, they defended their trade in the economic terms of the day. They claimed to be supplying a Chinese (American) demand that they had no hand in creating.[13] (It should be noted that after the Opium War, when the Chinese monopoly followed the British East India Company into the dustbin of history, opium sales increased.)

The Chinese did not care about the fine points of Britain's political economy. Should the coastal trade open up? The Chinese imperial court saw instead arrogant, dangerous smugglers, crafty and stubborn foreigners, who connived with the meanest elements of Chinese society. How could the court open the trade to such people? Chinese authorities saw foreigners who practiced and preached a foreign religion along the coast, areas already afflicted with heterodox, secret cults and with organized gangs. The 1820s found more reports reaching the capital of foreign vessels in coastal waters, of foreign coins in areas along the coast. By 1830, reports indicated that peasants in the Chinese interior were planting opium poppies in their fields. This development was accompanied by increasing concern about the economy and the drain of silver along the coast. Thus, when the governor-general of Guangdong and Guangxi forwarded a British petition requesting open trade, the emperor was not so inclined to think of these foreign petitioners as gentlemen.[14]

In 1828, when a certain Bai Weiyi appeared at the headquarters of the Beijing Commander of the Army claiming that he had been kidnapped by Christians (whom he called the Western White Lotus Sect), men who had drugged him and carried him off through Anhui and Hupei provinces, his story brought about an extensive investigation from the highest levels of government, especially after he turned over foreign coins as proof of his ordeal. He accused Ling Xianli of Zhejiang province of having lured him to his house pleading illness (Bai was a doctor and a seller of paintings by profession), where, he claimed, Ling tried to convert him. Only after thorough questioning by provincial authorities, only after Ling's house was searched for unfit volumes, and only after Ling tread on a cross and ate meat and drank wine in public court was he released. Ling admitted that his grandfather had been a Christian but had renounced his faith. It is not known whether Christians drugged Bai. Bai was found guilty of fabricating the story; because he had a history of mental disease, he was released to his family's custody.[15]

Who used opium in China? There were no surveys, and literature extolling the virtues of mind expansion was far in the future. Yet opium use was not limited to the lowest classes. In 1830, for example, authorities discovered that Zhang Jinfu, a palace eunuch, had been selling opium within the imperial palace itself. Investigations implicated a certain Moslem prince, Kekesebuku, who was serving as an imperial guard. Kekesebuku was not as lucky as Jimmy Carter's aide Hamilton Jordan. Kekesebuku was charged under the opium laws, denounced for engaging in lewd behavior with eunuchs, and sentenced to wearing the wooden collar for three months, given one hundred blows with the bamboo, and stripped of his job. Li Hongbin, the governor-general of Guangdong and Guangxi also lost his job. When a minority group, the Yao, rebelled in the southern border regions, Li had been placed in charge of pacification. In 1832, reports surfaced that the operation was going slowly because soldiers under Li's command were using opium. Li was dismissed.[16]

Between 1830 and 1839, the growing perception of the breakdown of Chinese control of its borders created a crisis in the capital and led to the determination in 1839 to take every measure possible to eliminate the opium traffic once and for all. As a consequence, the Chinese emperor appointed a Lin Zexu, a man who was the epitome of the Chinese culture, a brilliant scholar, an able administrator, a member of an influential literary and political discussion club, to go to Guangzhou with full authority to do whatever was necessary to rid the country of opium. Lin arrived in March 1839 and began prosecuting all cases of those implicated in the opium traffic. He locked the foreign merchants in their trading compounds until they turned over to him twenty thousand chests of opium, which he then publicly destroyed. This action brought his country into a shooting war with Great Britain, which China lost.

The astounding economic success of these crafty and stubborn foreigners, who were loud and lacking in the manners of civilized society, sparked debates in the capital and along the China coast that challenged long-held Chinese beliefs. How does one control the traffic—through pouring money into military technology or through moral suasion? Was it foreigners who forced opium on the Chinese, or did blame lie within China, where demand for the commodity grew so great that Commissioner Lin believed that one out of every one hundred Chinese had tried the drug? How can a country stop the dramatic and unchecked loss of silver leaking out of the empire in the boats of smugglers? Would it be in the interest of the nation to leaglize opium and bring it under government control? Or should there be a more rigorous application of antiopium law? Should foreigners, whose country expounded the virtues of legal procedures and trial by jury, be subject to the rigors of the Chinese laws they were breaking? The Chinese never solved these problems. Since the 1840s, no one else has either.

Points of Comparison

Similarities between the Chinese and American cases are worth noting. First of all, the boats were similar. Narcotics enforcement creates the tactical problem of barriers. Legal restrictions dictate the conditions under which traffickers must operate; they demand that the product be produced elsewhere, be brought close to the point of entry, and be stored while distribution arrangements are made, then run through the barriers, quietly, quickly, and at night. Barriers inflate the price of the commodity when it finally reaches its destination, creating strong incentives for innovation. Some of the high profits must be reinvested into the smuggling enterprise because better equipment increases the probability of success. Drug traffickers have the money and the motivation to stay on the cutting edge of marine technology.

In the spring of 1987, Luis Gustavo García sat in the U.S. Senate office building and described a successful marijuana and cocaine trafficking enterprise he had carefully built up in the Bahamas. Kojak, as he was called because of his neatly shaved head, developed the Bahamas as an offshore base of operations through well-placed bribes given to a receptive government. The Bahamas was the perfect location. Situated close to Miami and offering many deserted harbors and cays, Kojak maintained his fleet of cigarette boats and planes, safely transferred cargo coming from Colombia, and reduced the length of the most dangerous leg of the journey. He told the senators, "You got the stuff right 50 miles away from you and, you know, then the odds change completely. The risk can be taken." Carlos Lehder also used these islands for the same purposes.[17]

Kojak's entry into the trade came through his ability as a boatman and mechanic. He began running the blockade into Miami using boats; only later did the profitability of his endeavor allow him to purchase a fleet of planes, with the radar and radio equipment to accompany it. Like most of his fellow smugglers, he did not skimp on hardware. Profits of the trade easily allowed Kojak to afford the $150,000 price tag of a boat made of fiberglass with twin 440-horsepower turbo engines, high-capacity fuel tanks built narrow for speed, and with a shallow draft, making it possible to run quickly from open ocean into shallower inland waterways. Called cigarette boats by the company that makes them, or "go-fasts" because of their obvious attraction to smugglers, they are tough to catch.[18]

The ostensible solution is to provide the police with the same sort of fleet. And so the U.S. Customs Service acquired *Blue Thunder,* a thirty-nine-foot catamaran with 450-cubic-inch Merc-Cruiser engines, designed and built by the same man who designed cigarette boats. But these boats are dangerous at high speeds. Policemen and customs agents, who do not make as much in a year as the pilots of the go-fasts do in one delivery, tend to be more cautious, even when they do not take bribes.[19]

In China, the smugglers were equally crafty. At first, smugglers brought opium right into the city of Guangzhou with them, unconcerned about restrictions. But after 1821, when the Daoguang emperor ordered Ruan Yuan, then governor-general of the Guangdong area, to correct the opium situation, the ensuing crackdown forced smuggling operations to the offshore island of Lintin, where deals were done in receiving ships. On these ships native smugglers and brokers bargained in relative safety for their share of each cargo. The smugglers who made the last and most dangerous part of the journey, from Lintin along the coast, past the coastal defenses, and up the rivers of China, made increasing profits as the cost of opium rose during the 1820s. They bought for themselves sleek vessels, called "fast crabs," which were long and narrow and lined on each side with oars. When fully manned, they could move like the wind. Government patrol boats could not catch them.

In the seventh year of the Daoguang emperor, 1827, local officials suggested the government fund the building of seven fast patrol boats designed along the same model as the fast crabs. Stalking the fast crabs was dangerous work. Drug smugglers armed their people and the boats came equipped with chain-mesh guards to repel government weapons. The soldiers who manned the oars of the government boats earned room board and between four- and six-tenths of an ounce of silver per day, a nice salary, but not as high as the rewards that must have passed among the bandits who staffed the fast crabs. These government men, whose jobs took them into the terrain of the smugglers, were subject to many temptations to augment their incomes. And so they did. In 1839, when Lin Zexu made his investigation of corruption in Guangzhou, he found that the officer in charge of the fast-crab fleet was securely in the pay of the smugglers.[20]

Second, barriers create a climate in which corruption must grow. In

1839, when Lin Zexu came to Guangzhou to eradicate the smuggling problem, he knew he was walking into a breeding ground of vice. He would have felt equally at home in Miami. In 1985, the Miami River police case brought the questionable reputation of the Miami city police to national attention. A group of police officers had regularly been stealing drugs found in the cars they stopped for traffic violations and selling the goods to increase their salaries, perhaps hoping to maintain the stylish image flashed to the world on "Miami Vice." They soon broadened their activities to include intercepting drug deliveries and selling the catch rather than turning it in. They got caught attempting to hijack a boatload of cocaine moving up the Miami River. When three of the boatmen jumped overboard and drowned, the situation became impossible to conceal. Subsequent investigations indicated that the corruption exposed by the mishap on the Miami River was only the tip of the south Florida iceberg. Within a year, seventy-two other Miami police officers were dismissed or suspended. Rumors circulated that one hundred to two hundred more officers were under investigation.[21]

Miami Police Chief Clarence Dickson blamed the situation on indiscriminate hiring that took place in the early 1980s—in response to institutional racism that had been part of the department for several decades. The Liberty City riots in the summer of 1980 and the influx of Cubans from the Mariel boatlift forced a restructuring and expansion of the department. This policy coincided with the remarkable increase in cocaine and cocaine money in the southern Florida economy. The combination of intense racial bitterness in the face of so much money put the temptation far beyond mere lack of professionalism.[22]

In South China foreign drug kingpins, denied access to Chinese territory by restrictive laws, had to rely on native marketing networks. They found their Chinese counterparts to be most helpful at all levels of society. Many of their allies came from the *Danjia,* a minority group who clung to the rivers for their residences and their livelihoods and who met only with disapproval on the land. But these were not the only Chinese involved in the trade. When the opium came inland, after it ran the barriers on the fast crabs, it went to distribution points called *yaokou,* where the purchasers broke up the chests of opium for redistribution. Then it was taken inland in different ways. British merchants on the China coast claimed that one of the best means of getting the opium to the inland market was aboard the tribute ships carrying tax grain to the capital from the south—clearly an operation in official hands. Because of their imperial status, tribute ships rarely suffered government inspections, and those serving as officials or attendants on the voyages north could make profits with little concern for the law. Foreign opium traffickers were so convinced of official connivance in the trade that they tended to explain away the periodic crackdowns ordered by the central government as being excuses for bureaucrats to renegotiate their percentage of the illicit profits.[23]

Not all of the highest bureaucrats were corrupted by opium money; in fact, many were scandalized by what they saw as the moral erosion of their system. But the considerable profits made by participants in the illegal traffic allowed them to buy a certain measure of protection from the system whose laws they were breaking. In America drug barons buy the best legal advice; in China they purchased rank. When Lin arrived in Guangzhou, he drew up a list of most-wanted native traffickers. Among these was Wang Zhengao, a native of Fanyu County, just outside the city. Wang had made enough money through operating a fast crab and a *yaokou* to purchase a commission in the navy and command a government patrol boat. From this splendid position he was able to shield other traffickers and dealers. The middle-ranking employees in government service, the scribes, clerks, and errand-runners of the local officials appointed by the capital, had access to information that smugglers needed. They could also supply counterfeit seals of office, which made running the barriers easier.[24]

Third, money concentrates around the entry points of drug traffickers. Kojak told Senate investigators about standing ankle-deep in a room littered with currency. Drug barons are known to weigh money because counting it becomes tedious. In the same way, one reporter from a Calcutta newspaper of the 1820s described tripping over bags of silver on board a receiving ship off Lintin. The U.S. Federal Reserve Bank for Florida reported a $5.5 billion dollar cash surplus in 1981 as narcodollars flooded the southern Florida economy. In China, reports that the ratio of copper to silver was out of balance came from every point in the empire. Yet Guangdong maintained the old rates. If the imbalance was caused by silver scarcity, then the numbers showed Chinese silver settling in Guangdong like sand in a funnel. The Chinese economy had weaknesses that were caused by conditions other than opium; the official perception that silver was leaking into the ocean was based on a phenomenon they could see. The American economy has many problems, but the public hears little about the impact on it of narcotics traffic. Perhaps on this point the United States could learn from China.[25]

Fourth, uncontrolled illegal traffic involves large amounts of money and corruption, whether in China or in the United States. Therefore, as the economy and disregard for the law got out of hand, some people in both places questioned the wisdom of creating barriers in the first place.

In China, the debate over legalization emerged primarily from the economic conditions that opium created for the empire. In the mid-1830s a small but influential group of officials, many of whom had held posts in Guangdong and so had experience to back their convictions, called for legalization of opium. The best-known representative of the legalizers was Xu Naiji, who had been a provincial judge for Guangdong. In 1834 he became an imperial censor in the capital, giving him good access to the throne. In 1836, after several of his colleagues wrote tentatively about possibly easing opium restrictions without incurring imperial wrath, Xu submitted a memorial of his own recommending legalization.

Xu argued that China should return to the earlier practice of taxing opium as a medicinal herb. Then when it came into port, he said, it could be traded for tea and other goods on a barter system. In this way the price of opium and the loss of Chinese silver in the exchange could be controlled. He advocated taxing opium but making the tariff low, to discourage smugglers. Xu pointed out that the results of interdiction had only been to increase both the sales and the price of the drug. As the laws grew more severe, the smugglers had only become craftier. The illegal traffic weakened the empire by bringing corruption into every area it touched. He cited examples of bandits dressed as government agents using opium searches as an excuse to rob people, and instances of actual government agents planting opium on victims and blackmailing them. Miami had a similar rash of such incidents. At the same time that the Miami River cops were using their badges to relieve speeders of their stash, there was a wave of burglaries conducted by thieves dressed in police uniforms, driving the highways in mock patrol cars. This led one Miami paper to comment: "The great existential question in Miami today is 'Who is a real cop (and is he a drug wholesaler?) and who is a fake cop (and is he a "Miami Vice" actor or a home burglar?).' "[26]

Xu Naiji's response to such a climate was to recommend easing the restrictions on opium. He urged the emperor to revise the law codes so that opium once again could legally enter Canton. Yet he did not advocate free use of opium throughout the empire; he recommended instead a ban on smoking among government officials and soldiers. In the summer of 1836, it seemed that Xu's proposals might be adopted. The foreign traders, though, greeted this news with caution. Hearing that the new regulations would soon go into effect, they assumed that China could not change course so easily. They reasoned that too many high-level officials were making too much money in bribes to allow such a reform to take place.[27]

The legalizers time of influence was short. Xu's memorial drew criticism from numerous law-and-order Confucian officials. Huang Juezi, for one, responded to the idea of legalization by calling instead for stricter laws and even the death penalty for those who trafficked in opium. (The conditions of Chinese prisons were such that overcrowding would not have been a problem. No one advocated flogging because one hundred blows with the bamboo was considered a light sentence.)

The great debate over legalization of opium in 1836 should sound familiar to readers of recent American editorial pages. The points of the arguments have become more complex over the century, as has the trade, but the core is the same. American legalizers, such as Ethan A. Nadelmann, contend that it is the laws that create the problems associated with drugs, not the drugs. Interdiction reduces the supply, making what does slip through barriers more valuable. Barriers force traffickers to be craftier, leading to more refined, and therefore more dangerous, drugs in this age of modern chemistry: heroin rather than opium; crack rather than cocaine. The drug laws also benefit those traffickers most able to consolidate their operation because they increase their profits. The police weed out any inefficient competition. No border can be entirely controlled. Abbie Hoffman pointed out that about 300 million people a year pass through customs, as do 150 million tons of cargo. Efficient law enforcement can only cover so much of the border, and the traffickers will adapt. In 1836 Yu Kun raised much the same point, claiming that if Guangzhou were completely sealed off, the barbarians would only move somewhere else along the coast.[28]

Those who argue for legalization point to a time in the not-so-distant past when most Americans turned to opiate-laden patent medicines for everyday afflictions. Make opium, cocaine, and marijuana legal again and they will become inexpensive commodities to be taxed and controlled. Like Xu before them, most Americans are not calling for widespread drug use but for a controlled legalization, and with it control of a large, but hidden, area of the national economy.[29]

Those who would currently legalize narcotic drugs, and some of those who would not, consider the erosion of America's cherished legal protections to be one of the casualties of the war on drugs. The image of the cocaine addict from the inner city, unable to fund his habit, sometimes armed, usually black, always desperate from the craving, breaking into the suburban household, repeats itself in newspaper reports and on television dramas. Many Americans now perceive drug-related crime to be so serious that they seem ready to set aside the legal restrictions allegedly hampering law enforcement officials. Public safety, they claim, demands the invasion of privacy. Absurdly symbolic of this, the last years of the 1980s brought the right to control one's own urine before the Supreme Court in cases such as *National Treasury Employees Union v. Von Raab,* which permitted urine tests of applicants for certain jobs. Urine tests of employees is already practiced in many companies and increasingly in schools.[30]

But the legal problems of narcotics are not merely domestic. Drug traffic involves borders, and therefore it involves adjoining jurisdictions. Crossing national sovereignties is a sensitive procedure. It is just this problem that makes borderlands dangerous places of opportunity. The recent phase of America's war on drugs has brought the politically explosive issues of sovereignty and jurisdiction to the foreground by raising the question of extradition. To Americans the problem seems simple. Certain known people have broken U.S. laws; why should they live safely and in style in Colombia? Yet many Latin Americans become suspicious when enthusiastic authorities from the north want to cross international legal barriers. For Colombians, this issue is viewed against a history of U.S. interference in the region. Even those not sympathetic to cocaine kings question the extent and nature of U.S. encroachment on domestic sovereignty. It is easy for them to see hidden agendas in U.S. drug policy, easy enough that it became an issue in Colombia's recent presidential campaign. They have cause to question U.S. intent when they see U.S. forces invade Panama, capture General Manuel Noriega, and jail him in Florida, while Washington Mayor Marion Barry, who was videotaped smoking crack, goes free after a public trial. Perhaps the suspicions on their part come from cultural misunderstanding of the American legal system. Perhaps they think that Latin Americans, especially Colombians, are unduly taking the blame for a domestic American problem. When U.S. war ships sail ominously close to Colombian waters threatening to carry out interdiction only weeks after the invasion of Panama, one can hardly blame President Virgilio Barco Vargas for protesting undue interference from Washington.

On the China coast some 150 years ago, the question of legal jurisdiction hovered at the edges of the opium questions as well: officials working within the framework of Chinese law had more leeway to act on their suspicions when investigating cases than their American counterparts of the present age; nor were they fettered by as many legal restrictions when questioning suspects. Cruel punishment was usual, yet opium continued to be sold. British traffickers considered Chinese law to be barbaric; they did not look beyond the sanctioned use of torture to understand the fine points of Chinese jurisprudence. Yet the native judicial system, which had been in place for over a thousand years, was more than the brutal, arbitrary thing the British extraditables made it out to be. It was based on legal precedent, on judicial investigation, and on the logical presentation of evidence in public court. It was not frivolous, as foreign merchants on the China coast claimed it was. It had bodies of rules; it had produced legal scholars of note as well as beloved judges of popular fiction. It was corruptible; all legal system are. But perhaps it is to its credit that when Chinese dynasties were on the decline, one of the first complaints would be that evil people had corrupted the courts, implying, if you will, that the general public expected the courts to be fair. It was a system that worked well—even without lawyers.[31]

The British extraditables did not appreciate the subtle traditions of Chinese law, which aimed to deter crime through stringent justice. British merchants had many chances to observe Chinese justice at work. Even before Commissioner Lin arrived in Guangzhou, local officials had made public examples of convicted opium dealers, hoping to cut off the trade. Early in 1837, for example, A-ming, an employee of one of the firms designated to handle foreign goods appeared in the streets of Guangzhou wearing the wooden collar after being convicted of smuggling money abroad. The next year officials publicly strangled a certain He Lanxin in front of the foreign factories for selling opium from his wine shop. The public harshness of the punishments was meant to stop foreign smugglers. It did not.[32]

While demonstrations of the vigor of Chinese law did not deter men like Lancelot Dent or James Innes, it did make them wary of Chinese courts. If the case of A-ming had not been example enough, they all remembered the Terranova case of 1821, when an American sailor who had murdered a Chinese subject was strangled by Chinese authorities. These British extraditables berated the system that they helped to corrupt and called it uncivilized. After Lin Zexu's actions brought war, and after that war was won by the force of British arms, one clause in the Treaty of Nanking gave British residents of the newly opened Chinese ports the gift of extraterritoriality. This diplomatic creation meant that those who might have been strangled had the war been lost had the right to be tried by their own consuls when and if they were indicted. During the hundred years following the Opium War, various Chinese governments tried both legalization and prohibition to control opium use. During the time of prohibition, beginning in 1906, extraterritoriality became a haven for smugglers. For instance, the Japanese diplomat Ishii Itarō tells in his memoirs of his assignment early in his career to the consular court in Tianjin. When he sentenced a drug smuggler under his jurisdiction to two months of hard labor, he gained the reputation as a tough judge.[33] Commissioner Lin Zexu would not have been amused.

Money, Culture, and Power

I composed some final thoughts while sitting in front of the Shibuya subway station in Tokyo, drinking a can of *JIVE* coffee. At the time, prospects for a peaceful resolution to the Persian Gulf crisis were remote. Nonetheless, the Shibuya shopping frenzy continued unabated. The only sign of the times was the three Buddhist priests who were chanting sutras in the spot where a right-wing sound truck usually sat.

Readers unfamiliar with Asia should know that Shibuya is a favorite shopping and restaurant district located in the southwest of Tokyo. For myself and millions of other residents of the metropolitan area, it is a transfer point from the Tokyo subways to the suburban lines. There always seems to be incredible energy here. The lights on the neon signs never seem to burn out. The people at Shibuya are always fashionably and expensively dressed, even when they affect a "punk" style. Considering the numbers of people and the quantities of money that pass through this square every hour, Shibuya is clean and relatively crime-free, at least it seems so to those of us who come from more restive locales.

Many Americans regard Japan as being free from drug abuse. Perhaps they would even agree with those Japanese officials who constructed on Formosa at the turn of the century a colonial opium monopoly modeled after the British opium monopoly in India. Those men claimed that the product of their new bureau would never spread into Japan because culturally and physically the Japanese were, and would remain, a sake-drinking people not given to drugs.

Japan is, however, a highly addicted society. I know from the stories of friends that just across from Shibuya Station, down the central lane that twists between the brightly lit department stores, there are places where the discerning shopper can purchase marijuana, cocaine, or, more likely, amphetamines—the drug of choice in this high-pressure society. Amphetamines have been in Japan for a long time. The original compound was isolated in the Tokyo University labs in 1887. During the years of the Pacific War, the imperial army dispensed it freely so that soldiers might stand longer watches. At the war's end, the surplus supply found its way to the general public and helped fuel the process of rebuilding Japan. Amphetamines became illegal only in 1951, at which time their use declined. Yet the last two decades have seen amphetamine abuse return to the immediate postwar level, assisted by examination stress and by the press of overwork. Amphetamine abuse seems natural in a country where one is never more than a block away from vending machines selling canned coffee and tea—hot or cold—or vitamin drinks in small brown bottles.

Do the Japanese have a cultural propensity to consume stimulants? Or is it that they have too much money? Is amphetamine use only the first step toward a broader range of drugs in Japan, or is it the wave of the future for all nations?[34] Answering these questions requires an understanding of the nexus of drugs with money, culture, and power—which turns our attention, again, to China.

There exists some consensus among Western historians of China that opium was not the fundamental cause of the Opium War of 1839–42. The war came about, they argue, because of cultural differences between East and West and because of the Chinese government's inability to come to terms with a new world order, one which demanded that China open its ports to trade, permit foreigners to travel inland, and provide for a corps of diplomats to reside in Chinese cities to negotiate problems between China and the outside world. The Chinese were slow to accept this new reality because they looked at the world from a rigid notion of superiority which had come from being so successful for so long. Any change would seem like a defeat. These same accounts, while acknowledging opium as the source of the prosperity of men like Jardine, Matheson, and Dent, portray these same men as bad boys on a lark, whose pranks managed to advance modern civilization.[35]

Chinese society faced great difficulties at the beginning of the nineteenth century and interference from the outside world was, at best, untimely. One problem was the inability of the government to enforce one of its laws. Looking at opium through the Chinese eyes of the time, instead of from the viewpoint of the swashbuckling William Jardine, that rugged individualist and proponent of free trade, Jardine becomes a man the officials of the day called the "Iron-Headed Old Rat" with the same vehemence that some call Noriega "Pineapple Face." Just as the Bush administration finally could not abide dealing with a government dominated by such a man, many in the Chinese government could not easily suffer the opium trade in order to help create the future world order. Instead, they saw a loud, arrogant, oafish, inelegant people with a strong body odor, whose sailors were given to drunkenness and violence.

Until the crisis in the Gulf diverted attention, Americans were telling pollsters that ending drug abuse should be a national priority. This concern with narcotics ought to elicit a reconsideration of both the Chinese and American experiences in one of two ways. Either imperial China had a serious problem with drugs or American society has grave structural problems and is too rigid to deal with them creatively. Even after having enrolled in the most recent phase of the war on drugs, do Americans really understand drug abuse, let alone its connection with budget deficits? And in the confusion, some Americans seem willing to do away with the kinds of political and legal guarantees, liberties and freedoms, that men like Jardine and Dent, in their own way, sought to represent.

Obviously, the differences between America and China of a century and a half ago are profound. Chinese were collective; Americans are individualists. Americans are industrial; Chinese were agricultural. Despite, or perhaps because of, such differences, the similarities in the two situations are compelling. The continuity lies not in different cultures, economies, or times but in the culture of the trade itself. Narcotics trafficking has a history that coexists with the course of modern development. The players have changed, as have the locations, but the history of the trade contains some of the most successful businessmen and enterprises in the world of finance. They have adapted quickly to ever-changing restrictions. The captains of this industry were, and continue to be, rugged and colorful individuals no matter what their culture or race. At great risk, they market a product for which they cannot make use of standard advertising or distribution systems. In a world where formal diplomacy breaks down into charge, countercharge, and war, traffickers build networks across hostile borders through which they move quantities of money and produce. The Sino-British problems of the 1830s may have been caused by cultural misunderstanding, but such hindrances did not affect transactions off Lintin Island. George Bush may have his differences with governments in South America, but cocaine keeps moving. And the great profits to be made are helping some North Americans and their Latino business partners, through their own cultural bonds, to transcend other cultural barriers and former resentments passed down through time.

Narcotics use is ultimately a problem of affluence, not one of poverty. Drug traffic goes where money accumulates, and it plays a role as instrumental as any bank or stock exchange in moving that money around. That is power. If there are similarities between modern America and China of the past, those similarities are caused by the uneven distribution of affluence within systems that for the most part work fairly well and by attempts of certain groups, both domestic and foreign, to redress lack of access to that affluence because for one reason or another they cannot fit the pattern for success. City street gangs with their gold chains and expensive athletic shoes—reminiscent of the Chinese triads, who also wore gold—provide a familiar group for those who are not smart enough or disciplined enough or prepared from birth to grab their share of the legitimate pie. Gangs and triads moved drugs and thus did well for themselves as they responded to the lure of power. It would be wrong to think of these groups as antisocial; they are remarkably cohesive. They are successful and powerful because they participate in the demand economy.

The union of money, culture, power, and drugs is not new. Coming to terms with its influence compels a historical awareness of the support that illicit transactions provide to a weak, legitimate economy. In other words, would the British tea trade have done so well in the nineteenth century without the opium monopoly to back it up? And what was the influence of cocaine sales and the money it generated on American prosperity in the 1980s? The presence of fast crabs and cigarette boats in the two eras, respectively, suggests answers that can only be regarded as troubling.

Lafayette College

Notes

1. For a discussion of the wealth and well-being of imperial China, see Rhodes Murphy, *The Outsiders: The Western Experience in India and China* (Ann Arbor, 1977); Susan Naquin and Evelyn S. Rawski, *Chinese Society in the Eighteenth Century* (New Haven, 1987).

2. David F. Musto, M.D., *The American Disease: Origins of Narcotic Control,* expanded ed. (New York, 1987).

3. Jay Stevens, *Storming Heaven: LSD and the American Dream* (New York, 1987); Hunter Thompson, *Hell's Angels* (New York, 1988); Alfred McCoy, *The Politics of Heroin in South East Asia* (New York, 1972).

4. "Man in Motion," *Newsweek,* 14 April 1969. In the early 1970s major tobacco companies, in anticipation of imminent legalization, reportedly had taken out copyrights on the names Panama Red and Colombia Gold.

5. *New York Times,* 25 August 1979.

6. Paul Eddy, Hugo Sabogal, and Sara Walden, *The Cocaine Wars* (New York, 1988); Guy Gugliotta and Jeff Leen, *The Kings of Cocaine: Inside the Medellín Cartel—An Astonishing True Story of Murder, Money, and International Corruption* (New York, 1989).

7. *New York Times,* 5 September 1989 and 10 March 1990; "Drug Kingpins Deserve to Die, Edgar Declares," *Chicago Sun Times,* 11 November 1989; Dana G. Rinehart, Mayor, City of Columbus, *Changing Attitudes: The Columbus Consensus on Drug Policy,* Draft Proposal.

8. "Bill in Delaware Seeks Revival of Whipping Post," *New York Times,* 29 January 1989; "Congressman wants Drug Felons Sent to Faraway Pacific Islands," *Columbus Dispatch,* 18 September 1990. Flogging, as we shall see, was standard punishment for drug cases in China. Few were deterred by it.

9. Jonathan Spence, "Opium Smoking in Ch'ing China," in Frederic Wakeman, Jr., and Carolyn Grant, eds., *Conflict and Control in Late Imperial China* (Berkeley and Los Angeles, 1975).

10. Yu Ende, *Zhongguo Jinyan Faling Bianqian Shi* [History of Chinese Opium Prohibition Laws], (Shanghai, 1934).

11. Susan Naquin, "The Transmission of White Lotus Sectarianism in Late Imperial China," in David Johnson, Andrew Nathan, and Evelyn Rawski, eds., *Popular Culture in Late Imperial China* (Berkeley and Los Angeles, 1985). It is interesting that the earliest

punishments against opium were modeled after the punishments prescribed for those preaching heterodox religions.

12. Library of Congress, Washington, D.C., *Fanyu Xianzhi* [Gazetteer of Fanyu county].

13. The diplomacy of the Opium War has been extensively described in several monographs. See Hsin-pao Chang, *Commissioner Lin and the Opium War* (New York, 1964); Peter Ward Fay, *The Opium War, 1840–1842* (New York, 1975).

14. *Ching Shih Kau Chiao Chu* [Draft on Ching Dynasty Documents], Xuan Cengcheng Huangdi Shilu [Historical Record of Emperor Xuanceng cheng (Daoguang)], (Beijing, 1986), vol. 35, Chuan 163, 527.

15. Gugong Bowuguan, compiler, *Qingdai Waijiao Shiliao Daoguang Chao* [Source Materials on the Foreign Policy of the Qing Dynasty Reign of Daoguang] (Taibei, Taiwan, 1968), 283–85, 267–71. The officers of the court made Ling tread on the cross for obvious reasons. They made him eat meat and drink wine because the White Lotus practitioners abstained from both. Throughout the document the vocabulary describing Christianity was taken from popular Daoist/Buddhist practices. Officials whose names appeared on the memorials as being chief officers in the investigations including Qiying, who later negotiated the treaty with the British opening ports to trade, and Deng Tingzhen, who later was the governor-general of Guangdong and Guangxi during the Opium Wars.

16. The standard sentence for opium possession was two months in the wooden collar. Kekesebuku [I have transliterated the Chinese characters but do not know what his real name might have been] was given an extra month in the collar because the emperor was angry. *Ching Shih Kau Chiao Chu*, vol. 35, Chuan 200, 1144. Chang, *Commissioner Lin*, 36.

17. U.S. Congress, Senate, "Drugs, Law Enforcement and Foreign Policy," *Hearings before the Subcommittee on Terrorism, Narcotics and International Communications, Committee on Foreign Relations*, 100th Cong., 1st sess., 27 May 1987, part 1, 12.

18. "Running Scared," *Motor Boating and Sailing*, February 1986.

19. Eric Sharp, "Chasing Smugglers on Blue Thunder," *Motor Boating and Sailing*, September 1985; Eddy, *The Cocaine Wars*.

20. Liang Tingnan, *Yuehai Guanzhi* [Gazetteer of the Guangdong Customs], vol. 20, 18–20.

21. Eddy, *The Cocaine Wars*, 219–33; Volsky, "Wide Miami Inquiry into Police Is Seen," *New York Times*, 13 December 1987.

22. Eddy, *The Cocaine Wars*; Gugliotta and Leen, *The Kings of Cocaine*.

23. *Canton Register and Price Current*, 19 February 1829 and 2 September 1831.

24. Lin Zexu, *Xin Ji Lu* [Letters and Records], in Zhongguo Shixue Cengshu [Collected Writings on Chinese History], (Taibei, Taiwan, 1973), 9–10.

25. Testimony of Charles Kimball, Real Estate Economist, Miami, Florida, U.S. Congress, Senate, "Illegal Narcotics Profits," *Hearings before the Permanent Subcommittee on Investigations of the Committee on Governmental Affairs*, 96th Cong., 1st sess., December 1979, 183–90. Frank H. H. King, *Money and Monetary Policy in Nineteenth Century China* (Cambridge, Mass., 1965), 141. King argues that the favorable rate of copper to silver exchange in the Guangzhou area shows that foreign trade was not the cause of China's economic woes at the time. I prefer to trust the Chinese officials of the day. There were other, domestic problems, but if silver was leaving the country, it naturally was collecting at the point where it was leaving.

26. Yao Tingfang, *Yapian Zhanzheng Yu Daoguang Huangdi, Lin Zexu, Qi Shan, Qi Ying* [The Opium War and the Daoquang Empire, Lin Zexu, Qi Shan, Qi Ying] (Taibei, Taiwan, 1970), 84–19; "Drugs and the Law," *Rolling Stone*, 23 March 1987.

27. *Yapian Zhanzheng Yu Daoguang Huangdi*, 84–91; *Canton Register*, 12 July 1836; *China Press*, 23 July 1836.

28. Ethan A. Nadelmann, "Drug Prohibition in the United States: Costs, Consequences, and Alternatives," *Science* 245 (1 September 1989), 939–47; Abbie Hoffman, *Steal This Urine Test: Fighting Drug Hysteria in America* (New York, 1987).

29. For example, Eric Sterling, who worked as a congressional staffer writing anti-money-laundering legislation before he founded the Criminal Justice Policy Foundation, advocates controlled legislation as a way to recognize and address the dangers of both interdiction and drug abuse.

30. Nadelmann, "Drug Prohibition in the United States"; Hoffman, *Steal This Urine Test.*

31. *Canton Register and Price Current,* 3 January 1837 and 18 December 1838.

32. Ibid.

33. Ishii Itarō, *Gaiko kan no Isshō* [My Life as a Diplomat] (Tokyo, 1972), 32–34.

34. Ōki Kōsuke, *Mayaku, Nō, Bunmei* [Narcotics, The Brain, Culture] (Tokyo, 1990).

35. These men are depicted as romantic heroes, such as in James Clavell's novel *Tai Pan* (New York, 1983). One cannot help but think that the day will come when Manuel Noriega or Pablo Escobar are so presented in fiction.

JONATHAN MARSHALL

Opium, Tungsten, and the Search for National Security, 1940–52

If Indochina goes, several things happen right away. The Malayan Peninsula, that last bit of land hanging on down there, would be scarcely defensible—and tin and tungsten that we so greatly value from that area would cease coming. . . . So, when the United States votes $400,000,000 to help that war, we are not voting for a giveaway program. We are voting for the cheapest way that we can to prevent the occurance of something that would be of the most terrible significance for the United States of America—our security, our power, and ability to get certain things we need from the riches of . . . Southeast Asia.—President Dwight Eisenhower, speech to Conference of Governors, 4 August 1953.[1]

National security is an infinitely plastic concept, capable of rationalizing policies—from support for dictatorships abroad to suppression of basic liberties at home—that offend cherished national values. One cause repeatedly sacrificed in the name of national security is the immensely popular but fruitless effort to rid American society of drugs. U.S. policymakers have subverted that aim time and again in favor of containing communism—often by making drug traffickers covert allies rather than targets of foreign intelligence operations.[2]

The origins of this "government-gang symbiosis"[3] go back at least to World War II, when Naval intelligence and the Office of Strategic Services (OSS) forged a now-notorious alliance with the American and Italian mafia. An equally significant, though still largely unknown, alliance of U.S. intelligence with world-class Chinese drug traffickers helped ensure East Asia's continuing role as a leading source of heroin and powerfully shaped the postwar political development of China, Japan, and their neighbors.

At the center of that secret relationship were two strategic materials: tungsten and opium. For both the United States and Japan, tungsten was a scarce metal vital to their war economies, and opium was a preferred means of payment in its major country of supply: China. For China's Kuomintang (KMT) government in turn, tungsten supplies helped ensure Washington's commitment to the war effort in the Far East. And opium was not only a valuable currency that resisted depreciation in a hyperinflationary environment, but also was a source of central government power against the centrifugal forces of warlordism, revolution, and foreign invasion.

Tungsten and opium, seemingly so different, had one other thing in common besides their extraordinary value: to reach their ultimate consumers during wartime, both had to be smuggled. That fact put a premium on finding successful criminal organizations able to mobilize their operatives to move those materials where needed. In vying for China's tungsten, both Japan and the United States turned to gangsters for help, setting in motion a political dynamic that would peak some years later during the Cold War.

Tungsten and the War Economy

The United States has fought three major wars in Asia in the last half century. All, in significant measure, were struggles for control of the vital resources of the Pacific Basin. One of the most important of those materials was tungsten, prized by the military and by civilian industry for its unequaled tensile strength and for its use in critical steel alloys. Tungsten is indispensable for everything from electric light filaments to armor-piercing shells.

American consumers may now take tungsten for granted, but policymakers have not always had that luxury. In 1940 the Army and Navy Munitions Board listed the metal as one of fourteen "strategic materials," which one authority termed "so closely knit into our modern industrial structure that the whole trend of modern life would be disorganized without them."[4] The War Department's Planning Branch noted that of the various resources it deemed of "major importance to our national welfare," tungsten was among the four that occupied a "position of highest priority because of their importance in industry and the problems involved in assuring an adequate supply in an emergency."[5]

At that time, outside of the United States, nearly all the noncommunist world's supplies of tungsten ores came from the Far East. China dominated the market, with lesser deposits found in Burma, Korea, and the Malay states. American industry depended heavily on these distant sources. The Senate Military Affairs Committee concluded, after studying the availability of tungsten and other critical materials, that "the United States would find itself at a grave disadvantage in the event that war or other emergency should close the sea lanes or block the normal sources of supply."[6]

The United States was not alone in needing the metal. Nazi Germany secretly stockpiled huge quantities of Chinese tungsten during the 1930s, and once embarked on war, it paid as much as $50,000 per ton for ores from neutral Spain and Portugal.[7]

Japan's invasion of China in the 1930s, followed by its encircling movement into Southeast Asia, threatened to cut the U.S. economy off from its chief suppliers of tungsten and other vital raw materials—contributing to the Roosevelt administration's increasingly hostile and provocative reaction to Japanese aggression. President Roosevelt, in late July 1941, mentioned tungsten in explaining why he imposed the oil embargo on Japan that would lead to war less than six months later:

> The importance of [southern Indochina] lies in the fact that geographically Indo-China was at a hub, from which any attack can be made in a number of directions. It is only a very short distance from there to the Philippines in the east. It is a relatively short distance from there down to the Dutch East Indies, which is the most industrial part—southwest there is Singapore—fortified. To the west there is the Malay Peninsula, parts of Thailand, parts of the Malay Straits. . . . Only a short distance from here, of course, lies Burma, and the entry—the bottleneck to the Burma Road, a short distance from Siam. We are getting a very large proportion of our supplies—rubber, tin, etc.—from that whole area of southwestern Pacific, and we are getting out over the Burma Road—the two-way road—we are getting a large amount of very important material, such as tungsten.[8]

A State Department analysis of the coming U.S.-Japan conflict, prepared that September, noted that "most of our supplies of tungsten" and several other strategic materials came from East Asia. "And if Japan were to gain control of that whole area," it warned,". . . she would be able to withold these supplies from us, from Great Britain and from other countries, to supply them exclusively to her allies, or to dictate to us in what amount and on what terms we might have them."[9]

No less revealing were drafts, from late November 1941, of a speech

President Roosevelt planned to deliver to the nation to explain the need for war against Japan. The issue of raw materials loomed prominently in them. The State Department's version declared, "To permit Japanese domination and control of the major sources of world supply of tin and rubber and tungsten would jeopardize our safefy in a manner and to an extent that cannot be tolerated."[10] Japan's attack on Pearl Harbor relegated the speech, but not the concerns behind it, to the archives.

Alarmed by this perceived threat to America's economy, the White House assigned the Metals Reserve Company, a subsidiary of the Reconstruction Finance Corporation (RFC), to buy up Chinese tungsten. In June 1940, just before the Japanese takeover of French Indochina, RFC chief Jesse Jones contracted to buy a huge quantity of Chinese tungsten stored in the colony. As one chronicler has noted, "The transaction was completed in twenty-four hours, no doubt one of the quickest transactions of such magnitude ever consummated between two nations."[11]

By late 1940 Jones had arranged to purchase China's entire tungsten output. After the closing of the Burma Road, tungsten was flown out over the Himalayas, a testament to the metal's vital importance to America's war economy.[12] The Japanese takeover of most of China and Southeast Asia cut the United States off from 61 percent of its supplies of tungsten ore, according to the War Production Board.[13]

A contemporary account conveyed the urgency with which the American government viewed the growing tungsten crisis. "Tank warfare has made tungsten more valuable than diamonds," wrote the journalist Bradford Huie in 1942. "Tungsten carbide is as hard as diamond, and can penetrate armor plate better than any other substance. The ideal anti-tank shell is made of steel and tipped with tungsten carbide. . . . We have always got it from the Chinese interior. Donkeys brought it out of the mountains to our ships. But now we can get it only with the greatest of difficulty. We need cargo planes not only to carry supplies into China, but to bring out that precious tungsten. . . . A little thing like a [fleet of cargo planes] flying out of Shangri-La [each] with six tons of tungsten may determine the winner and the loser in this war."[14]

Vital materials were not all that U.S. planes flew out of China "over the hump," however. Some also carried opium, as pilots for the CIA's Air America were alleged to have done on occasion during the Vietnam War.[15] Other planes hauled prostitutes, gold, cigarettes, gems, and precious goods worth millions of dollars. An investigation by the Army Inspector General implicated General Claire Chennault, founder of the Flying Tigers, but no official action was taken because he was politically untouchable.[16] As we shall see, Chennault would later found Civil Air Transport, which supplied displaced Nationalist Chinese forces engaged in tungsten and opium trafficking in Burma.

The RFC bought the tungsten from China's National Resources Commission. The broker on these transactions was Wah Chang Trading Corporation, an American company headed by the immensely wealthy expatriate Chinese businessman K. C. Li.[17] Li represented a crucial link between the U.S. and Chinese governments, their respective secret intelligence agencies, and underworld smugglers of illicit narcotics and profitable strategic materials.

Li enjoyed extraordinary access to the regime of Chiang Kai-shek, having been a major finanical backer and political supporter of the Kuomintang in the United States. He helped lead a fundraising committee of New York City Chinese to support Chiang's Nineteenth Route Army against the Japanese in early 1933. He also became the American agent for the Nanking government's arms purchases during the turbulent 1930s, when warlordism and Japanese imperialism threatened the survival of Chiang's regime.[18] For a time he sat on the board of directors of the Central Bank of China.[19] As a result, Li had a direct pipeline to the Generalissimo—and indeed claimed to communicate with him in a personal code.[20]

Stanley Hornbeck, the State Department's chief political adviser on Far Eastern affairs, described Li as "one of the most successful and probably the best known Chinese businessmen in the United States. He was sometime ago offered the post of Minister of Commerce by the Chungking Government, which offer he declined. . . . His opinions carry weight with various high Chinese officials and in Chinese business circles both in this country and in China."[21] U.S. government agencies considered Li's company to have "quasi-official status" in Washington.[22]

Li's association with tungsten went back to 1911, when, as a young mining engineer prospecting for tin in southwest China, he stumbled across the purest outcropping of tungsten ore (wolframite) anywhere in the world.[23] His Wah Chang Corporation became the largest trader and producer of tungsten in this country. Its interests spread from mines in Brazil to import-export companies in Thailand.[24] During World War II, Li's refineries processed 90 perent of the tungsten used by the Allied armies.[25]

Thus it was only natural that agencies of the U.S. government most concerned with tungsten supplies—the Board of Economic Warfare, the War Production Board, and the Metals Reserve Company—turned to Li for help in procuring Chinese tungsten during the war from under the noses of the Japanese. Li adopted the role of smuggling agent with Washington's blessing.[26]

Washington's Underworld Ally

From the meager evidence available, it is clear that Li had help at the highest level of China's smuggler aristocracy—from none other than Tu Yueh-sheng, leader of the "Green Gang," China's most powerful secret society and underworld organization. Tu controlled a criminal empire based on extortion, smuggling, and, above all, trade in narcotics extending from Shanghai up the strategic Yangtze River to Chungking. Tens of thousands of Green Gang members took his orders. His immense wealth and a large army of followers made him a natural ally when Chiang Kai-shek came looking for support in 1927 against the Communists in Shanghai. Tu's massacre of the Reds in advance of Chiang's army won him the Generalissimo's everlasting gratitude—and official protection for his nationwide opium trade. To cement their alliance, Chiang even appointed Tu head of the Shanghai Opium Suppression Bureau, a post the gangster used to monopolize the drug business with official sanction.[27] Wealth opened many doors. Tu's nearly endless résumé noted his achievements as a philanthropist, including vice-president of the Chinese Red Cross, labor leader, president and director of numerous banks and industrial and transportation firms, and managing director of three newspapers.[28] He even owned the Southwestern Transportation Company, which controlled most of the traffic on the Burma Road, including U.S. Lend-Lease supplies, before the Japanese seized that strategic route.[29]

For Chiang, opium was nothing less than a strategic material. Monopolizing its trade became a matter of both personal and national security. Outside his control, opium offered a financial base for regional rivals who impeded China's unification. Under Chiang's control, opium was the key source of revenue that brought him to power in the late 1920s, consolidated his position against warlords in southwest China, and let him undertake military campaigns against both the Japanese and the Communists. It was a vital weapon in his campaign to build a central state capable of governing his ancient and glorious but now dilapidated nation.[30]

As the then-obscure U.S. military attaché in China, Joseph Stilwell, observed in 1935, Chiang's nationwide opium "suppression" campaign was really designed to "secure domination of the opium traffic to increase the political power of the National Government over provinces whose allegiance is doubtful. . . . [O]pium is the chief prop of all power in

China, both civil and military. No local government can exist without a share of the opium revenues. If the Central Government can control the opium supply of a province, that province can never hope to revolt successfully."[31]

Chiang's agents in the nationalist cause, Tu and Li, may have become acquainted in any number of ways. Their paths crossed often enough in the war against Japan. Both were active supporters of the anti-Japanese Nineteenth Route Army, which trafficked in hundred-ton quantities of Persian opium. Both were key participants in the Nationalist government's purchase of American aircraft with cash raised from narcotics sales. Both got an inside track on the purchase of lucrative U.S.-dollar savings certificates issued by the Chinese government. And Tu followed Li into the tungsten trade.[32]

During the war, Tu Yueh-sheng aided the Nationalist cause in coordination with General Tai Li, the ruthless leader of China's vast secret police apparatus and arguably the second most powerful leader after Chiang Kai-shek. Tai Li had earned Chiang's favor in 1927, when he acted as an advance scout for the KMT armies and sewed up the support of Tu's Green Gang for Chiang's victorious entry into Shanghai.[33] In the 1930s he headed the Blue Shirts organization, recruited largely from the ranks of the Green Gang and much feared for assassinating liberal intellectuals and other opponents of the regime.[34] As his power grew, Tai earned a widespread reputation as the "Chinese Himmler." In 1942, the U.S. naval attaché in Chungking reported that this "Gestapo chief" controlled "all subversive activities ranging from terrorism to smuggling." The report described Tai and his associates as "astonishingly narrow-minded men who are essentially anti-foreign. . . . Their power behind the government scene is insidious and tremendous."[35]

After Shanghai fell to the Japanese in 1937, Tai recruited the Green Gang's vast underworld army for intelligence and guerrilla operations. From his base in Hong Kong and then Chungking, Tu financed sabotage and assassination campaigns against the Japanese and their Chinese collaborators in Shanghai and other occupied cities. But he played a complicated game, selling opium from southern China and other sources to Japanese authorities, including the Special Services under General Doihara Kenji. For a time Tu even retained effective control of occupied Shanghai's opium monopoly. As late as August 1941, for example, Tu arranged an enormous shipment of opium from Yunnan and Szechwan provinces to the city aboard a Japanese freighter.[36]

The Japanese played along with Tu for the same reason Chiang did: they could not govern the Yangtze River basin without him. In particular, they could not control the foreign concessions in China's coastal cities that, prior to 1940, remained unoccupied by the Japanese army. As one American intelligence official explained, the Japanese

> have been wanting to secure the cooperation of the underworld influences for a long time. They believe this is the best way to secure control of the foreign areas for once they can secure these underworld forces, they will be able to create disturbances to harass the police, arrest anti-Japanese elements and Chinese Government agents, attack Chinese Government banks, law courts and anti-Japanese newspapers and damage the stability of the Chinese currency. This means they could control the foreign areas through these gangsters without resorting to occupying them by force. The only weapons left for the Japanese to secure the cooperation of these gangsters are opium and gambling business.[37]

Tu could not have shipped so much opium so easily to the enemy without the active support of Tai Li, who doubled as head of China's Smuggling Prevention Bureau. U.S. Navy Commander Milton Miles, who led intelligence operations with Tai during the war, wrote, "It has never been learned where General Tai obtained all of the required funds to operate his organization. In common with other central government agencies the BIS [Tai's Bureau of Investigation and Statistics] financing was grossly inadequate. . . . He once [said] that the secret of financing the BIS must await the end of the war before it could be revealed."[38]

Other Americans, however, were either better informed or less coy about Tai's finances. They knew that his agents protected Tu's huge opium convoys, many to Japanese-held territory, and derived tens of millions of dollars in profits from them, backed by loans from the country's four official banks of issue.[39]

This arrangement amounted, as before the war, to an effort by Chiang and the KMT leadership to monopolize the country's narcotics traffic, even to the point of trading with the enemy. Their opium policy was no different than their approach to any other profitable business. Graham Peck, a journalist, recalled that

> the Kuomintang used the Japanese invasion to increase its nationwide monopolies, of economic, political and military power. Even before the war, this regime had shown that it wanted most of China's basic industry and trade to be controlled by monopolies belonging either to the government or its state banks. Later it used the disloca-

tions of war to give its monopolies such a stranglehold on China's economy that private business was plunged into a state of extreme depression and began to die out.[40]

The United States aided this process indirectly through support for the Sino-American Cooperation Organization (SACO), a joint project of Tai and Commander Miles, who had been sent to China by OSS chief General William Donovan. To Donovan's disgust, Miles soon became Tai's right-hand man rather than his master. Though supplied with American matériel and training, Tai froze the OSS out of his intelligence operation and left Donovan's men in the dark. Miles worked closely not only with Tai but with Tu Yueh-sheng, despite his criminal reputation.[41]

Tu made other contacts with U.S. intelligence through K. C. Li as well. One of Miles's associates, OSS Major Preston Goodfellow, approached Li to explore means of carrying out sabotage behind Japanese lines. Li steered him into backing the gangster, according to a record of their conversation:

> The leader (of the anti-Japanese guerrillas) in Chungking is a man named Y.S. Doo (Doo Yu Sen), who has agents in Shanghai, Hankow, and all principal cities. Mr. Li said that this is a dirty type of work which has to be carried out by men of the gangster type, but it is possible to arrange for payment after delivery; in other words, after sabotage has been carried out. Mr. Li thought a great deal more could be accomplished if Doo had larger amounts of money to work with, but he said the Chungking Government had such heavy demands . . . that not much was available for this particular branch of work. Mr. Li did think it would be extremely important to spend more money.

Li also noted in passing that Tu's forces were already "supported by wealthy Chinese in this country," but he did not say whether he was among them.[42]

Li apparently gave similar advice to other top officials in OSS. Before Quentin Roosevelt, grandson of Theodore Roosevelt, flew to Chungking in 1944 as Donovan's personal representative to the Chiang government, he approached Li for advice. Li in turn introduced him to one of Tu's three sons then attending school in the United States. Li gave a letter on Quentin's behalf to the son to pass back to Tu. When Quentin arrived in Chungking, Tu promised full cooperation and the two in fact succeeded in coordinating their activities closely, thanks to Li's intervention.[43]

Tu also seems to have been in touch with John C. Caldwell, a young employee of the Office of War Information sent by the U.S. Army to evaluate the feasibility of enlisting China's fierce coastal pirates—many of whom were directly affiliated with the Green Gang—for intelligence gathering and attacks on Japanese fishing. Caldwell convinced the authorities in Chungking that the pirates could be won over, or bought off, and succeeded in calling off air strikes on their junks in order not "to antagonize potential allies." Caldwell later recalled, "The basis for an understanding with the pirates had been laid." SACO soon began supplying the pirates with arms, ammunition, training, and money. The pirates in turn collected weather information, laid mines, rescued downed American pilots, and, when the Japanese finally surrendered, helped Tu and Tai Li crush Shanghai's Communist underground.[44] One senior OSS official involved in the effort to organize the Chinese pirates was K. C. Li's confidant, Preston Goodfellow.[45]

The U.S. intelligence connection with these pirates extended all the way across the Pacific. When it came time for U.S. Naval Intelligence to determine the characteristics of one pirate bay where "no white man has ever been" (except as the victim of an attack), it turned, through the OSS, to Dr. Margaret Chung, an intimate of Mme. Chiang Kai-shek living in San Francisco. As head of the "Bastards Club," an informal association of flyers, submariners, and other veterans of action in the Far East, Chung was well connected to the highest ranks of the U.S. military, all the way up to Fleet Admiral Chester Nimitz. She was equally close, however, to notorious American gangsters and was a suspected narcotics trafficker in her own right. Dr. Chung volunteered that she could supply detailed information on the bay "from some of the smugglers in San Francisco."[46]

The Japanese employed many of the same mercenaries at the same time and for the same purposes: to supply information and patrol the coast. Japanese forces offered them freedom from naval interdiction and sold them opium, which the smuggler armies in turn marketed at a huge profit along the Chinese coast.[47] The Japanese also used them to acquire Chinese tungsten. Through lavish bribery, Japan succeeded in tapping the output of smaller mines nominally under the control of the Chinese government's National Resources Commission (NRC)—to the great annoyance of American and British officials, who believed the NRC was not devoting sufficient resources to deny this precious metal to the enemy. Chinese military forces traded opium and tungsten to the Japanese in exchange for cotton cloth, yarn, and other basic necessities in short supply—as well as refined narcotics.[48]

The Japanese began organizing their tungsten smuggling network as early as 1932 by tapping the expertise of the Bias Bay pirates on the South China coast, about thirty miles northeast of Hong Kong. The pirates "stole and/or bought up the tungsten ore inland and smuggled it down to the coast near Bias Bay," according to one OSS officer. "In fact I have been reliably informed that the ease with which the Japanese marched from Bias Bay to Waichow and on the Canton in 1938 was in large part due to their connections with this pirate-bandit tungsten smuggling gang, who in turn had been paying their way with certain Chinese army groups."[49] This channel was lucrative for all concerned; by 1942 the Japanese were said to be shipping as much as 5,000 tons of wolfram annually from southern China.[50]

The Kodama Agency

The connection between tungsten and narcotics went far beyond coastal smuggling. The Japanese Army handled much of its materials procurement in China through the Showa Trading Company, headed by a reserve army colonel, Sanya Hori, who obtained his financing from the War Ministry and Japan's three biggest corporations: Mitsui, Mitsubishi, and Okura. According to a postwar investigation by U.S. intelligence officials, Showa Trading Company's job included "the collection of intelligence information, the shipment of narcotics, and the shipment of war material to cultivate friendship with foreign nations." It also "acquired tungsten, scrap, copper, magnesium, mercury and brass from China, mostly in exchange for narcotics, opium and heroin."[51]

One of Showa's chief agents was Yoshio Kodama, a right-wing terrorist active in ultranationalist secret societies. U.S. occupation authorities described him as a "plotter of assassinations, [a] seditious and inflammatory pamphleteer." Orphaned at eleven, he was sent to Korea to live, but returned to Japan in 1927 at the age of sixteen to make his fortune. He quickly joined the first of many extreme anti-Communist organizations. In the early 1930s he plotted to murder the emperor's cabinet, but the plot failed and he was imprisoned until 1937. After his release, Kodama began associating with imperialists inside the government. By 1941 he had become chief of the East Asia Section of Ryoichi Sasagawa's Kokosui Taishu To (National Essence Masses Party), which agitated for southward military expansion.[52]

Kodama worked for Showa in 1940, when it was founded by the Japanese Army in case the United States embargoed vital war supplies.

Kodama told his postwar interrogators, "This company was one of the means of preparing for the Greater East Asia War." He explained, "What was most important for the Japanese war effort was Tungsten. In order to obtain Tungsten this company used heroin for trading purposes." Many ends were served by this secret operation, Kodama recalled: "The Army also planned on deriving Y2,000,000 to Y3,000,000 in secret funds from the Showa Trading Company. . . . Through this company they could obtain material illegally for preparing the war and, furthermore, the officers at the War Ministry would be able to use secret funds derived from such sources. . . . There was a great margin of profit . . . and the Army gained its purpose in having tungsten in its possession, plus the profit." With the authorization of the Army's General Staff Headquarters, Kodama acquired heroin from Japanese pharmacists and turned it over to Hori, who shipped it for sale to Canton. Hori told Kodama that "heroin was the only material with which they could purchase tungsten because the people in southern China did not want money. They had use for military currency and heroin was the most welcome exchange."[53]

Kodama parlayed that experience into an extraordinarily successful wartime career in supply and intelligence. From November 1941 to July 1943, he commuted between Tokyo and Shanghai on procurement missions, this time for the Navy. Then he opened his own Shanghai agency, Kodama Kikan, with a broader agenda. American authorities called him a "purchaser of colossal supplies for the Navy" and the "greatest of war profiteers" in Shanghai. He also operated tungsten mines in Japan and Korea for the Navy, ran a huge spy ring in China with as many as ten thousand agents, and financed the Japanese secret police office in Shanghai.[54]

The secret of Kodama's success was in employing the methods he learned from Showa Trading Company. He paid for goods and services in China with narcotics, then a mainstay of Japanese as well as Chinese government finance.[55]

Kodama was a close associate of Yoshihiko Satomi, a notorious Shanghai-based narcotics dealer working for the Japanese army. Satomi used Mitsui to ship opium into the city for sale, using supply sources in both China and Iran that had been developed by the Japanese opium monopoly on Formosa.[56] Satomi was said by one U.S. intelligence report to have "contributed huge funds to fanatic militaristic societies" and to the Japanese Gendarmerie Intelligence Fund. He reportedly engaged in illicit missions, including extortion and bribery, for Japanese army and navy purchasing teams.[57]

U.S. occupation forces rounded up Kodama after V-J day and imprisoned him as a suspected Class "A" war criminal. Before his arrest,

Kodama managed to hide a pile of cash and several truckloads of industrial diamonds and platinum, loot from his Shanghai procurement days, in a Tokyo basement. Kodama delivered much of his fortune to Karoku Tsuji, a powerful, right-wing financier who controlled underworld gangs and political strong-arm squads. Tsuji, known as "Japan's Al Capone," in turn used the money to found the Liberal Party, which merged to form the ruling Liberal Democratic Party in 1955.[58]

Kodama walked out of Sagumo Prison a free man in December 1948. The U.S. decision to release him, indeed not even to charge him with war crimes, flew in the face of a military intelligence (G-2) assessment that

> his long and fanatic involvement in ultra-nationalist activities, violence included, and his skill in appealing to youth, make him a man who, if released from internment, would surely be a grave security risk. In addition, there is the outstanding probability to be reckoned with that as a result of his hearty cooperation with the war effort, he has a large fortune to back up whatever activities he might see fit to undertake. His success in the difficulties of securing supplies for the Navy mark him as one who could very easily become a big time operator in Japan's reconstruction period. Persistent rumors as to his black market profits in his Shanghai period, plus his known opportunism, are forceful arguments that he would be as unscrupulous in trade as he was in ultranationalism.[59]

Why was such a man released? One possibility is that he had unnamed friends within the U.S. intelligence community who intervened on his behalf. Former Central Intelligence Agency agent Miles Copeland claimed that Kodama "had been a 'contact' (not quite an 'agent') of Paul Blum's 'Chrysanthemum' group which operated, first, under the American military attaché before Pearl Harbour and later, under General [Charles] Willoughby when he became G-2 on [General Douglas] MacArthur's staff. Kodama was released as soon as his identity was known."[60]

Another possibility is that Kodama or his friends used his fortune to grease the right hands. Corruption was hardly unknown among the American occupiers. According to one Japanese account, wartime construction magnate and rightist boss Ando Akira "opened a nightclub chain in downtown Tokyo exclusive to high officials of MacArthur's General Headquarters (GHQ) and Japanese bigshots. There, cash, as well as jewelry and women, was used to bribe the GHQ officials in favor of the emperor system. Among the guests was Lt. Gen. A. Eichelberger and Tokyo

Tribunal's U.S. Prosecutor [Joseph B.] Keenan. . . . The nightclub was soon turned into the pro-Emperor lobbying center."[61]

The most plausible explanation, however, is that the American desire for revenge and social reform had given way by 1948 to a view that Japan must be revived as a conservative bastion against Communist expansion in Asia. The crumbling of China dashed hopes that America's wartime ally would ever become the pillar of regional power envisioned when it joined the United Nations Security Council. Instead, the United States would have to turn to its wartime enemy for a secure foothold off the Asian mainland. And that, in turn, meant restoring the rights and privileges of some of Japan's most notorious rightists—just as in Europe, even earlier, the cause of anti-Communism and Soviet containment had justified resurrecting former Nazi war criminals in the service of U.S. intelligence.[62] Soon after his release from prison, indeed Kodama became a confidant of G-2 (headed by the former tungsten miner and right-wing zealot, Maj. Gen. Charles Willoughby) and its political surveillance arm, the Counter-Intelligence Corps (CIC).[63] He engaged in U.S.-sponsored operations to intimidate and destroy the Japanese left, acting as an intermediary between G-2 and the Yakuza, or Japanese mob. He was in the unique position of enjoying the trust of both the underworld and the occupation authorities.[64] Kodama later boasted of being the "boss over Tokyo's yakuza world," adding, "We are united in our opposition to Communism. The same blood runs in our bodies."[65]

Kodama's Korean experience came in handy in recruiting Korean gangsters for the same cause. Hisayuki Machii, a Korean-born Japanese, was one of his first postprison contacts, "courtesy of the CIC," according to one-Japanese report.[66] Machii's street thugs and access to guns and other weapons made him useful in controlling the Japanese population. As one American business partner said of Machii, his "strongarm" tactics were used to "break up Communist demonstrations, kind of like union busting. It was illegal in the pure sense, but it was done under the quasi-jurisdiction of our occupation forces."[67]

During the American occupation, both Kodama and Machii worked with a CIC network headed by Col. J. Y. Cannon. Some journalists have suggested that the recruitment of gangsters into this ring left its mark on CIC's operational style:

> Through the Counter-Intelligence Corps (CIC), the G-2 organized intelligence activities throughout Japan, composed of former military, intelligence, and rightwing figures. . . . The most well known of the CIC groups was one organized by intelligence officer Lt. Col.

> [J. Y.] Cannon which, with the assistance of second-generation Japanese-American Victor Matsui, engaged in drug smuggling and kidnappings. (Matsui's name later came up on a list of CIA-connected persons related to the attempted coup against Sihanouk in Cambodia in 1959.)[68]

Kodama was also associated in 1949 with a plot, likely supported by elements within MacArthur's command who favored rolling back communism in Asia, to smuggle Imperial Army veterans into Taiwan to bolster Chiang Kai-shek's beleaguered forces. Kodama was joined in this effort to help Japan's former enemy by the prewar ultrarightist Mikami Taku. Their effort was set back, however, by the notorious *Kairetsu-go* Incident. On 17 August 1949, Japanese police discovered a group of men unloading illegal contraband, including drugs, from the KMT-financed Chinese ship, *Kairesu-go.* Fourteen people were indicted for smuggling, including Mikami and Iida Seisei, who had served with the Japanese secret service in China. They were financing Kodama's recruitment effort, but their reliance on smuggling discredited the whole operation.[69]

Kodama was too useful to American authorities to drop because of a drug scandal, however. He emerged more important than ever as a U.S. intelligence operative during the Korean War. Kodama was in Seoul for unexplained reasons as part of the U.S. military on 25 June 1950, the day the war broke out. He also helped recruit Japanese officers for illegal service in the fighting.[70]

Even more important was his wartime experience as a smuggler. With former members of the Kodama Agency in Shanghai, he founded a firm called Tokyo Rare Metal, which supplied the occupation General Headquarters with tungsten during Korean war. As in World War II, supplies of the strategic metal were both scarce and precious, thanks to the shutdown of trade with Communist China.[71] By 1951–52, half the world's production of tungsten was in Communist hands, and the price had tripled.[72] The Senate Preparedness Subcommittee called the tungsten shortage "little short of desperate."[73] Tom Wilder of the Emergency Procurement Service, which handled stockpiling of strategic materials following enactment of the Stockpiling Act of 1946, later recalled that when the Korean War began, "one of the most critical items of all was tungsten. Requirements exceeded available supply, and the stockpile inventory was meager in terms of a substantially increased objective." With price literally "no object," Wilder added, "tungsten became an item of international concern in the free world."[74]

According to the *New York Times,* Kodama "received some $150,000 from the American Embassy to smuggle a hoard of tungsten out of mainland China on Nationalist warships and deliver it to United States authorities in Tokyo." The story goes that the ship carrying the ore sank, but Kodama kept the commission anyway.[75]

The United States had other "assets" besides Kodama for its tungsten projects. In early 1951 it called upon Eugene Dooman, the former head of the Japan desk at the State Department who had become a private businessman and active lobbyist for rebuilding Japan's strength. Financed with a special grant from the General Services Administration, the CIA advanced Dooman at least $2.8 million to "get busy buying tungsten" through a Japanese intermediary. The tungsten had been secretly stockpiled throughout Japan by former members of the Japanese military, including Kodama's associates in naval procurement. Profits from the resale of the metal would in turn allow Dooman's group to "carry out some undercover operations in the fields of intelligence, propaganda, and transportation." But the tungsten ore Dooman procured was allegedly low grade and the project collapsed. Seeking a settlement with the U.S. government, which demanded repayment, Dooman threatened to expose damaging secrets, including allegations that the CIA had kidnapped two Japanese Communists and that "CIA employees were caught smuggling narcotics."[76]

Beyond China and Japan

China and Japan were not the only sources of tungsten in the Far East. Korea itself was the third largest world producer after China and the United States. Indeed tungsten was South Korea's most valuable mineral product. The State Department declared in April 1951 that "potential Korean production [was] essential" owing to the metal's "desperately short supply."[77] The most important mines, at Sangdong, were located just south of the 38th parallel. Washington ordered the Far East Command to see to their rehabilitation and classified as secret all information about their operation. But work at the mines was impeded by the raging civil war, South Korean political corruption, and marauding southern troops who looted the facilities.[78]

The Korean tungsten business attracted no American more than Preston Goodfellow, deputy director of the OSS during World War II and, as noted, K. C. Li's confidant regarding Tu Yueh-sheng. Goodfellow was "the official in charge of the American operation that moved Syngman Rhee into Korea" in 1945.[79] After the war he headed the mysterious "Overseas Reconstruction Corporation," a likely intelligence front. Wearing his business hat, Goodfellow became involved in tungsten deals with World Commerce Corporation, a postwar firm established by the heads of several Allied intelligence organizations, including General Donovan.[80] "By early 1949," notes historian Bruce Cumings, "Goodfellow was with Donovan's World Commerce Corporation, seeking to become Rhee's principal American adviser and pursuing the typical Donovan combination of business and clandestine activities. From the fall of 1949 to the mid-1950s, Goodfellow in becoming a key agent for Korean-American business deals" and, it would appear, intelligence operations involving both the United States and Nationalist China.[81] The tungsten trade continued to hold his attention, even after supply shortages eased. In 1954 Goodfellow arranged with Kenneth D. Mann, former head of propaganda operations in the OSS, to import Korean tungsten for the U.S. stockpile, Mann noted, "After a talk with General Donovan [then U.S. Ambassador to Thailand], I am quite sure that we can restrict the production from Thailand to insure world market stability."[82] Tungsten indeed became one of Korea's chief foreign-exchange earners during the 1950s, accounting for 17 percent of its total exports.[83]

Yet another important but politically troubled source of tungsten was northeastern Burma. In this portion of the notorious Golden Triangle, rebel armies clashed for control of the rugged mountainous terrain and the profitable opium trade routes passing through it. Those armies included not only ethnic minorities seeking autonomy from Rangoon's chauvinist rule but also KMT units that retreated from China in the wake of the Communist victory in 1949. 'With help from the CIA, those KMT soldiers mounted occasional forays into the People's Republic, only to get bloodied and battered. Soon they began devoting their energies to opium trafficking instead.

In clear violation of Burmese sovereignty, and in spite of Burma's protests to the United Nations, these lawless KMT forces were supplied by Civil Air Transport (CAT), founded after the war by Claire Chennault and subsequently controlled by the CIA.[84] By 1948 it had become the largest cargo-carrying airline in the world.[85] Before the fall of China, it shipped out tungsten through its trading subsidiary, International Suppliers Corporation (ISC). This was a political as well as a commercial venture; ISC developed CAT's contacts with northern Chinese warlords, who, Washington hoped, could be reinforced to resist the spread of communism.[86] Soon thereafter, Chennault was flying military cargo missions for the U.S. military in Korea. He was also a confidant of Korean President Syngman Rhee, who invited him to Korea in November 1949 to present plans for building a Korean air force.[87] He may thus have been part of the many, poorly understood intelligence intrigues surrounding Willoughby, MacArthur, Chiang, and Rhee that were attempting to trigger a U.S. military confrontation with the Chinese Communists.[88]

Fragmentary evidence suggests that CIA support for the opium-smuggling KMT army in Burma may have been designed not only to tie down Communist Chinese forces that might otherwise have fought in Korea but also to facilitate Western control of Burma's tungsten resources. In October 1951, Karen rebel forces seized three years' worth of tungsten output from the British-owned Mawchi mine 270 miles north of Rangoon. Before the Korean War, that mine alone supplied 10 percent of the world's needs. Now, fortunately for Washington, the Karens began smuggling the ore across the border into Thailand. To move the wolfram they turned to the CIA's KMT allies.[89]

Several thousand soldiers of the former Nationalist Chinese army moved into Mawchi to join the local Karen insurgents. Reports of this move began surfacing in the American press by the fall of 1951.[90] By 1953 Americans could read that these forces were being armed against the Burmese government in exchange for "a regular flow of opium" and that the KMT-Karen alliance was "based on the exchange of the Karen-controlled wolfram for modern arms provided by the Chinese Nationalists."[91] And, one might add in retrospect, provided by the CIA.

Liaison between U.S. intelligence and the KMT was handled at least in part by Alvin Snell, a CIA representative with experience in the Japanese occupation. He traveled under cover as a representative of the General Services Administration to Thailand in 1951 to procure tungsten for the United Nations forces fighting in Korea. His chief area of operations was the northern town of Chiang Mai, famous as a center of narcotics distribution and smuggling.

But with the world price of tungsten at record levels, there was too much temptation for corruption. A rival tungsten dealer charged that Snell was taking kickbacks from the producers with whom he was contracting—in particular from a company whose board of directors included the Queen Mother's business agent and four top officers from the Thai army—including Major General Thanom Kittikachorn, a CIA asset who would, years later, seize power in a coup and become known as a protector of the drug trade. Representatives of this company countercharged that the allegations were fabricated by K. C. Li's Wah Chang Company, which still had a choke-hold on the world tungsten market.

Wah Chang was said to pull strings in Washington to determine where GSA let its tungsten ore contracts. And Snell himself charged his chief accuser with "running dope from Hong Kong to Korea to the troops."

U.S. inspectors never could resolve the matter. They could not even get to the scene to inspect the mines in question because Thai border police and KMT guerrillas—both deeply implicated in opium trafficking and both CIA-supported—made the area unsafe for passage. And U.S. Ambassador William Donovan, a close associate of the CIA, stepped in to quash the investigation.[92]

These violent years provided extraordinary opportunities for clandestine entrepreneurs and intelligence agents who operated under a mantle of national security to control and exploit strategic resources like tungsten and opium. The subterranean traffics associated with both substances established covert alliances between ostensible foes: governments and gangs, warring armies, victors and vanquished.

Those alliances have had enduring consequences for the growth and spread of the worldwide drug traffic. Thus KMT forces that trafficked opium during World War II with the direct support and tacit approval of the U.S. government later moved their trade, again with Washington's direct support and tacit approval, to the Golden Triangle, where they established the world's largest center of opium production. The Japanese Yakuza, who today distribute methamphetamine and other drugs throughout the Pacific Basin, enjoy a criminal empire that is traceable to the collaboration of American occupation authorities. Such precedents guided subsequent covert U.S. cooperation with Afghan *mujahedeen*, Nicaraguan *contras*, anti-Castro Cubans, Panamanian strongmen, corrupt Mexican intelligence officials, and other forces implicated in drug trafficking.[93]

But the significance of these traffics and alliances should concern more than criminologists. The combination of enormous profits, the involvement of intelligence agencies, and the aura of national security has given these smuggling networks unusual influence in the political development of nations where they operate. Opium and tungsten were the wirepullers' secret weapons, representing sources of finance for political movements and providing the keys to state power.

In China, an obscure Shanghai stockbroker named Chiang Kai-shek rose to power in alliance with the Green Gang and its opium riches.[94] Opium was the resource Chiang Kai-shek and his lieutenants tried to monopolize in order to consolidate their personal power, squeeze their enemies, and accelerate the building of national institutions. Tungsten was also a valuable commodity capable of buying support from both the United States and

Japan when needed. But the Faustian bargain Chiang made with the underworld to promote these lucrative traffics also fostered rampant corruption, treason, warlordism, political extremism, and ultimately national disintegration, paving the way for the Communist victory.[95]

Access to and control of both materials helped a former terrorist rise to political heights in Japan, profoundly shaping that country's postwar political development. Yoshio Kodama's fortune, built of profits from tungsten and opium, established the party that today rules Japan. Until he was discredited in the Lockheed bribery scandal of the mid-1970s, Kodama stood at the apex of what journalist Koji Nakamura called Japan's "gangster-rightist clique." As Nakamura described this circle, "With entree to virtually every postwar prime minister, their financial power and ideological rigidity have bolstered reactionary attitudes within the ruling (conservative) Liberal Democratic Party [LDP], and helped fuel within it the feeling that Japan must one day abandon its democratic constitution and revert to the authoritarianism of the defeated empire."[96]

His investment of extraordinary wealth in national politics propelled Kodama into his notorious role as the chief backroom kingmaker, or *kuromaku,* in postwar Japan. Kodama forged political alliances that culminated in Ichiro Hatoyama winning the premiership in 1954. He also used his influence to ensure the election of Prime Minister Nobusuke Kishi, his friend and fellow inmate of Sagumo Prison, in 1959.[97] He allegedly helped win the premiership for Kakuei Tanaka in 1972, in part by lining up support from a future prime minister, Yasuhiro Nakasone.[98]

Last but not least, Kodama contributed to the pervasive corruption of Japanese politics by steering huge corporate contributions into the coffers of favored LDP members. This pattern culminated in the Lockheed scandal, which revealed that multi-million-dollar payoffs by American aerospace firms had swayed key procurement decisions by Japan's national airline and defense establishment and raised the possibility that the CIA had used Kodama and corporate funds to influence Japanese politics.[99] The money-laundering channel used for Lockheed's bribes was favored both by the CIA and international drug traffickers.[100]

Kodama achieved this exalted status as *kuromaku* not only because of his wealth, ambition, and drive but above all because he enjoyed extraordinary support from U.S. military and intelligence authorities. His recruitment into the inner sanctums of the American occupation in Japan—despite, or perhaps because of, his reputation as a political extremist, war-crimes suspect, and corrupter—shaped not only the history of organized crime in Japan but the politics of the world's second largest economic power.

Washington's alliance with Kodama also had an impact on Korean politics, extending far beyond the Korean War years. With the Korean-born gangster Machii Hisayuki and Japanese business tycoon Kenji Osano (another key figure in the Lockheed scandal and a part owner of Korean Air Lines), Kodama used his influence to achieve the normalization of Japan–South Korea relations in 1965. Indeed, the South Korean dictatorship decorated both Kodama and Osano for "contributions to promoting Tokyo-Seoul relations."[101] The whole process was rife with hints of aid kickbacks, political corruption, and payoffs to organized-crime interests. As Harvard Professor Jerome Cohen noted, "Premier Tanaka and businessmen allied with him, and former prime ministers Sato and Kishi and others, have very close economic ties to the Park regime in South Korea. It is said that these political leaders have amassed enormous wealth from rebates on aid to the ROK."[102] One member of the Japanese Diet, Tokuma Utsunomiya, charged that Japanese trading companies operating in Korea paid commissions on their deals of up to 20 percent to the Korean CIA (KCIA), some of which returned to Japan in the form of kickbacks to leading politicians. The two most prominent Japanese figures implicated in that wholesale purchase of influence were Kodama's protégés Kishi and Tanaka.[103]

The corruption in Asia by the former narcotics peddler Kodama invaded America as well. Tongsun Park, a Korean wheeler-dealer close to both the KCIA and to Kodama, was but the most notorious political agent in the United States of the regime of South Korean President Park Chung Hee, which conspired to bribe its way into the good graces of Congress.[104] As in Japan, the vehicle was recycled money. Some of it came from corporations like Gulf Oil, which made secret payments of $4 million to the Park regime from 1966 to 1970. And some came directly from the American taxpayer, in part through the sale of subsidized rice to Seoul. In 1977, when the so-called Koreagate scandal was at its height, reporter Tad Szulc disclosed:

> Massive but largely unwarranted economic aid to South Korea, much of it politically motivated and often provided in secret by the Johnson and Nixon administrations, is the "original sin" behind the Korean bribery scandals now under investigation by a federal grand jury. . . . The aid to Seoul, running into hundreds of millions of dollars between 1969 and 1975, not only kept the dictatorial regime of President Park Chung Hee solvent and politically stable; it also helped to finance his formidable lobby here, as well as covert intelli-

> gence operations against Korean dissidents living in the United States.[105]

Strong evidence suggests that the Nixon administration knew that its aid and subsidies to the Park regime were laundered back into the United States for lobbying and illegal payoffs, but was content to see its own foreign-policy objectives advanced by this indirect channel.[106]

The common nexus between narcotics, intelligence, ultraright nationalism, organized crime, and respectable politics in Asia has thus had ominous parallels in the United States.[107] The fostering of such forces in the name of national security has hindered not only narcotics control and law enforcement but constitutional governance. Current scholarship in this field is scanty, hindered by enormous challenges of documentation. But the riches that surely lie below the surface justify more concerted exploration by those seeking to understand our nation's recent past.

Notes

1. *Public Papers of the Presidents: Dwight D. Eisenhower,* 1953, 540.

2. For an overview of the many cases illustrating this point, see Jonathan Marshall, *Drug Wars: Corruption, Counterinsurgency, and Covert Operations in the Third World* (Forestville, Calif., 1991).

3. I have borrowed the term from Peter Dale Scott, a pioneering researcher in this field.

4. Quoted in Jonathan Marshall, "The Road to War: Raw Materials and America's Far Eastern Policy, 1940–41," honors thesis, Stanford University, 1976, 25.

5. Quoted in ibid., 24.

6. Ibid.

7. K. C. Li, *Tungsten* (New York, 1955), xv.

8. *Pearl Harbor Attack,* Exhibits, XIX, 3503, cited in Marshall, "Road to War," 198.

9. Quoted in Marshall, "Road to War," 32.

10. Ibid., 187.

11. Li, *Tungsten,* xiv. The quantity involved was 5,940 tons of wolframite and 5,670 tons of antimony. See "Purchase of Chinese Wolfram (Tungsten) and Antimony," 5 July 1940, box 56, Herbert Feis papers, Library of Congress.

12. Li, *Tungsten,* 50, 52. Between 15 May and 15 July 1942, American planes hauled seventy-nine tons of tungsten ore out of China; *ONI Weekly,* 26 August 1942, 27.

13. War Production Board, Statistics Division, Materials Branch, "Major Losses of Sources of War Materials," 25 October 1942, 111.1 Raw Materials-Sources, RG 179, Records of the War Production Board, National Archives, Washington, D.C.

14. Bradford Huie, "Ten Ways to Lose the War," *American Mercury,* October 1942. State Department Political Advisor Stanley Hornbeck commented that the article was "of considerable current significance." 9 September 1942 memo, Box 466, Stanley K. Hornbeck papers, Hoover Institution, Stanford, California.

15. *North China Daily News,* 4 September 1947.

16. Barbara Tuchman, *Stilwell and the American Experience in China, 1911–1945* (New

York, 1970), 477; Paul Frillmann, *China: The Remembered Life* (Boston, 1968), 152; Israel Epstein, *The Unfinished Revolution in China* (Boston, 1947), 338; Graham Peck, *Two Kinds of Time* (Boston, 1950), 474; Gilbert Stuart autobiography, ms., Box 1, Gilbert Stuart papers, Hoover Institution; Drew Pearson, *Diaries, 1949–1950* (London, 1974), 60.

17. "Purchase of Chinese Wolfram (Tungsten) and Antimony," 5 July 1940, in Feis papers, Box 56. Li may have been the wealthiest Chinese citizen in the United States. See *Washington Post*, 9 March 1961.

18. U.S. Congress, Senate, Special Committee Investigating the Munitions Industry, *Munitions Hearings*, 73d Cong., 2d sess., (4–14 September 1934, 1990, 2069; on military aircraft, cf. Joseph C. Green memo to Hornbeck, 13 June 1939, and memo of conversation between Hornbeck, K. P. Chen, K. C. Li, and Hu Shih, 2 August 1939, in Hornbeck papers, Box 16.

19. *Washington Post*, 9 March 1961.

20. Herbert Feis memo of conversation with K. C. Li re tungsten smuggling in China, 4 January 1943, in Division of Defense Materials lot file, Box 25, Record Group (RG) 59, Records of the Department of State, National Archives.

21. Stanley Hornbeck memo to Hull, 26 May 1943, Box 467, Hornbeck papers.

22. H. Trueblood, State Department Economic Affairs section, memo of 21 August 1941, in Box 278, Hornbeck papers.

23. Li, *Tungsten*, xii.

24. *Washington Post*, 9 March 1961.; OSS report A33480, 27 July 1944, RG 226, OSS records, Modern Military Records, National Archives, on the early history of Wah Chang.

25. *Business Week*, 21 November 1953.

26. K. C. Li cable to Chungking, n.d. (December 1942 or January 1943), Box 417, Hornbeck papers.

27. Jonathan Marshall, "Opium and the Politics of Gangsterism in Nationalist China, 1927–1945," *Bulletin of Concerned Asian Scholars* 8 (July–September 1976): 31–34.

28. *Who's Who in China*, 5th ed. (Shanghai, 1936), 237–38; Howard L. Boorman, ed., *Biographical Dictionary of Republican China*, 3 vols. (New York, 1967–79), III: 329. For a list of his many positions in public organizations, education, finance, media, utilities, paper-making, flour-milling, textiles, fisheries, trading, and other industries, see the special supplement to *Shang Pao*, 29 August 1947, on the occasion of his sixtieth birthday. He also controlled the Chinese Association of Labor, which represented China before the International Labor Organization; see Nym Wales, *The Chinese Labor Movement* (New York, 1945), 122n, and Randall Gould, *China in the Sun* (Garden City, N.Y., 1946), 358. At the same time, Tu was also on the payroll of the American-owned Shanghai Power, apparently to keep its labor force in check; see Edgar Snow, *The Battle for Asia* (New York, 1941), 79. Milton Miles wrote that Tu "organized the workers of Shanghai so thoroughly that, in many ways, he held the running of the city in his hands. His 'associations' . . . included all the carriers—the stevedores, cargo boatment, 'carry-cary' coolies, and rickshaw men. He had also organized the employees of the public utilities—the street railway, the telephone, the telegraph, the water works, and the electric power and gas companies." Miles also noted that Tu's men "succeeded in protecting the public utilities from several attempts to blow up Shanghai's generators and other important equipment." See Milton Miles, *A Different Kind of War* (Garden City, N.Y., 1967), 508, 527.

29. Memorandum for A-7 files, 3 July 1945, Milton Miles papers, Center of Naval History, Washington, D.C.

30. Marshall, "Opium and the Politics of Gangsterism."

31. Joseph Stilwell, "Political Issues and Problems, The Narcotics Situation," G-2 report, 5 March 1935, 893.114 Narcotics/1547, RG 59, National Archives.

32. Marshall, "Opium and the Politics of Gangsterism," 33, 36–37, 41 [Nineteenth Route Army and aircraft]; Treasury memorandum to Henry Morgenthau, 21 April 1945, in U.S. Congress, Senate, Judiciary Committee, *Morgenthau Diary (China)* (Washington,

D.C., 1965), II:1486–88 [Chinese bonds]; Randall Gould, *China in the Sun* (Garden City, N.Y., 1946), 359 [Tu and tungsten].

33. Boorman, *Biographical Dictionary of Republican China,* III:209.

34. Office of Naval Intelligence, "Background Study of Lt. General Tai Li, Chinese Army," no date, in Chapter 38 file, Miles papers, Center of Naval History.

35. Naval attaché report, 7 April 1942, Box 159, Hornbeck papers. Not all judgments were so harsh. One U.S. assessment admitted that he "has not hesitated to kill or maim" and was "definitely cruel and barbarous," but added with satisfaction that he "has actively sought to learn our methods." It judged Tai Li to be "exactly as fascistic and evil as J. Edgar Hoover." And it noted that he was well liked by, among others, Admiral Charles Cooke, General Claire Chennault, and Col. John Coughlin of OSS (ONI, "Background Study," Miles papers, Center of Naval History). The chief of naval intelligence, Thomas Inglis, termed Tai Li an "ardent admirer of the U.S. Navy" and concluded that his possible appointment as China's navy secretary "would be highly advantageous except for the fact that his public reputation identifies him chiefly as the head of the Chinese National Secret Police." (Thomas B. Inglis, chief of naval intelligence, memo for Secretary of the Navy, no date, Miles papers, Center of Naval History.) Tai Li's chief American admirer and wartime liaison, Navy Commander Milton Miles, reflected in 1950, "I am certain in one thing that if Tai Li were alive today there would not be any Red China today. As you know, he was my best friend; and as you also realize, he was ruthless and capable of engineering a great deal of things of importance to free peoples, even if in the engineering there was a slight amount of killing here and there" (Milton Miles letter to Captain C. D. Smith, 6 July 1950, Box 1, Milton Miles papers, Hoover Institution. After Tai Li was killed in a plane crash in 1946, the Navy insisted that he be given the Distinguished Service Medal, a proposal whose political implications distressed General George Marshall. See John Robinson Beal, *Marshall in China* (New York, 1970), 236.

36. Marshall, "Opium and the Politics of Gangsterism," 38–40; E. Jacobson report, 28 July 1941, 893.114 Narcotics/3074, RG 59; E. Jacobson report, 18 August 1941, 893.114 Narcotics/3085, RG 59, National Archives.

37. Quoted in Marshall, "Opium and the Politics of Gangsterism," 40.

38. "General Tai Li," in Chapter 38 file, Miles papers, Center of Naval History.

39. Marshall, "Opium and the Politics of Gangsterism," 41–42; Memorandum for A-7 files, Subject: Tu Yueh-sen, 3 July 1945, Miles papers, Center of Naval History.

40. Peck, *Two Kinds of Time,* 38.

41. Marshall, "Opium and the Politics of Gangsterism," 42. Despite Tai's drug smuggling, SACO also enjoyed training assistance from experts from the FBI and FBN (*New York Times,* 14 September 1945).

42. Memorandum, 14 May 1942, Box 3, Preston Goodfellow papers, Hoover Institution.

43. Yang Wei, *I tai hao-hsia Tu Yueh-sheng* (Hong Kong, 1968), 85–86; cf. Shih-i [pseudonym for Hu Hsu-wu], *Tu Yueh-sheng wai-chuan* (Hong Kong, 1962), 109–10. Another OSS agent who had extensive contact with the Green Gang, though perhaps not with Tu himself, was Oliver Caldwell. See Elizabeth MacDonald, *Undercover Girl* (New York, 1947), 102; Oliver Caldwell, *A Secret War: Americans in China, 1944–1945* (Carbondale, Ill., 1972).

44. Marshall, "Opium and the Politics of Gangsterism," 42; "War Diary of SACO Camp 8, 12 July 1944–15 August 1944," in Chapter 26 file, Miles papers, Center of Naval History; MacDonald, *Undercover Girl,* 194–95. The former French intelligence officer Thyraud de Vosjoli recounted how "Tai Li granted the monopoly for smuggling along a certain part of the coast to two leaders, Chang Kuei Fang and Chang Yi Chiu, who ruled over more than 25,000 pirates. In exchange, they kept him informed on everything in their area and occasionally agreed to carry out jobs for him." See P. L. Thyraud de Vosjoli, *Lamia* (Boston, 1970), 86. Caldwell later become an avid member of the right-wing China lobby. Another OSS contact of the pirates, Thibaut de Saint-Phalle later served as a CIA agent in French Indochina; MacDonald, *Undercover Girl,* 194–95.

45. Goodfellow memorandum to General Le, no date, Box 3, Goodfellow papers.

46. OSS CID 126155, 19 April 1945, RG 226. Cf. David Hanna, *Virginia Hill, Queen of the Underworld* (New York, 1975), 148–50; Hank Messick, *Secret File* (New York, 1969), 215.

47. Marshall, "Opium and the Politics of Gangsterism," 42; Naval attaché report (Chungking), 4 May 1945, OSS CID #XL10551, RG 226.

48. John Carter Vincent memos, 24 December 1942 and 15 January 1943, Foreign Economic Administration (FEA) Intelligence file #457282; C. E. Gauss to Secretary of State, 21 December 1942, FEA Intelligence file #418813; Harrison Matthews (London) to Secretary of State, 22 January 1943, FEA Intelligence file #424428, all in RG 169, records of the Foreign Economic Administration, National Archives. Cf. Randall Gould, *China in the Sun* (Garden City, N.Y., 1946), 193; Consul General M. S. Myers dispatch from Canton, 28 July 1941, 893.114 Narcotics/3070, RG 59.

49. R. D. Wolcott, OSS, to Mahlon F. Perkins, Department of State, 22 September 1942, in Box 15, Division of Defense Materials lot file, RG 59; cf. FEA Intelligence file, #494107, RG 169.

50. C. E. Gauss dispatch to Secretary of State, 21 December 1942, FEA #418813, RG 169.

51. "Report on the Showa Trading Company" by Lt. Eric W. Fleisher, Investigative Division, 25 July 1947, RG 331, Office of the Military Government, United States (OMGUS) files, Washington National Records Center, Suitland, Md.

52. G-2 memo to Lt. Col. R. E. Rudisill, 24 May 1947, RG 331.

53. William Edwards's interrogation of Kodama Yoshio, 21 and 23 July 1947, RG 331.

54. Edwards's interrogation of Kodama, 21 July 1947; G-2 memo to Lt. Col. R. E. Rudisill, 24 May 1947, RG 331; "Curriculum Vitae of Kodama, Yoshio," U.S. army compilation, RG 331; *Los Angeles Times,* 6 February 1976 [tungsten mines]; *Japan Times Weekly,* 14 February 1976 [spy ring]; David Kaplan and Alec Dubro, *Yakuza* (Reading, 1986), 65 [Kempei Tai].

55. G-2 report on Kodama Yoshio, #18930, 24 May 1947, RG 331; Lt. Col. William T. Hornsday's interrogation of Kodama, 14 March 1946, RG 331; cf. Statement of Home Minister in puppet Nanking regime, International Military Tribunal for the Far East [IMTFE], *Proceedings,* 4912–13.

56. M. R. Nicholson report, 14 November 1939, 893.114 Narcotics/2673 1/2; Nicholson report, 15 November 1939, 893.114 Narcotics/2683 1/2; Nicholson report, 8 May 1940, 893.114 Narcotics/2787; Shanghai police report, 26 March 1940, 893.114 Narcotics/2756; Richard P. Butrick (Shanghai) to Secretary of State Cordell Hull, 28 March 1940, 893.114 Narcotics/2724; Stuart Fuller's remarks to Opium Advisory Committee, 20 May 1939, 893.114 Narcotics/2718, all in RG 59.

57. "Report on Investigation of Kodama, Yoshio, ex-Class "A" Suspect," RG 331; IMTFE *Proceedings,* 4881–4913.

58. Liberal Party secretary general Ichiro Kono cashed in the diamonds by pressuring wealthy rice brokers to buy them. See *Los Angeles Times,* 6 February 1976; *Japan Times Weekly,* 21 February 1976; *Parade,* 28 March 1976.

59. G-2 memo to Lt. Col. R. E. Rudisill, 24 May 1947, RG 331.

60. *New Statesman,* 21 May 1976. Blum, born in Yokohama, became a high-level OSS officer in World War II.

61. *Ampo,* April-September 1976, 19.

62. John Loftus, *The Belarus Secret* (New York, 1982); Christopher Simpson, *Blowback* (New York, 1988).

63. On Willoughby's tungsten venture, see Bruce Cumings, *The Origins of the Korean War: The Roaring of the Cataract, 1947–1950* (Princeton, 1990), 99.

64. Kaplan and Dubro, *Yakuza,* 68.

65. Donald Kirk, "Crime, Politics and Finger Chopping," *New York Times Magazine,* 12 December 1976, 91.

66. *New Asia News,* 16 April 1976.
67. Kaplan and Dubro, *Yakuza,* 62.
68. *Ampo,* October–December 1975, 58.
69. Ian I. Morris, *Nationalism and the Right Wing in Japan: A Study of Post-War Trends* (London, 1960), 45–46, 228–29; *New Asia News,* 16 April 1976. This group was close to Gen. Ho Ying-chin and enjoyed the support of Chiang Kai-shek. The whole mission sounds suspiciously like that of Admiral Charles Cooke, described in Cumings, *The Origins of the Korean War,* 132–34, 140–41, 510–53.
70. *Japan Times Weekly,* 8 May 1976.
71. Ibid.
72. *New York Times,* 10 November 1952.
73. *New York Times,* 5 July 1951.
74. U.S. Congress, House, Government Operations Committee, hearings, *Investigation of United States Government Contracts for Purchase of Tungsten in Thailand,* 83 Cong., 1st sess., 30 November 1953 to 5 February 1954, 324.
75. *New York Times,* 2 April 1976.
76. Dooman correspondence, cited in Prof. Howard Schonberger, "The Japan Lobby and the CIA: A Smoking Pistol," unpublished ms., and conversations with Professor Schonberger. I am grateful to him for sharing the results of his research in progress. One kidnapping case that Dooman may have had knowledge of, involving both G-2 and the CIA, is discussed in Kaplan and Dubro, *Yakuza,* 60.
77. Cumings, *The Origins of the Korean War,* 148.
78. *Engineering and Mining Journal* (October 1952): 132.
79. Bradley F. Smith, *The Shadow Warriors* (New York, 1983), 408.
80. Letter from Harold Wendel Lady (Office of the President, Republic of Korea), 2 March 1949, Box 1, Goodfellow papers.
81. Cumings, *The Origins of the Korean War,* 136, 515–19.
82. Memo to Goodfellow, 27 April 1954, Box 1, Goodfellow papers.
83. Cumings, *The Origins of the Korean War,* 147.
84. For a good overview of the airline's history, see William M. Leary, *Perilous Missions: Civil Air Transport and CIA Covert Operations in Asia* (University, Alabama, 1984).
85. *CAT Bulletin,* August 1953.
86. ISC memorandum, Political Analysis of the Leading Figures in N.W. China, no date. Box 1, Whiting Willauer papers, Seeley G. Mudd Library, Princeton University. Willauer, Chennault's partner in CAT, had a commission in U.S. Naval Intelligence before World War II. He was later named ambassador to Honduras in 1953 thanks to Under Secretary of State Walter Bedell Smith, former head of the CIA. See "Oral History of CAT," Box 1, Willauer papers.
87. U.S. Congress, House, Committee on Un-American Activities, *International Communism: Consultation with Major General Claire Lee Chennault* (Washington, D.C., 1958), 8.
88. See Cumings, *The Origins of the Korean War,* passim, on this angle.
89. *New York Times,* 10 November 1952; ibid., 20 January 1953; Catherine Lamour and Michel R. Lamberti, *The International Connection: Opium from Growers to Pushers* (New York, 1974), 95.
90. *New York Times,* 23 September 1951.
91. Tibor Mende, "Report from the Burma Border," *Reporter,* 12 May 1953, 17–21; cf. *New York Times,* 20 January 1953.
92. House Government Operations Committee, *Investigation of United States Government Contracts for the Purchase of Tungsten in Thailand,* passim. On the Thai Border Patrol Police and KMT activities, see Alfred McCoy, *The Politics of Heroin in Southeast Asia* (New York, 1972), 130–35. On Narong Kittikachorn, see *Washington Post,* 12 April 1976.
93. For an overview of this history, see Marshall, *Drug Wars.*
94. Many sources remark on Chiang's early relationship with the Green Gang in the

days when he was a broker in Shanghai. See, for example, Boorman, ed., *Biographical Dictionary of Republican China,* I:319; Mark Gayn, *Journey From the East* (New York, 1944); 338; O. E. Clubb, *Twentieth Century China* (New York, 1972), 144; Harold Isaacs, *Tragedy of the Chinese Revolution* (Stanford, 1951), 81; Theodore White and Annalee Jacoby, *Thunder Out of China* (New York, 1946), 120–21.

95. To take just the claim of political extremism, Tu Yueh-sheng's money was an essential element in the the post–World War II rise of the right-wing CC-Clique (named after powerful brothers Chen Li-fu and Chen Kuo-fu), which controlled the KMT's secret political police and "opposed all of Marshall's efforts at compromise." Its rigid stand helped ensure the relatively swift and total loss of power by the Nationalists on the mainland of China. See Beal, *Marshall in China,* 23, 27, 96, 252; OSS CID 15501–217, RG 226. Joseph Stilwell noted in his 1935 G-2 report that the "intimate connection between opium and militarism is a cause of two of China's great sorrows—the tremendous size of her so-called armies and their utter worthlessness for national defense." See note 31.

96. *San Francisco Chronicle,* 12 January 1975.

97. *New York Times,* 2 July 1974. The Kishi government arranged the Japan–U.S. Security Treaty, signed in 1960, Kodama organized a force of 15,000 rightists and gangsters to break up planned anti-Kishi and anti-Eisenhower demonstrations. See *Far Eastern Economic Review,* 20 February 1976.

98. *New York Times,* 11 May 1976.

99. *New York Times,* 1 March 1976 and 2 April 1976; *Ampo,* March 1976, 6–9, 12; Kaplan and Dubro, *Yakuza,* 79; Tad Szulc, "The Money Changers," *The New Republic,* 10 April 1976, 10–12; John Roberts "America and the Making of Japan Inc.," *Nation,* 13 February 1982, 175. There is a narcotics connection here, too. One figure in the Lockheed payoff channel was Shig Katayama, president of ID Corporation, which kept an account at the Castle Bank in the Bahamas, where notorious gangsters and drug traffickers parked their money. According to an unconfirmed Japanese source, Katayama did intelligence work for the occupation in the 1940s and then in the next decade went on "to handle narcotics for the US intelligence work." See Yamakawa Akio, "Lockheed Scandal," *Ampo,* April–September 1976, 3. Castle Bank was headed by Paul Helliwell, former head of OSS in China, a key backer of Chennault's Civil Air Transport and one of the organizers of the CIA program of support for the KMT army in Burma.

100. Marshall, *Drug Wars,* 55.

101. *Japan Times,* 22 May 1976 and 21 February 1976; *Ampo,* March 1976, 17.

102. Quoted in *Ampo,* Winter 1975, 40.

103. *International Herald Tribune,* 19 February 1977; *Newsweek* (international edition), 7 March 1977.

104. On Tongsun Park's representation of the interests of Kodama and Machii Hisayuki in Japan Lines, see Takaoka Susumu, "South Korea Buys Politicians in Japan, Too," *New Asia News,* 12 November 1976. Kodama was also a prime mover behind two other KCIA-sponsored agents of influence in the United States: the Unification Church of Sun Myung Moon and the World Anti-Communist League (WACL). The American head of WACL, retired Gen. John Singlaub, was deputy CIA chief in South Korea during the Korean War, where he may have known Kodama. See Scott Anderson and John Lee Anderson, *Inside the League* (New York, 1986), 125, 151; *Congressional Quarterly,* 1 April 1978. Singlaub, WACL, and the Unification Church became leading promoters and sponsors of the Nicaraguan *contras* in the mid-1980s. In the White House, another such promoter was Donald Gregg, national security adviser to Vice President Bush. Gregg had been CIA station chief in South Korea from 1973 to 1976, during the height of Korean influence peddling in the United States.

105. Tad Szulc, "Too Much Rice, the Original Sin," *The New Republic,* 29 January 1977.

106. *San Francisco Chronicle,* 22 November 1976; *International Herald Tribune,* 9 June 1977; *San Francisco Examiner,* 31 July 1977; *Washington Post,* 22 December 1979.

107. For but one exploration of this theme, see Hank Messick, *John Edgar Hoover* (New York, 1972). See also various works by Peter Dale Scott, beginning with *The War Conspiracy* (Indianapolis, 1972). Bruce Cumings also makes an impressive effort in this direction in the second volume of his *The Origins of the Korean War.* The Iran-*contra* affair brings many of these elements together; see Jonathan Marshall, Peter Dale Scott, and Jane Hunter, *The Iran-Contra Connection: Secret Teams and Covert Operations in the Reagan Era* (Boston, 1987).

DOUGLAS CLARK KINDER

Shutting Out the Evil: Nativism and Narcotics Control in the United States

The general public in the United States has been inundated during the 1980s and early 1990s with information about narcotics abuse, trafficking, and control. From journalists, politicians, law enforcement officials, and the medical community, the American populace ascertained that illicit drug use and trading have recently become among the nation's most intractable problems. Repeatedly, those sources reported that the consumption of cocaine, especially "crack", had reached epidemic proportions, that drug-related violence overran the country's major cities, that youths should (according to First Lady Nancy Reagan) "just say no" to the purveyors of addictive substances, and that Presidents Ronald Reagan and George Bush had declared war on drugs. Americans learned too that only partial gains had been made against narcotics abuse and trafficking. Such a realization proved difficult for them to fathom following the 1988 presidential election campaign with its antidrug rhetoric, after the enactment by Congress of the Omnibus Drug Act of 1988 (which created a cabinet-level "drug czar"—the director of the office of National Drug Control Policy in the Executive Office of the President), and given the stormy two-year tenure of William Bennett in that post. Of greater concern by 1991, evaluations of the nation's antinarcotics endeavors by the press, government authorities, and other informed observers indicated that the fundamental strategy of drug control was in dispute. Notwithstanding compelling arguments which insisted that the narcotics problem would continue until the domestic demand for drugs ended, federal government efforts have generally sought to eliminate foreign narcotics production and the smuggling of those substances into the United States.[1]

Concern with widespread drug abuse and trafficking, contrary to the image projected over the past ten years, has existed in America since the mid-1800s. Similarly, for more than a century antinarcotics advocates largely ignored the domestic causes of substance misuse and contended that other countries and certain undesirable ethnic groups within the United States engendered the nation's drug difficulties. Because they perceived addiction as a serious and growing problem that could be corrected only by purging habit-forming products from this country, a small group of social reformers, physicians, pharmacists, diplomats, and muckraking journalists launched a narcotics-restriction movement between 1840 and 1914. The proponents of drug limitation enjoyed little success, however, until they promoted a drug hysteria with fear-provoking accounts of other nations overcultivating opium and other narcotics and of domestic ethnic minorities abusing drugs. Thus by asserting that the narcotics problem was "foreign," both in terms of source as well as use, restrictionists exploited nativistic feelings in America and justified a series of laws collectively establishing a nonmedical drug prohibition in the country and entrusting narcotics control to the federal government.[2]

Although the ad hoc drug limitation campaign of the nineteenth and early twentieth centuries built a popular consensus against narcotics through uncritical arguments about foreign drug sources and users generating narcotics misuse in the United States, post-1914 federal drug-restriction officials adopted nativistic attitudes for additional reasons. A defender of the nation's cultural values, the government bureaucracy, aside from indiscriminately employing xenophobic rhetoric, frequently viewed addicts and traffickers, whatever their ethnicity, as foreign because they behaved amorally, asocially, irresponsibly, and criminally. With various regions of the world supplying illicit drugs to the country's habitués, narcotics-control authorities also believed that global overcultivation of opium and coca threatened the security of the United States. After 1919, by updating the nativistic allegations of earlier antidrug reformers, federal narcotics officials explained as well the necessity for harsh supplemental antinarcotics laws, for budgetary requests, and for enhanced authority.[3]

The zenith of such practices occurred following the creation in 1930 of America's first separate national drug law enforcement agency, the Federal Bureau of Narcotics (FBN) within the Treasury Department. Directed by Harry J. Anslinger, the nation's original antidrug czar, the FBN for the next thirty-two years implemented countrywide narcotics proscriptions, regulated legitimate, medicinal drug trading, and participated in all facets of narcotics-control diplomacy. With regard to the use of nativism, Anslinger, officially designated as the commissioner of the Federal Bureau of Narcotics, issued literally hundreds of unsubstantiated accusations in books, films, professional journals, magazines, newspapers, and congressional testimony. Disregarding abundant contrary evidence, for instance, he claimed in the 1930s and 1940s that one marijuana cigarette (supposedly often peddled to American teenagers by foreigners) could create "a mad insensate or a murderer" and that the Japanese military used opiates as weapons during World War II. Likewise during the Cold War era, he charged that a cohesive Italian-American "Mafia" conspiracy, with international ties, dominated American narcotics trafficking and that the People's Republic of China "dumped" drugs on the free world for ideological purposes and financial gain. The FBN chief's xenophobic rhetoric became his ally in blunting criticism (which contended that punitive law enforcement failed to reduce drug addiction in the United States), in actuating public demands for stricter narcotics control, and in obtaining assent from Congress and the executive branch for his bureau's budgetary requests and for additional strict antinarcotics legislation.[4]

Anslinger exerted his administrative expertise and the FBN's broad jurisdiction so well that he projected the agency as a vital part of American government. At the same time, he instituted a personal fiefdom in the federal bureaucracy. The commissioner secured these achievements by portraying his bureau as the best defense against the drug evil, by associating the FBN's narcotics-limitation efforts with the nation's attempts to solve other serious domestic and global issues, and by extending his role in the country's foreign policy beyond the FBN charter's definition. As he bolstered and expanded both his and his agency's position, Anslinger became an initiator of drug-restriction activity and improved international antinarcotics cooperation. In spite of strict budgetary constraints during much of his thirty-two-year tenure, he also managed the most efficient and effective federal drug-control program in U.S. history.[5]

Demonstrating the FBN chief's importance to American narcotics limitation even after his mandatory retirement at the age of seventy in 1962, his nativism has continued to color popular thinking on drug abuse and trafficking until the present. That influence endures because of the commissioner's authorship of many publications; the widespread reporting of his ideas in newspapers and magazines; the residual employment of Anslinger-trained antidrug officers; and the continuing validity of state and federal laws (until the 1970s) and international narcotics limitation conventions (to the present) based upon his perspective. In multinational drug-restriction endeavors, his influence was sustained for a number of years too as a result of his service as the nation's representative to the United Nations Commission on Narcotic Drugs between 1946 and 1970.[6]

Yet Anslinger's enduring ability to shape antinarcotics attitudes could not prevent a restructuring of the country's narcotics-control bureaucracy a mere three years after his retirement. Without his redoubtable personality in the FBN to advocate the limitation only of opium, cannabis, coca leaves, their derivatives, and their synthetic substitutes by a single integrated agency with both domestic and foreign responsibilities, a reorganization took place. Hence, to regulate hypnotic and stimulant drugs, federal legislation in 1965 established the Bureau of Drug Abuse Control in the Department of Health, Education, and Welfare. Three years later, in an effort to improve the restriction of narcotics and other habit-forming substances, Congress approved the creation of the Bureau of Narcotics and Dangerous Drugs (BNDD) in the Justice Department by merging the FBN and the Bureau of Drug Abuse Control. Then as a consequence of differing law-enforcement strategies in the BNDD (which emphasized the interdiction of drugs and the arrest of major traffickers) and the Office of Drug Abuse Law Enforcement in the Executive Office of the President (which urged operations against local offenders), the legislative branch and the chief executive combined the two entities and formed the Drug Enforcement Administration (DEA) within the Justice Department in 1973. Armed with ten times more manpower and a twenty-five-times-larger budget (in fiscal year 1974) than the FBN (in fiscal year 1962), the DEA performed just a part of the earlier agency's tasks. Other drug-control duties became the jurisdiction of the State Department, the Federal Bureau of Investigation, and about thirty additional federal government units.[7]

The proliferation of government agencies charged with regulating addictive substances caused more than the eradication of Anslinger's bureau. The reorganization of the United States drug-limitation system, for instance, brought about a lack of coordination among various federal antidrug entities, leading to the institution of a cabinet-level drug czar in 1988. Despite the new emphasis upon curbing demand, the restructured bureaucracy failed to reject the nativistic outlook espoused by narcotics restrictionists 150 years earlier.[8]

The original advocates of drug control blamed other nations and domestic minorities for encouraging addiction in this country. In reality, physicians had long overprescribed habit-forming substances, and the general public had bought unregulated opiates, cocaine, cannabis, and narcotic-laced proprietary medicines. Throughout the nineteenth century, the medical profession dispensed opium and morphine to arrest perplexing symptoms, to aid natural healing, and to relieve discomfort. Of perhaps greater import, untrained practitioners, druggists, general stores, and mail-order houses sold opium, morphine, heroin, cocaine, cannabis, and patent medicines virtually without limitations. Narcotics use was so widespread that opium importation rose more rapidly than the nation's population rate between the 1840s and the 1870s. Also, proprietary medicine consumption increased seven times faster than the population during the nineteenth century.[9]

In spite of America's largely unregulated drug practices and the emergence of a small, disorganized group of narcotics restrictionists, addiction generated little concern in the 1800s. Physicians sometimes realized that chronic opiate users needed increasing dosages to achieve the same results, but contemporary articles in professional journals, newspapers, and magazines insisted that narcotics consumers could enjoy normal lives. Even after the Civil War, medical practitioners misinterpreted the impact of drugs on the human body. Furthermore, narcotics abuse, unlike alcoholism, was seldom linked with irresponsibility, lust, or violence by the country's populace. In holding that view, it logically ignored sporadic warnings by medical authorities, social reformers, and the press that drugs were poisonous; that alcoholics, prostitutes, and the mentally ill were typical recreational narcotics consumers; that drug trafficking occurred in all of the nation's major ports and cities; and that abuse of habit-forming substances was an element of urban corruption and decadence.[10]

Even though Americans perceived narcotics as legitimate healing agents, pain relievers, and intoxicants, some progressive professionals inaugurated an antinarcotics movement. The reformers, trusting in the country's moral superiority, moral progress, and paternalism, wanted to protect racial minorities and "old stock" society from the drug evil. According to the activists, narcotics seductively led foreigners (and native-born citizens too closely associated with immigrants) to immorality, criminality, and death. The only way to save them was to purge habit-forming products from the nation. Prodded by new medical discoveries, a tiny coalition of young physicians and pharmacists asserted that excessive exposure to drugs caused mental and physical decay. They supported state pharmacy laws to control narcotics distribution. In the American Foreign Service, social reformers and medical experts, oversimplifying cultural differences, alleged that drug addiction plagued all countries and that the United States should lead an international campaign against narcotics abuse and trafficking. As these antinarcotics advocates attacked drug misuse, muckraking American newspapers and magazines published highly sensational reports of ethnic groups committing acts of passion and vendetta while abusing narcotics. Whatever their individual orientation, most drug restrictionists held or employed strong nativistic feelings. They feared that immigrant narcotics consumption would undermine cherished values, refused to recognize that native-born citizens could misuse drugs without foreign instigation, and endorsed strict antidrug laws directed against minorities.[11]

The nativistic perspective of the narcotics-limitation crusade received noteworthy expression through local and state measures in the late nineteenth and early twentieth centuries. By 1875, citing reports that associated Chinese-American opiate consumption with the poverty, crime, and unsanitary conditions of Chinatowns, social activists acquired the passage of a San Francisco city ordinance forbidding the practice of opium smoking. Based on negative accounts of drug peddling and abuse and on strident anti-Chinese passions, the antinarcotics crusaders persuaded eleven western states to enact similar antiopium legislation between 1877 and 1900. Early in the new century, during the height of racial segregation and lynching in the South, white newspaper reporters and police officers next charged blacks with immoderate drug use. Most southern cities and states, armed with accusations that cocaine use gave blacks superhuman strength, improved their marksmanship, and made them difficult to kill, approved harsh anticocaine ordinances; many southern police departments changed from .32 caliber to .38 caliber revolvers to ensure that black cocaine abusers could be controlled. After 1910, southwestern antinarcotics reformers began to link Mexican-American violence with marijuana smoking—just as Chinese immigrants were identified with opium smoking and as blacks were associated with recreational cocaine consumption. Most Anglo-Americans knew or cared little about marijuana until that time, when several officials and journalists from the region advocated antimarijuana legislation and claimed that the drug made Mexican-Americans "lust for blood" and "insensible to pain." Eighteen western states therefore adopted marijuana restrictions founded on racial prejudice and fear of the narcotic.[12]

While xenophobia sustained drug regulation in the West, South, and Southwest, small professional groups and reporters from mass-circulation newspapers and magazines promoted, through more genteel rhetoric, uniform state and national controls on the sale and administration of habit-forming substances; yet they also linked ethnic groups with narcotics abuse. By 1901, the American Medical Association (AMA), representing primarily urban M.D.s from the East, and the American Pharmaceutical Association (APhA), representing trained and licensed drug preparers and dispensers, realized that narcotics ordinances should be coordinated with the emerging professional standards of medicine and pharmacy. Because patent medicines contributed to the country's addiction problem, provided ethnic minorities with drugs, and competed with physicians and pharmacists, both the AMA and the APhA discouraged the consumption of proprietary substances and supported the limitation of narcotics-laden trademarked preparations. Seeking stronger drug restrictions, journalists from a number of newspapers and magazines, including the *Nation, Good Housekeeping,* and *Harper's Monthly Magazine,* simultaneously disclosed that many patent medicines without ingredient labels contained narcotics and that immigrants often used these products. They, along with an increasing number of general social reformers, urged the legislative branch to implement countrywide regulations for proprietary substances as well. The combined efforts of the AMA, the APhA, the press, and activists kindled the first national concern with drugs; nevertheless, most congressmen argued that a federal statute controlling trademarked products would exceed the government's constitutional interstate commerce power. The drug industry's lobbyists further dissuaded senators and representatives from formulating a measure to govern patent medicines. In enacting the Pure Food and Drug Act of 1906, Congress at least forced the manufacturers of proprietary preparations to list all contents, including narcotics, on each product transported across state boundaries.[13]

Legislative attention soon shifted to the Chinese habit of smoking opium. While the Pure Food and Drug Act apparently reduced trademarked substance sales and domestic antidrug proponents sought stronger laws to eradicate these products, other prominent Americans attempted to end opiate trafficking in the Far East. Indeed, nonmedical narcotics had been excluded from the Philippines while William Howard Taft served as the governor-general there and as secretary of war (the cabinet officer with responsibility for that area) between 1901 and 1908. The presence of numerous foreign spheres of influence on the Asian mainland complicated law enforcement, making drug limitation virtually impossible in China. Responding to that situation, Theodore Roosevelt's administration summoned the representatives of thirteen countries to an antiopium conference in Shanghai in February 1909. Realizing with much embarrassment that the United States had no federal narcotics restriction statute, the nation's delegates at the meeting requested the State Department to seek the rapid passage of such a law. Domestic antidrug advocates suggested that Congress amend the Pure Food and Drug Act to remove drug-laden patent medicines from interstate commerce. To their consternation, the State Department recommended a new, less controversial national antiopium bill. Congress quickly approved, and President Roosevelt signed the State Department's proposed act forbidding the importation of smoking opium. The Opium Exclusion Act of 1909, ironically, struck at a practice symbolically associated with the country's Chinese populace.[14]

Though few accomplishments—other than the smoking opium prohibition—can be credited to the international gathering in China, social reformers and medical experts in the State Department used it to justify a drug-control foreign policy. U.S. delegates to the Shanghai meeting, undismayed by its achievement of only weak recommendations to limit opiates and reevaluate narcotics regulations, convinced many congressmen and much of the public that drug restriction in other countries would eliminate the indigenous narcotics problem. The envoys likewise contended that this nation should establish statutes to provide an example for the rest of the world and that the nonbinding Shanghai agreements warranted more antidrug legislation at the state and federal levels.[15]

In fact, shortly after the international opium-control conference adjourned, a member of Washington's mission to the meeting, Dr. Hamilton Wright, lobbied both for additional multinational antinarcotics gatherings and domestic drug-limitation laws. Undaunted by the difficulties of his task, Wright sought and attained the U.S. government's participation in a series of international narcotics-restriction conferences at The Hague between 1911 and 1914. The Hague meeting of 1911–12 fashioned the Shanghai opium-control recommendations into a formal diplomatic agreement (the Hague Opium Convention of 1912); and the cooperating countries, at the request of Great Britain, discussed morphine, cocaine, and marijuana limitation. Nonetheless, the 1911–12 conferees, because of international rivalries over drug-generated revenue, failed to conclude a pact to regulate narcotics other than opium. They merely promised "to use their best endeavors" to suppress trafficking, could not define acceptable drug usage, and refused to endorse the restriction of opium at its source. After drafting the emasculated antinarcotics treaty, moreover, few of the participating nations ratified it. The United States attended two later gatherings (the Hague conferences of 1913 and 1914), which reduced the number of consenting countries necessary to implement the convention. Notwithstanding the opium-control accord's weakness, Dr. Wright and the State Department founded U. S. drug-limitation diplomacy through 1931 upon the first Hague agreement.[16]

Meanwhile, Wright urged a campaign for a comprehensive antinarcotics law at home. Suspecting that a drug-regulating statute would soon be enacted, the APhA and many of the drug trade associations in the United States pledged to cooperate with Dr. Wright in formulating a federal narcotics-restriction measure. Representative Francis Burton Harrison (D-N.Y.) also offered to introduce a drug-taxing bill; earlier attempts to compose legislation grounded on constitutional interstate commerce powers had failed. Equipped with these commitments and Senate ratification of the 1912 International Opium Convention, the State and Treasury departments and Wright prepared a bill during 1913 that the APhA, the drug trade organizations, the AMA, and the Internal Revenue Bureau (IRB) as major enforcer of the proposed law supported. Congressman Harrison then sponsored the proposal, and both houses of Congress and the chief executive approved the Harrison Narcotics Act in 1914.[17]

The statute, controlling opiates and cocaine alone (marijuana would not be restricted by the federal government until 1937), compelled all dealers in these narcotics to report transactions on standard order forms (which would be preserved for inspection). Furthermore, they had to register with the IRB and pay an occupational tax. To appease medical and pharmaceutical interests, the Harrison law exempted physicians "in attendence" of patients from recording drug distributions, required medical practitioners and retail druggists to pay only a one dollar per year occupational fee, excluded the trademarked preparation industry from revealing its distribution, sales, and narcotics procurements, and permitted proprietary substances to contain small amounts of opiates and cocaine.[18]

Anxiety about "un-American" drug abusers during and after World War I caused the Harrison Act to evolve from one with rather limited powers to one embracing nonmedical narcotics proscription. The measure authorized physicians to dispense habit-forming substances for medical purposes; hence, practitioners could distribute opiates and cocaine to their addicted patients, a practice that maintained narcotics habitués. In March 1915 the Treasury Department's IRB announced regulations obliging pharmacists to determine both the validity and legitimacy of physicians' prescriptions. At the same time, Justice Department prosecutors began to argue that an unregistered person possessing restricted narcotics, without a medical practitioner's approval, violated the 1914 law.[19]

The *United States v. Jin Fuey Moy,* 241 U.S. 401 (1916), Supreme Court decision nevertheless held that only failure to provide adequate records or pay the one-dollar annual tax constituted an infraction under the law. The identification of drug misuse with anarchists, radicals, and undesirable aliens and the fear that liquor prohibition would encourage more recreational narcotics consumption in 1919 induced the high court to reverse its earlier ruling. It claimed in *United States v. Doremus,* 249 U.S. 86 (1919), and *Webb et al. v. United States,* 249 U.S. 96 (1919), that the Harrison Act forbade drug maintenance and possession of opiates and cocaine by unlicensed individuals without a physician's written order. In that year, Congress, disturbed about un-American narcotics misuse, adopted amendments to the Harrison law proposed by Representative Henry T. Rainey (D-Il.). These revisions allowed the IRB to exact reports from patent-medicine manufacturers about their operations, to assess an excise on controlled drugs by weight, and to consider possession of untaxed opiates and cocaine not prescribed by a doctor as a violation of the statute.[20]

As the Harrison Act grew into the centerpiece of federal antinarcotics legislation, both the nation's habitués and the narcotics-limitation movement changed significantly, yet internal minorities and other countries were still blamed for the domestic drug problem. Unrestrained access to dangerous drugs in the nineteenth and early twentieth centuries had produced a large, socioeconomically and ethnically diverse addict population, but the typical habitué before 1914, according to most medical experts, was a middle-aged, middle-class white female from the southern United States. Paralleling late nineteenth- and early twentieth-century progressive reform campaigns to eradicate alcohol misuse and prostitution and to improve the lives of women, children, and the poor, a small ad hoc group of social activists responded to the nation's widespread narcotics consumption by launching a drug-restriction crusade. The antinarcotics movement, like the Prohibition campaign, associated substance abuse with poverty, crime, and disease. In so doing, drug reformers received low-keyed and sporadic support from the Anti-Saloon League and the Women's Christian Temperance Union.[21]

Although motivated by a progressive impulse to purify American society—indeed all societies—these antidrug advocates also believed or uncritically argued that foreign narcotics users and sources engendered drug misuse in the United States. The proponents of narcotics limitation portrayed, and many perceived, opiate and cocaine abuse as an activity alien to the majority of American citizens. They contended that outsiders must have introduced and encouraged recreational drug consumption in this country. Primarily because of its allegations that domestic ethnic minorities and global narcotics overcultivation created the nation's addiction difficulties, the drug-restriction movement caused narcotics to appear more evil, sinister, and powerful than they actually were. And the movement achieved a series of state ordinances, the Opium Exclusion Act, and the Harrison law that collectively banned nonmedical narcotics usage.

Effective drug control, even with the strengthening of the 1914 antinarcotics measure, required vigilant law enforcement, supplemental federal legislation, and a national narcotics foreign policy; such a program exceeded the capabilities of a tiny, decentralized reform group. Drug-limitation activities in the United States after 1914 became a function of the government bureaucracy and the Congress. Since the Harrison Act reduced the availability of opiates and cocaine to the general public (even as medical and social commentators viewed addiction throughout the 1900s as a serious and growing problem), post-1914 habitués were more likely to be young, lower-class, urban white males who chose escapist lifestyles. New bureaucratic or organizational antinarcotics advocates nonetheless increasingly asserted—as earlier drug-limitation proponents had—that foreign narcotics misusers, traffickers, and producers generated the country's recreational consumption.[22]

Accordingly, federal drug-control officials treated Harrison law violators as social lepers. Congress advanced this effort by establishing the Prohibition Unit within the Internal Revenue Bureau in 1919 and by doubling the antidrug appropriation. In 1922 it enacted the Narcotic Drugs Import and Export Act, which expanded the 1909 Opium Exclusion Act to regulate the importation of coca leaves and all varieties of opium, in spite of the AMA's opposition, which was based upon the belief that the legislation would increase government supervision of physicians and inflate the cost of medicinal narcotics. In 1927 the legislative branch created the independent Prohibition Bureau within the Treasury Department to administer the Harrison law as well as alcohol prohibition more efficiently. Thus, throughout the 1920s the Narcotics Division of the Prohibition Unit (the Prohibition Bureau after 1927) enforced a nonmedical narcotics ban. It confined so many opiate and cocaine addicts and peddlers that almost one-third of all federal prisoners at the end of fiscal year 1928 were drug-law violators.[23]

While the Narcotics Division's activities embraced the nativistic values of the earlier narcotics-control movement, at the end of the 1920s medical spokesmen and high-level government authorities were questioning its utility. Because of corruption, disunity, and mismanagement within the division, Congress eradicated it on 1 July 1930. At that time, the legislative branch and the president approved legislation that established an independent Treasury Department agency with jurisdiction over all aspects of drug limitation—the Federal Bureau of Narcotics.[24]

The broad authority of the infant organization complicated the selection of an administrator. The commissioner of the Federal Bureau of Narcotics would supervise the enforcement of domestic statutes and be accountable for regulating all legitimate traffic in drugs. If the United States participated in international narcotics-control forums, the commissioner would be an important delegate. Since the commissioner would be the country's leading antinarcotic authority, various governmental interests wanted a role in choosing him. Given the need for the FBN chief to coordinate domestic and diplomatic programs, both the State and Treasury departments insisted that they especially should have a vote in the selection process. State and Treasury agreed upon a widely experienced individual to head the organization, Harry J. Anslinger, who had worked in both departments. After serving as interim narcotics commissioner between July and September 1930, Anslinger received President Herbert Hoover's appointment and the Senate's endorsement as the commissioner of narcotics, an office he held until his mandatory retirement in 1962.[25]

Without experience as a drug restrictionist, the new commissioner had to create a forceful domestic and foreign narcotics policy. As he began his duties, Anslinger quickly disguised his deficiency. The antidrug chief believed that adequate drug limitation depended upon his bureau's maintenance, additional punitive national legislation, and world antidrug agreements. He, like many prominent advocates of control, concluded as well that an existing, popular antinarcotics consensus had to support the three-part scheme. Toward that end, the American public's drug-restriction attitude had to be sustained and amplified with fear-provoking, zealous, and moralistic reforming accusations. If he wanted the acceptance of earlier narcotics-limitation activists in the executive and legislative branches, moreover, Anslinger surmised that issuing vehement, crusading antidrug statements, similar to those of preceding restrictionists, would capture it. As such, he wrote scores of articles for professional journals, newspapers, and magazines fervently promoting narcotics control and linking certain ethnic, foreign, and ideological groups with the country's addiction problem. He supplied information and encouragement to other authors willing to produce likeminded books and essays; and he included the resultant narcotics-limitation rhetoric in his testimony before congressional committees. Anslinger's initiative, ardor, and skill with the press soon persuaded physicians, pharmacists, antinarcotics reformers, and the general public to sanction his administration of drug control. For the next three decades, he skillfully managed a drug-restriction program combining diplomacy (based on the country's broader objectives, including national security concerns), bureaucratic expansion, proficient law enforcement, and crusading xenophobic rhetoric.[26]

Anslinger's effort, for a variety of reasons, depended primarily upon an antidrug foreign policy. Since 1909 American narcotics-control advocates had promoted with some success world opiate and cocaine limitations. Because Commissioner Anslinger sought the approval of such drug restrictionists, he naturally concluded that an energetic narcotics-limitation diplomacy would earn it—much as his fear-provoking statements won him endorsements from nativistic drug-control reformers. Moreover, because antinarcotics activists had always deemed domestic drug restriction impossible without international cooperation, and because one of the FBN head's major legal responsibilities was to assist the State Department in conducting narcotics-limitation negotiations, Anslinger directed his energy toward drug-suppression diplomacy. He also had to be a leader in global opiate, cocaine, and cannabis control activities in order to lend credence to his accusations that other countries caused narcotics abuse in the United States. That is, success at the international level would virtually eliminate criticism of his methods. Throughout his tenure, then, the narcotics bureau's chief emphasized antidrug foreign policy over the other elements of his program.[27]

In stressing the vital role of U.S. narcotics-restriction diplomacy, Anslinger became its most important figure. He, like all of the nation's delegates to world antidrug forums, applauded the goal of eliminating nonmedical and nonscientific opiates, cocaine, and cannabis at their sources. But upon entering office in late 1930, the commissioner already shared the responsibility for determining the means of implementing that objective with the State Department's narcotics-control expert. At Anslinger's urging, he and the State Department officer—John Kenneth Caldwell between 1930 and 1932, Stuart J. Fuller from 1932 to 1941, and George A. Morlock between 1941 and 1954—established a broad drug-limitation foreign policy that pursued both bilateral and multilateral negotiations. A radical departure from earlier antinarcotics diplomacy based on either direct or multilateral contacts, the strategy restored the country's prominence in the global drug-restriction movement, something that had not existed since the Hague conference in 1914. As a part of this policy, the FBN head and Caldwell, Fuller, or Morlock represented the United States at meetings of the League of Nations Opium Advisory Committee and later the United Nations Commission on Narcotic Drugs and served on delegations to international antidrug treatymaking conferences.[28]

Though Commissioner Anslinger increased his influence steadily, overshadowed his State Department counterparts by the late 1930s, and almost singlehandedly managed U.S. narcotics-control diplomacy during and after World War II, the Treasury and State departments cooperated in cordial and effective drug-limitation operations. Indeed, FBN and Customs Agency Personnel and Foreign Service officials stationed abroad, as well as members of the Justice Department, military intelligence, and the Office of Strategic Services, acquired and exchanged information about world narcotics production and trafficking. Anslinger further expanded the participation of federal government entities as he personally administered U.S. antinarcotics foreign policy following the war. From then to 1970, when he retired as Washington's representative to the U.N. Commission on Narcotic Drugs, his diplomacy included both bilateral and multilateral negotiations; in the process he maintained the nation's leadership position in the international drug-restriction campaign.[29]

Interagency collaboration and the reestablishment of American hegemony in world narcotics control brought about little advancement in drug limitation. Between 1930 and 1970, Anslinger's fundamental task around the globe consisted of changing cultural attitudes, often within certain economic, political, and social milieus in which illegitimate drug cultivation, manufacture, trade, and use was traditional. The FBN commissioner could not induce such an unmitigated transformation. By employing coercive and often nativistic tactics, he actually encouraged national governments and their people to perceive U.S. narcotics-restriction efforts as encroachments by an alien society. Even though Anslinger and his State Department colleagues extracted commitments to international antidrug conventions and bilateral agreements from European, Near and Far Eastern, and Latin American administrations, Washington's authorities failed to secure any discernible improvement in narcotics control.[30]

The antidrug chief's domestic program yielded a similar result. During his lengthy tenure, Anslinger's conduct of federal narcotics law enforcement prevailed over numerous bureaucratic obstacles and attained a record of great efficiency; however, it could not eradicate drug abuse, addiction, and trafficking in the United States. Considerations of ultimate failure aside, the commissioner's management of the FBN was noteworthy. The bureau's annual appropriation averaged around $2 million (see Table 1); its agents—the lowest paid in federal service—usually numbered about 250 and could not carry firearms under all circumstances, make arrests without warrants, or perform wiretaps until 1956; and they depended upon the confiscated automobiles of narcotics traffickers for the bulk of their transportation needs. Despite these constraints, Anslinger's officers—working an average of fifty-three hours per week—accounted for more convictions per agent than any other federal enforcement unit, oversaw the activities of two hundred thousand manufacturers, wholesalers, pharmacists, and physicians registered to participate in the legitimate narcotics trade, and spoke to various church, civic, fraternal, and school organizations about the drug evil. The FBN also received the responsibility for medicinal narcotics procurement and distribution for this country and its allies during World War II and the Cold War, operated a two-week training school (after 1956) for local, state, and foreign law enforcement personnel, published copies of federal drug regulations for graduating medical, pharmacy, and veterinary students, and provided information to every state medical, pharmacy, and veterinary licensing board. Of equal significance, the commissioner di-

TABLE 1. Annual Budget Requests and Appropriations for the Federal Bureau of Narcotics, 1930–1962

Fiscal Year	Budget Request	Appropriation	Appropriation Change over Previous Year
1930	—	$1,411,260	—
1931	$1,611,260	1,712,998	+$301,738
1932	1,719,688	1,708,528	− 4,470
1933	1,632,800	1,525,000	− 183,528
1934	1,427,523	1,400,000	− 125,000
1935	1,194,899	1,244,899	− 155,101
1936	1,249,470	1,249,470	+ 4,571
1937	1,275,000	1,275,000	+ 25,530
1938	1,267,000	1,267,600	− 7,400
1939	1,267,600	1,267,600	0
1940	1,332,500	1,306,700	+ 39,100
1941	1,304,600	1,303,280	− 3,420
1942	1,289,060	1,283,975	− 19,305
1943	1,289,060	1,289,060	+ 5,085
1944	1,200,000	1,325,016	+ 35,956
1945	1,383,000	1,338,467	+ 13,451
1946	1,439,000	1,332,932	− 5,535
1947	1,331,000	1,300,000	− 32,932
1948	1,506,400	1,430,000	+ 130,000
1949	1,434,000	1,450,000	+ 20,000
1950	1,560,000	1,649,700	+ 199,700
1951	1,855,000	1,848,942	+ 199,242
1952	2,654,000	2,631,425	+ 782,483
1953	2,815,000	2,804,915	+ 173,490
1954	2,820,000	2,857,800	+ 52,885
1955	2,820,100	2,805,368	− 53,432
1956	3,040,100	3,366,504	+ 561,136
1957	3,609,565	3,355,995	− 10,509
1958	3,760,000	3,845,193	+ 489,198
1959	3,780,000	4,060,550	+ 215,357
1960	4,080,000	4,080,000	+ 19,450
1961	4,100,000	4,100,000	+ 20,000
1962	4,462,000	4,462,000	+ 362,000

Source: Compilation of U.S. House of Representatives, *Treasury Department Appropriations Hearings* (1931–63) and of U.S. Treasury Department, *Federal Bureau of Narcotics Annual Reports* (1931–63).

rected his bureau to promote the passage of uniform state antinarcotics laws, the enactment of more national drug-limitation measures, and co-operation with other federal entities and police officials in other nations. Anslinger's agency probably enjoyed the best possible results, with a limited budget, through a law enforcement method of narcotics restriction.[31]

The shortcomings of that approach, combined with bureaucratic exigencies, largely explain the FBN head's reliance upon nativistic allegations after he won public endorsement as an antidrug reformer in the 1930s. Faced with the unglamorous task of supervising the scrutiny of import and export certificates and monthly reports from narcotics manufacturers, wholesalers, and medical practitioners (a duty comprising nearly half the FBN's activities); periodic congressional investigations that considered dismantling the agency; and low budgets, Anslinger resorted to issuing xenophobic accusations in books, films, professional journals, magazines, newspapers, and congressional testimony. Such a tactic assisted him in justifying his agency's existence and independence when proficient law enforcement failed to end drug misuse and trading. By portraying the FBN as locked in a struggle against foreign traffickers with virtually unlimited resources, the commissioner persuaded members of many civic and fraternal groups to report cases of narcotics abuse and trafficking and to inundate the executive and legislative branches with letters supporting the FBN. Anslinger's use of nativism convinced some of the public of the dangers of illicit, recreational drug consumption, too. Whatever their precise impact, his assertions repeatedly appeared in the findings of congressional investigating committees as reasons for recommending new antinarcotics legislation, for expanding the FBN's authority, and for modest budgetary increases. The president and the full Congress usually responded by assenting to committee proposals.[32]

The antidrug chief's statements about marijuana, Japan's use of narcotics as weapons during World War II, and Mafia and Communist drug trafficking in the Cold War era brought the greatest benefit to his bureau. By producing hundreds of articles over a twenty-year period associating marijuana abuse with crimes of passion and vendetta and with undesirable ethnic groups, for example, Anslinger convinced Congress to approve without scientific evidence the Marihuana Tax Act of 1937 and created a "killer narcotic" that could account for enforcement difficulties. Exploiting wartime concerns between 1934 and 1945, he insisted that Japan employed opium to "soften" nations under attack, to pacify conquered peoples, and to support the war financially. That rhetoric helped the commissioner project his agency as an important element of the country's defense.[33]

Then before a 1950–51 special Senate committee investigating organized crime, chaired by Senator Estes Kefauver (D-Tenn.), and a 1955 subcommittee of the Senate Judiciary Committee examining American drug laws, chaired by Senator Price Daniel (D–Tex.), the commissioner and his agents discussed international Mafia and Communist narcotics conspiracies. Although the FBN had not presented any real evidence of a cohesive Mafia, the Kefauver committee adopted Anslinger's view of narcotics law enforcement and attributed the bureau's inability to solve the nation's drug problems to the Mafia. In order to combat that sinister organization, the committee further proposed the Senate version of the 1951 Boggs Act, which called for mandatory prison sentences for narcotics criminals, and suggested an increase in the FBN's budget and manpower. For fiscal year 1952, Congress endorsed the Kefauver committee's recommendation and passed the largest increase in the agency's annual appropriation during the commissioner's tenure (see Table 1). Four years later, Anslinger achieved still more by informing the Daniel subcommittee that the People's Republic of China was acquiring foreign currency and disrupting the Free World through narcotics sales. Meeting in the mid-1950s, when Americans frequently viewed the mainland Chinese as a fanatical horde, the subcommittee claimed that "subversion through drug addiction is an established aim of Communist China" and supported the FBN head's legislative agenda. It proposed and Congress assented to the Narcotic Control Act of 1956, which increased the length of mandatory prison sentences and permitted the death penalty in some cases. In the same legislation, the commissioner obtained as well the authority for his agents to carry firearms under all circumstances, serve warrants and subpoenas, employ wiretaps, and make arrests without warrants (the FBN simultaneously received another sizable budget increase). Shortly before his retirement as commissioner in 1962, at a time of heightened tension between Castro's Cuba and the United States, Anslinger even launched a rhetorical campaign against that Communist state.[34]

While corroborated only by allegations, the commissioner's nativism had far greater long-term influence in this country. It maintained and amplified widely held antinarcotics values. Long after Anslinger left the FBN and his post as the U.S. representative to the U.N. Commission on Narcotic Drugs, his publications, former associates, and contributions to state and federal laws and international treaties reinforced the notion that drug misuse and trafficking were foreign-inspired. If true, American narcotics control merely needed to urge other nations to eradicate opium and coca cultivation, to interdict drugs entering the United States, and to incarcerate domestic purveyors of narcotics. Anslinger's legacy assured government officials and the populace that doing so eventually would extirpate the drug evil.[35]

Yet post-1962 reorganizations of the federal narcotics-limitation system and apportionment of antidrug responsibilities among various agencies did not enhance the nation's ability to realize that goal. Changes to U.S. narcotics-restriction operations and laws engendered such a lack of coordination between federal entities that Congress and President Reagan sought to remedy it by authorizing a cabinet-level drug czar in 1988. Apart from that action, the federal government for the past twenty-nine years has remained committed to ending foreign narcotics production and the smuggling of those substances into this country. Much like Anslinger and the FBN, more recent drug-control authorities as well as journalists and politicians blamed America's narcotics problems upon the overcultivation of opium and coca in other nations, the trafficking of drugs by foreign or ethnic criminals (frequently portrayed as Colombian or African-American), and the consumption of heroin or crack cocaine by the urban poor. Though drug surveys indicated that 69 percent of cocaine misusers were white and that two-thirds of drug abusers were employed, the public statements of officials interested in narcotics limitation depicted illicit drug consumers as maladjusted. Therefore, U.S. antinarcotics policies since 1962, while lacking the integration of Anslinger's period, have continued to emphasize opium and coca control at points of origination and drug-law enforcement over activities concerned with reducing demand.[36]

Efforts to suppress the country's illicit narcotics use and trading have differed little since the mid-1800s. In spite of unreliable addict population statistics, especially before 1962, which prevented a precise understanding of the impact of drugs on American society, advocates of limitation, whether from the 1890s, the 1920s, or the 1980s, made the same assessment. They believed that narcotics misuse and trafficking were at epidemic proportions. Moreover, they customarily exploited the nation's nativistic feelings and explained the need for a nonmedical drug proscription by contending that the narcotics evil was foreign in origin. For Harry Anslinger and other federal drug-control authorities, the identification of certain countries and domestic ethnic minorities with illicit narcotics consumption in America provided a powerful argument for reliance upon law enforcement as the primary corrective. Since the mid-nineteenth century, the favored solution for drug abuse, addiction, and smuggling in the United States has been to shut out habit-forming substances and the proclivity to use them.

Ohio University

Notes

1. Bruce Michael Bagley, "The New Hundred Years War?: U.S. National Security and the War on Drugs in Latin America," Raphael Perl, "International Narcopolicy and the Role of the U.S. Congress," and Donald J. Mabry and Raphael Perl, "Concluding Observations and Policy Recommendations," in *The Latin American Narcotics Trade and U. S. National Security*, ed. Donald J. Mabry (Westport, Conn., 1989), 43–58, 89–102, 151–61; Elaine Shannon, "A Losing Battle," *Time*, 3 December 1990, 44–48. American law and custom define narcotics as opiates, cocaine, and marijuana. The legal community, restrictionists, and the general public in the United States used the words "narcotic" and "drug" synonymously until the mid-1960s, though the two are pharmacologically distinct. As have other historical studies about narcotics, this article will employ the two terms interchangeably.

2. Douglas Clark Kinder, "Bureaucratic Cold Warrior: Harry J. Anslinger and Illicit Narcotics Traffic," *Pacific Historical Review* 50 (May 1981): 169–91; David F. Musto, M.D., *The American Disease: Origins of Narcotic Control*, expanded ed. (New York, 1987), 1–63, 97–120, 135–40, 206–15, 245–48; H. Wayne Morgan, *Drugs in America: A Social History, 1800–1980* (Syracuse, 1981), 1–63, 88–90, 118–28; Richard J. Bonnie and Charles H. Whitebread II, *The Marihuana Conviction: A History of Marihuana Prohibition in the United States* (Charlottesville, Va., 1974), 5–28, 32–45, 106–11; William O. Walker III, *Drug Control in the Americas*, rev. ed. (Albuquerque, 1989), 3–6, 9–20, 27–35, 41–45, 47–57, 62–64; Arnold H. Taylor, *American Diplomacy and the Narcotics Traffic, 1900–1939: A Study in International Humanitarian Reform* (Durham, N.C., 1969), 3–122, 132, 157–59, 171–77, 183–85, 200–224, 230–32, 241, 302–5; Rufus King, *The Drug Hang-Up: America's Fifty-Year Folly* (New York, 1972), 69–71; Norman H. Clark, *Deliver Us From Evil: An Interpretation of American Prohibition* (New York, 1976), 1–5, 218–23; James H. Timberlake, *Prohibition and the Progressive Movement, 1900–1920* (Cambridge, Mass., 1966), 39–99; Herbert L. May, "The International Control of Narcotic Drugs," *International Conciliation*, no. 441 (May 1948): 301–71. Narcotics control in this country has always had an association with cultural conflict and nativism. The term "culture" will be used to describe the attitudes, customs, and values that comprise an ethnic group's perspective of the world. "Nativism" is both the preference for and the defense of a native culture. For a discussion of "culture," see Walker, *Drug Control in the Americas;* William O. Walker III, "Drug Control and the Issue of Culture in American Foreign Relations," *Diplomatic History* 12 (Fall 1988): 365–82; Michael H. Hunt, *Ideology and U. S. Foreign Policy* (New Haven, 1987), 12–13. This article examines the control of the opium poppy, coca leaf, and cannabis plant and their derivatives and synthetic substitutes.

3. Musto, *The American Disease*, 135–40, 206–14, 245–48; Bonnie and Whitebread, *The Marihuana Conviction*, 9–18, 20–28, 106–11; Clark, *Deliver Us From Evil*, 1–5, 221–22; Morgan, *Drugs in America*, 88–90, 118–28; Taylor, *American Diplomacy and the Narcotics Traffic*, 132, 200–209; Walker, *Drug Control in the Americas*, 14–20; Kinder, "Bureaucratic Cold Warrior," 169–91.

4. Kinder, "Bureaucratic Cold Warrior," 169–91; Douglas Clark Kinder and William O. Walker III, "Stable Force in a Storm: Harry J. Anslinger and United States Narcotic Foreign Policy, 1930–1962," *Journal of American History* 72 (March 1986): 918–27; various clippings, articles, and typescripts in files 7, 11, and 12 in Box 1, file 1 in Box 2, and files 1 and 15 in Box 5, Harry J. Anslinger Papers, Pennsylvania Historical Collections and Labor Archives, The Pennsylvania State University, State College (hereafter cited as HJAP/PSU); U.S. Congress, House, Ways and Means Committee, *Taxation of Marihuana: Hearings on HR 6385*, 75th Cong., 1st sess., 27–30 April and 4 May 1937 (hereafter cited as *House Marihuana Taxation Hearings*); *Los Angeles Examiner*, 15 February 1942; Harry J. Anslinger, "Opium After the War," *The Prison World*, May–June 1944, 10, 28–29; *Atlanta Constitution*, 19 August 1946; Harry J. Anslinger, "Narcotics and the Physician," *The West Virginia Medical Journal* 38 (October 1942): 373–78; U.S. Congress, Senate, Special Com-

mittee to Investigate Organized Crime in Interstate Commerce, *Hearings before the Special Committee to Investigate Organized Crime in Interstate Commerce, Pursuant to S. Res. 202,* 81st Cong., 2d sess. and 82d Cong., 1st sess., 2 May 1950 to 1 September 1951, pt. 2, 81–89, and pt. 12, 537, 662–68 (hereafter cited as *Kefauver Crime Committee Hearings*); U.S. Congress, Senate, Special Committee to Investigate Organized Crime in Interstate Commerce, *Final Report of the Special Committee to Investigate Organized Crime in Interstate Commerce, Pursuant to S. Res. 202 (as amended by S. Res. 60 and S. Res. 129),* 81st Cong., 2d sess., and 82d Cong., 1st sess., 1–6 (hereafter cited as *Kefauver Committee Final Report*); U.S. Congress, House, Ways and Means Committee, *Report of the Ways and Means Committee on Increased Penalities for Narcotic and Marihuana Law Violations,* 82d Cong., 1st sess., 1–9 (hereafter cited as *Boggs Committee Report*); U.S. Congress, Senate, Judiciary Committee, *Hearings before the Subcommittee to Investigate the Administration of the Internal Security Act and Other Internal Security Laws of the Senate Judiciary Committee,* 84th Cong., 1st sess., 8, 18, 19 March and 13 May 1955, 1–14 (hereafter cited as *Senate Internal Security Subcommittee Hearings*); U.S. Congress, Senate, Judiciary Committee, *Hearings before the Subcommittee on Improvements in the Federal Criminal Code of the Judiciary Committee, Pursuant to S. Res. 67,* 84th Cong., 1st sess., 2 June to 15 December 1955, 31–33, 93–96, 275–78, 701, 1,378–95, 1,431–42, 3,115–18, 4,011 (hereafter cited as *Daniel Subcommittee Hearings*); U.S. Congress, Senate, Select Committee on Improper Activities in the Labor or Management Field, *Hearings before the Select Committee on Improper Activities in the Labor or Management Field, Pursuant to S. Res. 74 and 221,* 85th Cong., 1st sess., 30 June and 1–3 July 1958, pt. 32, 11,219–51 (hereafter cited as *McClellan "Rackets" Committee Hearings*); Stanley D. Backrack, *The Committee of One Million: China Lobby Politics, 1955–1971* (New York, 1976), 52–55, 122–23; Musto, *The American Disease,* 135–40, 210–15; Morgan, *Drugs in America,* 118–28.

5. U.S. Congress, House, Ways and Means Committee, *Hearings before the Ways and Means Committe on H. R. 10,561, A Bill to Create in the Treasury Department a Bureau of Narcotics and for Other Purposes,* 71st Cong., 2d sess., 7 and 8 March 1930, 1–44 (hereafter cited as *House Bureau of Narcotics Hearings*); U.S. Congress, House, Appropriations Committee, *Hearings before the Subcommittee of the Appropriations Committee in charge of the Treasury Department Appropriation Bills* for 1931–63, 71st Cong., 2d sess., to 88th Cong., 2d sess, 27 November 1929 to 29 January 1962 (hereafter cited as *House Treasury Department Appropriation Hearings*); *House Marihuana Taxation Hearings;* H. J. Anslinger, with Courtney Ryley Cooper, "Marihuana: Assassin of Youth," *American Magazine* 124 (July 1937): 18–19, 150–53; *Kefauver Crime Committee Hearings,* pt. 2, 81–89, and pt. 12, 537, 662–68; *Kefauver Committee Final Report,* 1–6; *Boggs Committee Report,* 1–9; *Senate Internal Security Subcommittee Hearings,* 1–14; *Daniel Subcommittee Hearings,* 31–33, 93–96, 275–78, 701, 1,378–95, 1,431–42, 3,115–18, 4,011; *McClellan "Rackets" Committee Hearings,* pt. 32, 11,219–51; Backrack, *The Committee of One Million,* 52–55, 122–23; "Highlights: The Realm of Entertainment," *Altoona* (Pennsylvania) *Mirror,* 10 May 1965; Walker, *Drug Control in the Americas,* 70–73; Kinder, "Bureaucratic Cold Warrior," 169–83; Anslinger, "Narcotics and the Physician," 373–78; "Executive Order for Interdepartmental Narcotics Committee," 2 November 1951, File: Legislation 82d Cong., 1st sess. (Narcotics), Box 81, George M. Elsey Papers, Harry S. Truman Presidential Library, Independence, Missouri (hereafter cited as Elsey Papers); Executive Order 10302, "Interdepartmental Committee on Narcotics," 2 November 1951, *Code of Federal Regulations,* Title 3—The President, 1949–1953 Compilation (Washington, D.C., 1958), 831–32; Statements by Gordon Canfield, Hale Boggs, and J. Vaughn Gary, *Congressional Record–House,* 82d Cong., 1st sess., 30 June, 16 July, and 20 August 1951, 7,545–46, 8,195–98, 10,385–87. Anslinger's administration of American narcotics control surpassed that of all federal officials supervising the earlier Narcotics Division (within the Prohibition Unit and Bureau), the State Department's drug limitation endeavors, and more recently established agencies such as the Bureau of Narcotics and Dangerous Drugs

and the Drug Enforcement Administration. A variety of factors explain the superiority of the commissioner's and his bureau's antinarcotics program. First, through national laws, presidential executive orders, and the assumption of authority, Anslinger and the FBN obtained greater legal power for drug restriction than any other federal officers and agencies. The commissioner and the narcotics bureau for more than three decades conducted a majority of the country's narcotics-control diplomacy; encouraged the institution of international police practices that aided drug-law enforcement; executed federal antidrug laws; regulated legitimate narcotics transactions; mobilized an existing popular consensus against drugs in the United States and consequently convinced senators, representatives, and presidents to enact additional harsh antinarcotics legislation; and operated a lobbying effort to promote supplemental drug-control laws at the state and local levels. Second, Anslinger and his agency produced a remarkable record of law enforcement efficiency. Despite an annual budget averaging only about $2 million and a staff averaging only about 250 agents between 1930 and 1962, the FBN sent more criminals to jail per agent than any other federal law enforcement unit, avoided major scandals, and earned a reputation of cooperating well with international, national, state, and local police. Third, the commissioner and the narcotics bureau achieved more influence over the dissemination of drug-related information than other authorities and agencies in the country. Other federal entities—even the armed forces—submitted their statistics on narcotics use, addiction, and trafficking to the FBN; the commissioner, in turn, released the country's only official figures to the press. Such an arrangement allowed him to publicize statistics (criticized by some contemporary and virtually all later public health officers and social observers for falsely minimizing the American drug problem) that indicated both the need for the FBN and its law enforcement success. Anslinger also influenced public thinking about narcotics consumption and trading by writing books and articles and by providing information to other authors. The effect of his public relations effort was to create the image that the narcotics bureau would have eradicated drug addiction and trafficking in the nation if it were not struggling against numerous well-equipped, foreign "super criminals." On these issues, see the sources above and Kettil Bruun, Lynn Pan, and Ingemar Rexed, *The Gentlemen's Club: International Control of Drugs and Alcohol* (Chicago, 1975), 15–18, 20–21, 54–59, 87–88, 300–301; Bernard Barton to Dr. Winford H. Smith, 25 May 1944, Anslinger to Murray Kramer, 20 December 1944, and Anslinger to I. V. Sollins, 19 February 1945, Medical Supplies: UNRRA-Narcotic Requirements file, Box 59, Record Group 179, Records of the Combined Production and Resources Board, National Archives, Washington, D.C.; William Howard Moore, *The Kefauver Committee and the Politics of Crime, 1950–52* (Columbia, Mo., 1974), 115, 134; U.S. Bureau of Narcotics, *Circular Letters*, nos. 17, 75, 98, and 251, 15 August 1930, 10 March 1931, 28 April 1931, 10 November 1933, item T56.2, Box T1169, Printed Archives Branch, National Archives, Washington, D.C.

6. Kinder, "Bureaucratic Cold Warrior," 169–91; Kinder and Walker, "Stable Force in a Storm," 908–27; Harry J. Anslinger and William F. Tompkins, *The Traffic in Narcotics* (New York, 1953); Harry J. Anslinger and Will Oursler, *The Murderers: The Shocking Story of the Narcotics Gangs* (New York, 1961); Harry J. Anslinger and J. Dennis Gregory, *The Protectors* (London, 1964); Anslinger and Cooper, "Marihuana: Assassin of Youth," 18–19, 150–53; Broadcast over KIRO, Seattle, 31 July 1939, file 8, Box 1, HJAP/PSU; Anslinger, "Opium After the War," 10, 28–29; Harry J. Anslinger, "Your Part in the War on Narcotics," *The Christian Advocate*, 21 April 1951, 8–9, 23, 27; Harry J. Anslinger, "The Opium of the People's Government," in U.S. Congress, House, Committee on Un-American Activities, *Soviet Total War: "Historic Mission" of Violence and Deceit* (Washington, D.C., 1956), 759–63; Harry J. Anslinger, "Dope from Red China," *The Military Police Journal*, February–March 1961, 2–6; *Washington Herald*, 27 July 1938; Estes Kefauver, *Crime in America* (Garden City, N.Y., 1951), 19–22; Jack Lait and Lee Mortimer, *Washington Confidential* (New York, 1951), 107–17; Lee Mortimer, "New York Confidential," *New*

York Mirror, 13 May 1958; Rodney Gilbert, "Dope from Red China," *American Legion Magazine,* September 1954, 16–17; Jack Anderson, "Castro Has a New Weapon," *Washington Post Magazine,* 29 July 1962; Bruun, Pan, and Rexed, *The Gentlemen's Club,* 15–18, 20–21, 54–59, 87–88, 300–301.

7. "Harry Anslinger Dies at 83," *New York Times,* 18 November 1975; "Harry Anslinger, Narcotics Chief," *Washington Post,* 18 November 1975; "Harry Anslinger Ex Drug Official," *Philadelphia Inquirer,* 17 November 1975; Michael Kernan, "Pioneer Narc Chief Views Drug History," *Austin* (Texas) *American Statesman,* 31 October 1971; *New York Journal American,* 14 January 1964; Adolf Lande to Harry Anslinger, 23 September and 3 December 1963, file 3, Box 2, HJAP/PSU; Bruun, Pan, and Rexed, *The Gentlemen's Club,* 15–18, 20–21, 54–59, 87–88, 300–301; U.S. Congress, House, Appropriations Committee, *Hearings before the Subcommittee in charge of Appropriations for the Departments of State, Justice, and Commerce, the Judiciary and Related Agencies for 1975,* 93d Cong., 2d sess., 12 March 1974, pt. 1, 910–11; Musto, *The American Disease,* 238–41, 257; Mabry and Perl, "Concluding Observations and Policy Recommendations," 151–61. The total federal government expenditure for narcotics law enforcement in fiscal year 1974 was sixty-five times larger than the FBN budget in fiscal year 1962. Musto, *The American Disease,* 257.

8. Bagley, "The New Hundred Years War," 43–58; Perl, "International Narcopolicy and the Role of the U.S. Congress," 89–102; Mabry and Perl, "Concluding Observations and Policy Recommendations," 151–61; Shannon, "A Losing Battle," 44–48.

9. Musto, *The American Disease,* 1–61; Bonnie and Whitebread, *The Marihuana Conviction,* 1–13; Clark, *Deliver Us From Evil,* 218–20; Morgan, *Drugs in America,* 1–63; David T. Courtwright, "Opiate Addiction as a Consequence of the Civil War," *Civil War History* 25 (June 1978): 101–11. See also two works by James Harvey Young: *The Medical Messiahs: A Social History of Health Quackery in Twentieth-Century America* (Princeton, 1967) and *The Toadstool Millionaires: A Social History of Patent Medicines in America Before Federal Regulation* (Princeton, 1961).

10. Morgan, *Drugs in America,* 1–97; Walker, *Drug Control in the Americas,* 13–14; Musto, *The American Disease,* 1–61; Clark, *Deliver Us From Evil,* 1–5, 219–21; Courtwright, "Opiate Addiction as a Consequence of the Civil War," 101–11; Bonnie and Whitebread, *The Marihuana Conviction,* 1–15, 28, 32–45; Timberlake, *Prohibition and the Progressive Movement,* 39–99.

11. Clark, *Deliver Us From Evil,* 218–23; Bonnie and Whitebread, *The Marihuana Conviction,* 5–15, 28, 32–45; Timberlake, *Prohibition and the Progressive Movement,* 39–99; Taylor, *American Diplomacy and the Narcotics Traffic,* 3–122; Musto, *The American Disease,* 1–61; Walker, *Drug Control in the Americas,* 13–15; Morgan, *Drugs in America,* 27–97.

12. Musto, *The American Disease,* 6–8; Bonnie and Whitebread, *The Marihuana Conviction,* 14, 32–45; Walker, *Drug Control in the Americas,* 13–14, 100–102; Morgan, *Drugs in America,* 27–97; Clark, *Deliver Us From Evil,* 1–5. See also Robert S. Weppner, ed., *Street Ethnography: Selected Studies of Crime and Drug Use in Natural Settings* (Beverly Hills, Calif., 1977); John Helmer, *Drugs and Minority Oppression* (New York, 1975); Bruce Bullington, *Heroin Use in the Barrio* (Lexington, Mass., 1977); David T. Courtwright, *Dark Paradise: Opiate Addiction in America Before 1940* (Cambridge, Mass., 1982).

13. Bonnie and Whitebread, *The Marihuana Conviction,* 14–15; Clark, *Deliver Us From Evil,* 220–22; Musto, *The American Disease,* 13–23; Walker, *Drug Control in the Americas,* 14–15; Taylor, *American Diplomacy and the Narcotics Traffic,* 3–122; "Patent Medicine Crusade," *Nation* 81 (9 November 1905): 376; "Patent Medicines and Poverty," *Outlook* 83 (2 June 1906): 253–54; "Creating Customers for Dangerous Drugs," *Outlook* 82 (7 April 1906): 778–79.

14. Taylor, *American Diplomacy and the Narcotics Traffic,* 3–19, 28–83, 87–91, 96–120; Musto, *The American Disease,* 3–6, 22–28, 30–37; Clark, *Deliver Us From Evil,* 219–22; Walker, *Drug Control in the Americas,* 15; King, *The Drug Hang-Up,* 10–11; Bonnie and

Whitebread, *The Marihuana Conviction,* 9–15; May, "The International Control of Narcotic Drugs," 308, 310, 314, 320–21.

15. Musto, *The American Disease,* 30–40; Taylor, *American Diplomacy and the Narcotics Traffic,* 47–81; Walker, *Drug Control in the Americas,* 15–16.

16. Taylor, *American Diplomacy and the Narcotics Traffic,* 82–122; Musto, *The American Disease,* 37–53; May, "The International Control of Narcotic Drugs," 321–23; Walker, *Drug Control in the Americas,* 15–16.

17. Musto, *The American Disease,* 40–48, 54–62; Taylor, *American Diplomacy and the Narcotics Traffic,* 127–31; Bonnie and Whitebread, *The Marihuana Conviction,* 15–17; Walker, *Drug Control in the Americas,* 16.

18. Musto, *The American Disease,* 54–62; Bonnie and Whitebread, *The Marihuana Conviction,* 15–17; *United States Statutes at Large,* vol. 38, 63d Cong., 3d sess., pt. I, 785–90.

19. Musto, *The American Disease,* 121–26, 129–32; Bonnie and Whitebread, *The Marihuana Conviction,* 15–21; Clark, *Deliver Us From Evil,* 222–23; *United States Statutes at Large,* vol. 38, 63d Cong., 3d sess., pt. I, 785–90; *United States Treasury Department Decisions,* Decision Nos. 2,172 and 2,200, 9 March and 11 May 1915, 124–31 and 173–74.

20. Musto, *The American Disease,* 128–36; Bonnie and Whitebread, *The Marihuana Conviction,* 15–21; Clark, *Deliver Us From Evil,* 222–23; *United States v. Jin Fuey Moy,* 241 U.S. 401 (1916); *United States v. Doremus,* 249 U.S. 86 (1919); *Webb et al. v. United States,* 249 U.S. 96 (1919); King, *The Drug Hang-Up,* 21; Alfred R. Lindesmith, *The Addict and the Law* (Bloomington, 1965), 3–6; Anslinger and Tompkins, *The Traffic in Narcotics,* 187; *United States Statutes at Large,* vol. 40, 65th Cong., 3d sess., pt. I, 1,130–33. Also see *Daniel Subcommittee Hearings,* testimony of Rufus King, 1,380–82; Alfred R. Lindesmith, "Traffic in Dope: Medical Problem," *Nation* 182 (21 April 1956): 337–38; "The Superstition of Dope," *Literary Digest* 54 (30 June 1917): 1990.

21. Bonnie and Whitebread, *The Marihuana Conviction,* 9–10, 14–18, 20–21, 23, 27–28, 106–11; Clark, *Deliver Us From Evil,* 1–5, 221–23; Musto, *The American Disease,* 206–14, 245–48; Taylor, *American Diplomacy and the Narcotics Traffic,* 132, 200–209; Walker, *Drug Control in the Americas,* 14–18; Morgan, *Drugs in America,* 88–90. See also "Is Prohibition Making Drug Fiends?" *Literary Digest* 69 (16 April 1921): 19–20, and Sara Graham-Mulhall, "The Evil of Drug Addiction," *New Republic* 26 (18 May 1921): 357.

22. Bonnie and Whitebread, *The Marihuana Conviction,* 9–10, 14–18, 20–21, 23, 27–28, 106–11; Clark, *Deliver Us From Evil,* 1–5, 221–23; Musto, *The American Disease,* 206–14, 245–48; Taylor, *American Diplomacy and the Narcotics Traffic,* 132, 200–209; Walker, *Drug Control in the Americas,* 14–18; Morgan, *Drugs in America,* 88–90; "National Menace of the Dope Traffic," *Literary Digest* 76 (24 February 1923): 34–35; Nicholas and Lillian Segal, "The Drug Evil," *New Republic* 34 (7 March 1923): 41–43; Stuart H. Perry, "The Unarmed Invasion," *Atlantic Monthly* 135 (January 1925): 70–77. Traditionally, addict population statistics have been unreliable. According to best estimates, the United States had about one million drug habitués in 1900 and between 200,000 and 215,000 in 1915. A special Treasury Department committee in 1919 discovered, however, that assessments of the total number of American habitués ranged from 200,000 to four million; the committee determined that the nation had one million addicts. By the 1920s, the Narcotics Division of the Internal Revenue Bureau claimed that the Harrison law was so well enforced that America had only 100,000 habitués (the figure officially recognized by the federal government at that time). Yet, the New York City health commissioner argued simultaneously that there were nearly 100,000 addicts in that area alone. Other observers outside the IRB and later the Prohibition Bureau believed that the national habitué population was large and increasing. Recent drug experts generally have asserted that this country's opiate addicts numbered about 400,000 in each year since the mid-1800s. They have claimed as well that punitive narcotics restriction forced habitués into clandestine activities. Walker, *Drug Control in the Americas,* 13, 17, 19; Musto, *The American Disease,* 189–90; Taylor, *American Diplomacy and the Narcotics Traffic,* 47; Lindesmith, *The Addict and the Law,* 99,

105–6, 111; King, *The Drug Hang-Up,* 18; U.S. Treasury Department, *Traffic in Narcotic Drugs: Report of Special Committee of Investigation Appointed March 25, 1918, by the Secretary of the Treasury,* 6–7, 20–25 (hereafter cited as *Report of the Special Treasury Department Committee*); *New York Times,* 23 May 1923. Statistics of known addicts in 1915 indicated that women outnumbered men and that a number of the habitués were middle-aged, came from the middle and upper class, and resided in the South. Figures for later years reveal an addict population dominated by lower-class men. Walker, *Drug Control in the Americas,* 13.

23. Musto, *The American Disease,* 59–60, 135, 138–39, 184–90; Anslinger and Tompkins, *The Traffic in Narcotics,* 185–86; Lindesmith, *The Addict and the Law,* 141–42; *Report of the Special Treasury Department Committee,* 6–7, 20–25; U.S. Congress, House, Ways and Means Committee, *Report No. 852 of the Ways and Means Committee: Importation and Exportation of Narcotic Drugs,* 67th Cong., 2d sess., 27 March 1922, 1–11; *United States Statutes at Large,* 67th Cong., 2d sess., vol. 42, pt. I, 596–98; Walker, *Drug Control in the Americas,* 18–20, 29–30. To enforce the Harrison law, Congress set aside $515,000 in fiscal year 1920. Arrests for Harrison Act infractions went from 3,900 in 1920 to an average of 10,300 in 1924–26 to around 9,000 in 1927–28. Drug-law violations caused the incarceration of 2,529 of the 7,738 people in federal prisons at the end of fiscal year 1928. Walker, *Drug Control in the Americas,* 18–20, 29–30.

24. Walker, *Drug Control in the Americas,* 18–20, 63–67; Harry Cohen to Henry Stimson, 27 May 1929, Decimal File 800.114 N16/351, Record Group 59, State Department General Records, National Archives, Washington, D.C. (hereafter cited as RG 59, [decimal file]); Memorandum of Conference by John Kenneth Caldwell, 11 April 1929, RG 59, 811.114 N16-Porter Bill/1; Memorandum of Second Conference by Caldwell, 13 April 1929 [dated 15 April 1929], RG 59, 811.114 N16-Porter Bill/2; *House Bureau of Narcotics Hearings,* 1–44; *Washington Herald,* 7 March 1930; Memorandum of a conversation by Caldwell, 12 March 1930, RG 59, 811.114 N16-Porter Bill/24; *Congressional Record,* 71st Cong., 2d sess., 7 March 1930, 5,186; *New York Times,* 9 March 1930; Musto, *The American Disease,* 209; Taylor, *American Diplomacy and the Narcotics Traffic,* 132, 200–209.

25. *House Bureau of Narcotics Hearings,* 1–44; Caldwell to Cotton, 6 June 1930, RG 59, 811.114 N16-Porter Bill/41; Memorandum from Caldwell to Cotton, 7 June 1930, RG 59, 811.114 N16-Porter Bill/43; Cotton to George Akerson (Secretary to the President), 10 June 1930, RG 59, 811.114 N16-Porter Bill/46; Cotton to Undersecretary of the Treasury Ogden L. Mills, 10 June 1930, RG 59, 811.114 N16-Porter Bill/47; Akerson to Mills, 20 June 1930, Box 248, RG 56, Treasury Department General Records, National Archives, Washington, D.C.; Memorandum of a conversation with Harry Anslinger by Caldwell, 17 June 1930, RG 59, 811.114 N16-Porter Bill/50.

26. Musto, *The American Disease,* 206–14; Walker, *Drug Control in the Americas,* 63–69; Taylor, *American Diplomacy and the Narcotics Traffic,* 132; Kinder, "Bureaucratic Cold Warrior," 160–91; William Dufty and Fern Marja, "The Czar Nobody Knows," *New York Post Magazine,* 17 January 1958; *Christian Science Monitor,* 9 November 1933; *New York American,* 25 September 1934; *Washington Herald,* 11 July 1934; "The Three Horsemen," editorial in *Washington Herald,* 18 July 1934; "From the East as Well as the West," editorial in *Washington Herald,* 10 September 1934; Anslinger and Cooper, "Marihuana: Assassin of Youth," 18–19, 150–53; *Toledo Times,* 25 November 1945; *Kefauver Crime Committee Hearings,* pt. 12, 662–68; Moore, *The Kefauver Committee and the Politics of Crime,* 115–34; Anslinger and Tompkins, *The Murderers,* 7–10; *Daniel Subcommittee Hearings,* 1, 31–33, 93–96, 275–79, 701, 3,115–16, 4,011; Anslinger, "Narcotics and the Physician," 373–78; Anslinger, "Opium After the War," 10, 28–29; Kefauver, *Crime in America,* 19–22; Lait and Mortimer, *Washington Confidential,* 107–17; Gilbert, "Dope from Red China," 16–17; Anderson, "Castro Has a New Weapon"; Ralph Hayes to James A. Farley, 8 January 1954, file 11, Box 2; Adolf Lande to Anslinger, 23 September 1963, file 3, Box 1; Samuel Levine to Andrew Bernard, 27 July 1962, file 5, Box 2; and various letters concerning Anslinger's influence, files 8, 12, and 13, Box 2, the last four entries in HJAP/PSU. Early narcotics

restrictionists had, for example, linked drug misuse and trafficking to West Coast Chinese communities, to African-Americans in the South, to Mexican-Americans in the Southwest, and to the underworld in the nation's cities. Between 1930 and 1962 Anslinger updated such allegations for his purposes. Only three months after entering office as commissioner of narcotics, he directed FBN agents to provide him information about narcotics of foreign origin. Similarly, thirty-two months later, he ordered his officers to compile a list of drug violations associated with certain ethnic groups. At that time, he also accused Japan of using drugs to pacify Manchuria and charged ethnic gangs with smuggling Japanese narcotics into the United States. Over the next thirty years, Anslinger claimed that a Mafia conspiracy dominated domestic narcotics trafficking, that Communist China dumped opiates on the Free World, and that Fidel Castro's agents smuggled cocaine into the United States from Cuba. The commissioner employed these unsubstantiated statements to convince physicians, pharmacists, reformers, and the general public that his small agency was fighting a war against powerful traffickers. Given the supposed difficulty of that struggle, the FBN needed the support of U.S. citizens—much as military forces might desire popular support at home while they faced combat. If Anslinger portrayed foreigners as the cause of the country's intractable drug problem, then he could argue that law enforcement alone would eventually provide a solution. On Anslinger's directions to FBN agents, see U.S. Bureau of Narcotics, *Circular Letters,* No. 75, 10 March 1931 and No. 254, 22 November 1933, item T56.2, Box T1169, Printed Archives Branch, National Archives, Washington, D.C.

27. Taylor, *American Diplomacy and the Narcotics Traffic,* 82–122, 171–77, 183–85, 201–24, 241–67, 334; Musto, *The American Disease,* 37–39, 49–53, 214–16; May, "The International Control of Narcotic Drugs," 321–23, 329; Memorandum of a conversation by Caldwell, 17 June 1930, RG 59, 811.114 N16-Porter Bill/50; Walker, *Drug Control in the Americas,* 27–35, 47–51, 53–56, 62–67, 71–73, 176–79, 190; Kinder and Walker, "Stable Force in a Storm," 908–27; Kinder, "Bureaucratic Cold Warrior," 169–91; Bruun, Pan, and Rexed, *The Gentlemen's Club,* 15–18, 20–21, 38–45, 50–59, 87–88, 91–92, 300–301.

28. *House Bureau of Narcotics Hearings,* 1–44; various memoranda in RG 59, file 811.114 N16-Porter Bill; Kinder, "Bureaucratic Cold Warrior," 169–91; Walker, *Drug Control in the Americas,* 23–73, 130–33, 177–78; Taylor, *American Diplomacy and the Narcotics Traffic,* 146–267, 270–71, 291; Stimson to the Treasury Department for Anslinger, 1 June 1931, RG 59, 893.114 Narcotics/245; Anslinger's Report on the Third Session of the United Nations Commission on Narcotic Drugs, 15 July 1948, RG 59, 501.BD Narcotics/7-1548; Memorandum from John Foster Dulles to Dwight Eisenhower, 4 May 1953, folder: "85-P United Nations Commission on Narcotic Drugs," Official File, Box 332, White House Central Files, Dwight D. Eisenhower Presidential Library, Abilene, Kansas (hereafter cited as DDEL). Between 1930 and 1941 the State Department's antidrug official held the position of assistant chief of the Division of Far Eastern Affairs. Taylor, *American Diplomacy and the Narcotics Traffic,* 270–71. George A. Morlock served as the department's principal narcotics-control officer from 1941 to 1954; his post following World War II was chief of the Narcotics and Dangerous Drugs Section, housed in State's Division of International Labor, Social, and Health Affairs. Harry S. Truman to Harry J. Anslinger, 7 June 1946, folder: "OF 85-Q Commissioner of Narcotics," Official File, Harry S. Truman Presidential Library, Independence, Missouri; Memorandum from John Foster Dulles to Dwight Eisenhower, 4 May 1953, and Memorandum from Charles F. Willis, Jr., to Sherman Adams, 11 May 1953 folder: "85-P United Nations Commission on Narcotic Drugs," Box 332, Official File and Resumé of Harry J. Anslinger, folder: "10-L-1 Commissioner of Narcotics," Box 221, General File, DDEL.

29. John Kenneth Caldwell to Nelson Trusler Johnson, 22 September 1930 and Johnson to Caldwell, 28 January 1931, General Correspondence file, Box 13, Nelson T. Johnson Papers, Manuscript Division, Library of Congress, Washington, D.C.; M. S. Myers to

Johnson, 16 March 1931, RG 59, 893.114 Narcotics/209; Stimson to the Treasury Department for Anslinger, 1 June 1931, RG 59, 893.114 Narcotics/245; M. R. Nicholson, Treasury Attaché at Shanghai, to the Commissioner of Customs for Anslinger, 19 May 1932, RG 59, 893.114 Narcotics/359; Walker, *Drug Control in the Americas,* 60, 81, 86–92, 119–24, 126–29, 130–33, 140–51, 164–69, 177–78; George A. Morlock to the American Mission, Mexico City, 9 August 1947, RG 59, 812.114 Narcotics/8-947; Victor Hoo (Hoo Chi-tsai) to Anslinger, 1 October 1945, and Anslinger to Victor Hoo, 24 January 1946, Box 2, Victor Hoo Papers, Archives of Hoover Institution on War, Revolution, and Peace, Stanford, California; Anslinger's Report on the Third Session of the United Nations Commission on Narcotic Drugs, 15 July 1948, RG 59, 501.BD Narcotics/7-1548; "Remarks of Harry J. Anslinger, "United Nations Commission on Narcotic Drugs, 17th session, 8 May to 1 June 1962, file 8, Box 1, HJAP/PSU; "Report of the United States Delegation to the 18th session, United Nations Commission on Narcotic Drugs," 29 April to 17 May 1963, International Narcotics Control file, Box 1, Harry J. Anslinger Papers, Harry S. Truman Presidential Library, Independence, Missouri (hereafter cited as HJAP/HSTL).

30. Walker, "Drug Control and the Issue of Culture in American Foreign Relations," 365–82; Kinder and Walker, "Stable Force in a Storm," 918–19, 927; Walker, *Drug Control in the Americas,* 86–92, 119–33, 140–51, 161–78; Brunn, Pan, and Rexed, *The Gentlemen's Club,* 15–18, 20–21, 38–45, 50–59, 87–88, 91–92.

31. *House Treasury Department Appropriations Hearings* for fiscal years 1932–42, 1944, 1948–49, 1952–54, 1956–60, statements of Anslinger; *Kefauver Crime Committee Hearings,* statement of E. H. Foley, p. 4; *Daniel Subcommittee Hearings,* testimony of Harry Anslinger, 11–14.

32. George Gallup, "Dope Peddling to Teenagers Arouses Public Opinion; Stiff Punishment Favored by Majority," Public Opinion News Service, July 1951, file on Senate Crime Investigation, Box 186, Subject File: Crime Probe, Truman Library; Musto, *The American Disease,* 214; *Kefauver Committee Final Report,* 1–6; *Boggs Committee Report,* 1–9; Kinder, "Bureaucratic Cold Warrior," 169–91.

33. On Anslinger's antimarijuana campaign, see Anslinger and Cooper, "Marihuana: Assassin of Youth," 18–19, 150–53; *House Marihuana Taxation Hearings;* various clippings, articles, and typescripts in files 7, 11, and 12, Box 1; file 1, Box 2; and files 1 and 15, Box 5, HJAP/PSU. For statements about Japan, see *Washington Herald,* 11 July 1934; *Los Angeles Examiner,* 15 February 1942; Anslinger, "Opium After the War," 10, 28–29; *Atlanta Constitution,* 19 August 1946; Anslinger and Tompkins, *The Traffic in Narcotics,* 8–10.

34. Moore, *The Kefauver Committee and the Politics of Crime,* 5–24, 114–34; *Kefauver Crime Committee Hearings,* pt. 2, 81–89, pt. 4-A, 420; King, *The Drug Hang-Up,* 120–26; *Daniel Subcommittee Hearings,* pt. 1, 31–33, 96; U.S. Congress, Senate, Judiciary Committee, *Report of the Judiciary Committee on Illicit Narcotics Traffic,* 84th Cong., 2d sess., 1956, S. report no. 1440; Kinder, "Bureaucratic Cold Warrior," 178–88. The quote from the Daniel subcommittee appears in the Senate Judiciary Committee report cited above.

35. Kinder, "Bureaucratic Cold Warrior," 169–91; Kinder and Walker, "Stable Force in a Storm," 908–27; Bruun, Pan, and Rexed, *The Gentlemen's Club,* 15–18, 20–21, 54–59, 87–88, 300–301.

36. Bagley, "The New Hundred Years War," 43–58; Perl, "International Narcopolicy and the Role of the U.S. Congress," 89–102; Mabry and Perl, "Concluding Observations and Policy Recommendations," 151–61; Shannon, "A Losing Battle," 44–48.

WILLIAM B. McALLISTER

Conflicts of Interest in the International Drug Control System

The drug problem in the United States and elsewhere has historically received intermittent attention, most often when the problem has reached crisis proportions in a certain locale. In such times, one of the natural focal points of discussion has been the role that other nations play in supplying drugs. It has not been unusual for foreign states to be accused of being the source of the problem, while others have been identified, in varying degrees of culpability, as accessories. This often has created conflict, especially when an accused nation has viewed the issue differently. Under these circumstances, states have frequently attempted negotiations in hopes of reaching some sort of agreement that will accommodate all the affected parties.

Throughout the twentieth century there has been more diplomatic activity concerning drug issues than one might expect. The current rules and regulations concerning the international control of drugs are embodied in two major treaties: the 1961 Single Convention on Narcotic Drugs and the 1971 Convention on Psychotropic Substances.[1]

The circumstances that made these two agreements both necessary and possible, the manner in which they were negotiated, and the final shape that each took is the subject of this article. We will see that the actual resolution of the drug problem has been a concern of only secondary importance for most of the nations directly involved with the issue. The major players involved have consistently pursued policies designed to protect economic, social, cultural, political, and/or strategic interests, even when doing so has come at the expense of the stated objective of eliminating illicit drug use.

A relatively small, but powerful, group of industrialized nations, including the United States, Canada, Japan, and some Western European states, has repeatedly prevailed in this clash of interests. In section I, a historical overview will provide the background information essential to understanding why the 1961 Single Convention was necessary. Section II will explain the motivations of the states attending that meeting by dividing them into five general groups of interest. Section III will sketch the outcome of the conference. Section IV outlines the course of events leading up to the convening of the 1971 meeting. By undertaking an extensive comparison of the 1961 and 1971 treaties, including the deliberations surrounding them, section V will explain why and how this group of industrialized states has been able to use mechanisms of international conflict management to fashion a system of controls favorable to their interests.

I. *Historical Overview*

Drug abuse on a national scale was first recognized as a problem in nineteenth-century China. The treaties ending the Opium Wars of 1839–42 and 1856–60 forced China to accept unlimited opium imports, largely from India, where a government monopoly on the sale and distribution of opium created a powerful coalition of farmers, distributors, and government officials opposed to controls. By the 1880s addiction had become widespread and, to the Chinese, became one of the main symbols of Western encroachment. The Imperial Chinese government was unable to do anything about the problem, however, until it received help from, of all quarters, Western missionaries—themselves another great symbol of foreign influence in the Celestial Kingdom. British missionaries in particular blamed opium smoking for a lack of conversions to the cross. In conjunction with a general upswing in temperance activity in the 1880s, pressure was put on Parliament to end the exporting of opium from India to China. At length the anti-opiumists won and in 1906 the British and Chinese governments signed a bilateral agreement to eliminate the trade gradually over the next ten years. This arrangement worked well until 1912, when the Chinese revolution ended effective implementation.[2]

In the meantime, American missionaries, becoming increasingly active in the Far East after 1898, saw the problem as a regional, not bilateral, one. They began to agitate for a convention of all the powers with territorial holdings in the area. While the initial response of the U.S. government was to ignore the issue as the British had done, it became clear over time that advocating a multilateral solution to the opium problem might help improve Sino-American relations, especially after the Boxer uprising. With little direct interest in the trade, the United States could, with no real sacrifice of its own interests, curry favor with the Chinese by advocating elimination of the traffic. In this way the United States could gain economic concessions out of goodwill, in stark contrast to the more aggressive tactics used by the other powers. After much arm-twisting by the United States, the twelve-nation Hague Opium Conference was convened between December 1911 and January 1912.[3]

The basic strategies employed by parties favoring and opposing control in The Hague reveal the general pattern that has been followed at all subsequent gatherings concerned with drugs. In essence, both sides saw a threat to their interests, especially economic ones, but each felt the need to employ moralistic arguments to bolster its cause. Those in favor of no or few controls included governments that received revenue from the production, manufacture, and export of opium. The procontrol forces included the United States and China, some merchants that traded other kinds of goods, and missionaries. This group believed that opium use was contributing to Chinese disintegration and was therefore a threat to its financial and political interests, whether real or potential.[4] They depicted opium use as the root of all evil and purveyors of the substance as reprehensible corruptors of the Chinese nation.

At the Hague conference the anticontrol forces immediately and permanently lost the moral high ground to their opponents. Nevertheless, they were able to outmaneuver advocates of control tactically by expanding the agenda to include both drugs other than opium and the issue of controls on a global (rather than regional) scale. This action ensured that the final agreement would be weak, because no Western nation was willing to jeopardize the interests of even a small group of its nationals for the welfare of Asian addicts. The final document made each nation responsible for controlling its own domestic production and distribution. Procontrol advocates won a moral but meaningless victory because Germany, the major manufacturer of cocaine at the time, insisted on universal acceptance before it would ratify the document. Thus the Hague treaty of 1912 did not come into force until after World War I. At that time all signatories to the Paris peace accords were required to ratify the Hague Opium Convention as well.[4]

With the creation of the League of Nations a new chapter opened in the history of drug control. An international agency, the Advisory Committee on the Traffic in Opium and Other Dangerous Drugs, or the Opium Advisory Committee, was empowered to form the Opium Control Board (OCB). The OCB was to enforce the stipulations of the Hague

Convention. The countries represented on the board, however, were the nations that profited most from the trade. Consequently, enforcement of the treaty's provisions was not pursued vigorously.

By the mid-1920s, in addition to the abuse of locally produced opium, pharmaceutical concerns in Europe and the United States were manufacturing large quantities of heroin, morphine, and cocaine, most of which found its way to eastern Asia via smugglers. The drug companies disavowed all responsibility for their products once they left the factory and, in the absence of serious attempts at national control by their governments, little could be done. Consequently, the United States, still hoping to gain diplomatic advantages in China that would redound to the benefit of investors there, called for a new, more rigorous treaty.[6]

In 1925 two separate conventions were organized to meet in Geneva.[7] The first dealt only with opium in the Far East. Signatories agreed both to limit opium sales there to government monopolies and to eliminate the trade within fifteen years. This important agreement signaled the willingness of European governments, especially the British, to abandon, eventually, the business of purveying drugs.

The second convention was intended to create a tighter world system of controls over an expanded list of drugs. It called for statistics to be gathered on the production of raw materials, including opium, coca, and hemp; the fabrication and distribution of the manufactured drugs heroin, morphine, and cocaine; and consumption. The OCB was reconstituted with a more balanced representation as the Permanent Central Board (PCB). The PCB was charged with calculating the quantities of drugs needed by each state. The second convention also set up an import certification system to control drug traffic by limiting the amount that nations could legally import and empowered the PCB to monitor the certification system. The PCB was also given the authority to place other substances on the controlled list.

The Geneva document represented an improvement over the Hague treaty, but the United States and China refused to sign it because it was not strict enough. They retained adherence to the 1912 agreement instead. A few nations, including Turkey and Switzerland, refused to adhere to either document because they were too strict.[8] As the number of treaties multiplied over the next thirty years, this phenomena became more pronounced.

Controlling imports proved to be an incomplete solution because it was a relatively simple matter to transship drugs in and out of nonsignatory countries. Pharmaceutical companies continued to manufacture quantities of drugs far in excess of the world's legitimate medical needs. Another meeting was therefore called at Geneva in 1931 to set exact limits for the overall manufacture of heroin, cocaine, and morphine and to control exports among the signatory countries. The PCB was to determine the total amount to be produced, utilizing estimates of need provided by the signatory nations. Colonies, however, could be exempted from these regulations. Consequently, in conjunction with incomplete adherence, the resulting agreement was less effective than had been hoped by drug control advocates.[9]

With the completion of the 1931 treaty, one phase of the crusade to eliminate the scourge of drug abuse drew to a close. After fighting a long rearguard action, the governments of Western Europe, sensitive to the interests of large pharmaceutical firms, acquiesced in a set of international regulations that, to a certain extent, limited the importation and exportation of raw materials and manufactured drugs to the legitimate medical needs of the world. Together with agreements to phase out government monopolies over opium distribution and to eliminate opium smoking in Asia, advocates of control assumed that the drug problem would simply disappear as excess supplies dried up.

Perversely, the problem did not go away. People continued to desire drugs and clandestine manufacturers of controlled substances quickly filled in the gap created by the retreat of legitimate firms from the market. The trafficking and distribution of illicit drugs was taken over by a more professional and ruthless group of entrepreneurs willing to take the risks and reap the profits of the trade.[10] Additionally, during the late 1920s and early 1930s, some countries, including the United States, became increasingly worried about domestic drug use. It seemed that a tougher approach was necessary. Another convention was held in 1936 in Geneva, producing a treaty that instituted international standards for penal legislation.[11] World War II began a few weeks before this convention came into force, rendering it ineffective until that conflict ended.[12]

After the war, all League functions concerning drug control were transferred to the United Nations. The major responsibilities were split between the Economic and Social Council (ECOSOC) and the World Health Organization (WHO). The first postwar effort to enhance the international drug control system was made in Paris in 1948. A protocol was signed that gave the WHO more authority to place drugs on the list of controlled substances. It also initiated control mechanisms for drugs not included in the 1925 and 1931 treaties, mostly new types of synthetic opiates.[13]

A protocol devised in 1953 attempted to restrict the worldwide production of opium to legitimate medical needs by strictly controlling agricultural production. All nations, if they so chose, were allowed to continue to grow opiates for domestic medicinal purposes, but legal exportation was restricted to seven producer countries.[14] Nations were slow to sign this treaty, however, and by 1961 it had still not received the requisite number of ratifications necessary to bring it into force.[15]

With the provisions called for in the 1953 treaty, a truly comprehensive system of controls for drugs concocted from organic substances was in place—at least theoretically. There remained certain obstacles to be overcome if a workable system of drug control was to be realized. The first problem was that the provisions outlined above were embodied in nine separate multilateral agreements.[16] In order to become effective, the disparate elements of the international drug control system needed to be combined into one integrated document, which could gain adherence from the majority of concerned governments. Second, the measures of control called for in some of the treaties were weak, while others were more stringent. The disparity of language and provisions in the treaties would have to be rectified and made agreeable to a large number of states with widely varying interests. Without near-universal acceptance, the proliferation of drug treaties would continue to impair progress toward real control. Third, by the late 1950s, numerous bodies of the United Nations had acquired responsibility for some aspect of international control. If the number of agencies charged with the responsibility of controlling the global drug trade was not reduced, battles for administrative turf might leave the system less than optimally effective.

In an attempt to rectify this situation the Economic and Social Council began in 1948 to issue calls for a consolidation of the numerous treaties concerned with drug control.[17] With each new agreement the necessity for a rationalization of the system became more apparent. The process of creating an acceptable document began in the late 1940s, but not until 1961 was a third draft ready for consideration. After years of behind-the-scenes haggling, delegates from seventy-three states convened in New York on 24 January 1961 with hopes of overcoming their differences and creating a single convention to control the use of organic drugs.

II. Interest Groups at the 1961 Conference

Each state attending the 1961 conference came to the meeting with an agenda based on its own domestic priorities.[18] Just as in the international arena, conflicts of interest had to be managed within each state, for in every country there were individuals and groups both supporting and opposing substantive controls. The Iranian government, for instance, normally resistant to controls because of its dependence upon opium for revenue, became much more amenable to the U.S. position after the Mossadeq government was overthrown with American support in 1953. In fact, in 1955 Iran outlawed all production of opium, a move that can be directly attributed to American pressure.[19] In addition, at the 1961 conference, Iran's behavior was generally less obstructionist than it had been at past meetings.

In another example of conflicting interests, health officials in almost all countries were concerned about potential or actual drug abuse in their jurisdictions and favored strict limitations on the availability of drugs. On the other hand, medical researchers almost unanimously opposed any regulations that would hinder their work. Within each state opposing factions such as these had to be accommodated.[20]

This section discusses the general positions taken by delegations at the conference, although on any one issue, a certain state might take a position inconsistent with its basic stance. With this proviso in mind, the states attending the conference can be divided into five discernible categories: the "strict control" group, the "neutral states" group, the "organic states" group, the "weak control" group, and the "manufacturing states" group.[21]

The states interested in creating a strict regime of control were usually nonproducing and nonmanufacturing countries.[22] Thus they had no particular economic stake in the trade. Among the leaders of the strict control group were France,[23] Sweden, Brazil,and Nationalist China.[24] Most of the states in this category were also culturally biased against the use of organic drugs and did not view them in a favorable light.[25] In addition, some states in this group suffered from varying degrees of drug abuse and were sometimes referred to as "victim nations." The interests of this group would be best served if drugs were available only for medical and scientific purposes, but inadequate drug controls in neighboring countries and among trading partners made this goal difficult to achieve. The cooperation of other states in creating an effective system of international control was deemed to be absolutely essential if these countries were to reduce or prevent drug abuse within their own boundaries.

In order to achieve these aims, strict control states were generally willing to sacrifice the convenience of their constituents, to relinquish a degree of national sovereignty in favor of the competent supranational organs of the United Nations and to enhance the power of those organs. They hoped that other nations would be willing to do the same, but past experience had shown that any agreement including extremely stringent provisions was not likely to gain widespread adherence, thereby defeating the purpose of controls. This Achilles' heel of the strict control group, incomplete adherence, forced them to moderate their demands in order to attain the widest possible acceptance of the new treaty. Although the vast majority of states would normally be expected to fall into this category, the number that actively pursued stringent controls was relatively small.

The neutral states group included most of the nations of Africa, Central America, sub-Andean South America, and assorted others such as Luxembourg and the Vatican. These states had no particular interest in the subject beyond wishing to ensure access to adequate supplies and were primarily motivated by factors extraneous to the specific issue of drug control. Some were aligned with political blocs and voted accordingly. Other were more opportunist, willing to trade votes on this issue for concessions in other areas of more importance to them. Still others were genuinely neutral on the issue and could be swayed by the arguments for or against control. Members of this group tended to be passive, proposed ideas rarely, and when faced with an impasse, generally advocated compromise in order to facilitate the widest possible acceptance of the new document.

The nations that comprised the organic group favored weak controls in 1961 because it best served their peculiar interests. Led by states such as India, Turkey, Pakistan, and Burma, this group consisted of countries that produced organic raw materials—the coca-producing states of Indonesia and the Andean region of South America, the opium- and cannabis-producing nations of South and Southeast Asia, and the cannabis-producing states in the horn of Africa. The substances produced in these areas were essential for the world's drug supply, at least until synthetics became common after World War II.[26] As a result, these countries had traditionally been the focus of control efforts. In turn, organic states believed that they had shouldered an inordinately heavy share of the burden of control because efforts to limit producton and export directly affected large segments of their population.

Although lacking the power to oppose the schemes of the more control-minded nations directly, the organic group developed over time a successful strategy for protecting their vital interests. Their usual tactic was to dilute the language of treaties by injecting exceptions, loopholes, and deferrals into the wording. If a final document was too strict, they often declared numerous reservations or refused to ratify it altogether. The threat of such action was usually enough to force some sort of compromise among the various interests involved.[27]

States in the organic group were culturally predisposed to view organic drugs in a favorable light, having had daily experience with the substances for centuries. They saw no reason why they sould have to suffer economic and social dislocation for the sake of foreigners and wanted to receive technical and other types of aid to compensate for losses incurred from strict controls. This group advocated control efforts on a national scale, preferring to allow each state to enact the regulations that best fit local conditions. They were generally not in favor of a strong supranational body of control.[28]

The weak control states were led by the Soviet Union and often, but not always, included its client states in Europe, Asia, and Africa. Although the USSR and its satellites had little direct interest in the trade and virtually no significant internal drug abuse problem, these governments were determined to avoid any language in the treaty that would allow outside inspection or control. Drug control, like almost all other matters in the Soviet bloc, was considered to be a purely internal issue and internal issues were not subject to interference by outsiders. For this reason, this group favored national over international controls and was particularly opposed to any language in the treaty that would give a supranational supervisory authority any substantive jurisdiction over internal decisions.

The manufacturing group was comprised of a collection of industrialized, Westernized nations and their allies. The leading states in the group included the United States, Great Britain, Canada, Switzerland, the Netherlands, West Germany, and Japan. With no cultural affinity for organic drugs and suffering from greater or lesser drug abuse problems, this group wanted to enact very strict controls on the production of organic raw materials and favored the strongest measures to eliminate illicit trafficking. At the same time, these states were the major producers of the world's pharmaceuticals and did not want undue restrictions placed on the course of medical research or on the fabrication and distribution of manufactured drugs. They were willing to retain the import/export controls and limitations on manufacturing already in operation but rejected the more stringent provisions advocated by the strict control group. Additionally, manufacturing group members wanted to strengthen the powers of the supranational bodies responsible for drug control, but only if they could be guaranteed a high degree of control over the decision-making process within those bodies—something they had traditionally succeeded in doing. In short, their strategy was to shift as much of the regulatory burden as possible to the raw-material-producing states while retaining as much of their own freedom of action as possible.

III. Goals and Outcome of the 1961 Conference

Chakravarthi V. Narasimhan, acting president of the 1961 meeting, outlined three goals at the first plenary session.[29] These goals provided a good example of how the competing interests of the various participants were combined into a program of work. The first objective was to fashion a document to replace the numerous existing treaties. This was a goal that all could agree upon, both because the existing situation met the needs of few nations and because it offered the opportunity for revision of the current system.

Another goal was to reduce the number of international agencies that dealt with drug control. The strict control states saw this as an opportunity to strengthen the system by enhancing the power of those bodies then remaining in existence. The organic group and the weak control states hoped to take advantage of the conference to accomplish exactly the opposite result. The manufacturing states wanted to maintain or, if possible, increase their influence over the agencies in hopes of achieving their own ends. Additionally, in apparent contradiction of this goal, the conference was scheduled to discuss the formation of a new body to hear appeals of the decisions made by these agencies. While this conflicted fundamentally with the goal of streamlining the system, each group of states hoped to gain advantage by creating an appellate process favorable to their interests.

Finally, the conference was supposed to introduce regulations on the production of organic raw materials. This development might at first appear to be a clear victory for the strict control and manufacturing states groups, but the weak control and organic states groups in fact hoped to use the conference to moderate some of the more onerous provisions of the 1953 treaty, which had not yet come in to force.

The final result of the conference, predictably, was a compromise between the various interest groups. The strict control group got a single document that was relatively stringent. All the major control systems introduced in previous treaties were retained and the duties ascribed to the supranational control bodies were somewhat expanded and strengthened. The organic states group managed to expunge the provisions of the 1953 treaty that would have forced them to eliminate almost all production of raw materials. Also, it was agreed that the final court of appeal for decisions concerning drug control would be the full Economic and Social Council, a body that was becoming increasingly likely to view the plight of the organic states in a sympathetic light. The Soviet bloc's weak control group successfully deflected attempts to strengthen significantly the supranational bodies of control, thereby achieving its most important objective: the protection of internal policy from outside interference. However, the biggest winners, as in the past, were the manufacturing states. They continued to be overrepresented in the supranational bodies, thereby ensuring that their interests on matters of substance were protected.

As for important, specific decisions, all cultivation of cannabis was to be eliminated, the first time any drug had been completely proscribed. Yet the cannabis-producing states were allowed a grace period of twenty-five years after the convention came into force before they had to meet this requirement. Furthermore, controls on the production and movement of organic raw materials continued to be more rigorous than those on the fabrication and distribution of manufactured drugs. And most important, the manufacturing states defeated an "insurrection" led by the organic states to place synthetic drugs under the same set of controls that were being applied to organic drugs.[30] This idea was anathema to the industrialized nations of the West and was rejected with only minimal discussion. It was, however, a harbinger of things to come.

IV. Trading Places

In the decade after the signing of the Single Convention, drug abuse became a societal matter of great concern, particularly in the industrialized West.[31] The problems experienced were caused for the most part by a plethora of synthetic drugs, most of which had been invented since 1945. Reminiscent of the conditions of the 1920s with respect to organic drugs, there was no systematic international control over the manufacture and distribution of synthetic drugs. As a result, many dangerous substances were easily attainable, and countries that wished to prohibit or control their importation were beset with smuggling and trade problems.

The widespread phenomena of synthetic drug abuse and the question of how to deal with it became focal points of discussion among those states active in the international drug control system. The strict control group continued to maintain its position in favor of the most stringent regulations that would achieve widespread acceptance. The stance of the neutral states also remained basically unchanged. Likewise, the weak control group of states continued to maintain the attitude that some modicum of controls was acceptable, but no outside interference in internal affairs would be allowed.

The states of both the organic group and the manufacturing group, however, completely reversed the positions they had traditionally held concerning international drug control. The organic group thus became the allies of the strict control states. They advocated, with great relish, that the same system of controls they had been compelled to accept be applied to synthetic drugs. On the other hand, states of the manufacturing group espoused the positions previously held by the organic group: that national controls were preferable to international ones, that strict limitations on the fabrication and distribution of synthetic drugs would cause economic hardship, and that supranational agencies should not be allowed to usurp the prerogatives of sovereign states. With this turn of events, the weak control states became the natural allies of the manufacturing states. After much foot-dragging by the manufacturing group, a plenipotentiary meeting charged with producing a treaty to control synthetic drugs was convened in Vienna on 11 July 1971.

Delegates to the Vienna conference used the text of the 1961 Single Convention as a guide in preparing a draft document for discussion. The final text, which came to be called the "1971 Psychotropic Convention," adopted many of its predecessor's features, including provisions calling for import/export controls, limitations on manufacture and distribution, schedules of control, and penalties for those involved in illicit trafficking. In addition, the supranational control bodies established to supervise the 1961 Single Convention were authorized to act in the same capacity under the new treaty.

Upon first reading, there would appear to be little difference between the two treaties. A closer examination of the texts reveals significant differences, however. The following section will compare selected provisions of the documents along with the proceedings of the two conferences. By doing so it will become apparent that the manufacturing states managed to forge, as they had many times in the past, a document that was weighted in their favor.

V. Comparison of the 1961 and 1971 Treaties

The Preamble. Composed last but read first, preambles are intended to express the overall goals and spirit of an agreement. This is certainly true in the case of the 1961 and 1971 treaties:

1961 Single Convention on Narcotic Drugs[32]

The Parties,

Concerned with the health and welfare of mankind,

Recognizing that the medical use of narcotic drugs continues to be indispensable for the relief of pain and suffering and that adequate provision must be made to ensure the availability of narcotic drugs for such purposes,

Recognizing that addiction to narcotic drugs constitutes a serious evil for the individual and is fraught with social and economic danger to mankind,

Conscious of their duty to prevent and combat this evil,

. . . Hereby agree as follows:

* * *

1971 Vienna Psychotropic Convention[33]

The Parties,

Being concerned with the health and welfare of mankind,

Noting with concern the public health and social problems resulting from the abuse of certain psychotropic substances,

Determined to prevent and combat abuse of such substances and the illicit traffic to which it gives rise,

Considering that rigorous measures are necessary to restrict the use of such substances to legitimate purposes,

Recognizing that the use of psychotropic substances for medical and scientific purposes is indispensable and that their availabilty for such purposes should not be unduly restricted,

. . . Agree as follows:

There was little discussion about the preamble during plenary sessions of the 1961 convention.[34] Most important, there was no objection to characterizing addiction to organic drugs as a "serious evil." The discussion primarily concerned whether to accept even tougher language introduced by the United States, the Netherlands, and Pakistan designating abuse of organic drugs as a "grave evil" and proposing to limit the use of these substances exclusively to medical and scientific purposes. The final wording of the treaty, as rendered in the slightly diluted version reproduced above, was proposed by a cosmopolitan group of states including Brazil, Canada, France, Ghana, India, and Poland. The organic group of states managed to avoid an outright condemnation of the substances controlled in the treaty, but the final wording remained strong. The general tone of the preamble is stringent, stating only that "adequate provision must be made to ensure the availability" of organic substances for the relief of pain and suffering.

The 1971 preamble is a weaker statement of purpose. It makes no reference to addiction, using instead the word "abuse," implying a less serious problem. Not all synthetic substances were defined as giving rise to abuse, and abuse was not characterized as an evil. Also, the preamble fails to mention the economic consequences of abuse. Finally, the general tone of the 1971 preamble is more lenient, stating that the availability of synthetic drugs for medical and scientific purposes "should not be unduly restricted."

The wording of the preamble received considerable attention during the 1971 proceedings.[35] The working draft prepared for the conference referred to the "spreading abuse" of psychotropics and that these substances should be "rigorously restricted to medical and scientific requirements." Various versions of this type of wording were supported by Mexico, France, Liberia, Togo, the Soviet Union, Australia, the Vatican, Ghana, and Turkey. The Turkish delegate, arguing in favor of the more restrictive text, attempted to establish a link between the 1961 and 1971 treaties by stating that they were both part of the same control mechanism and that they should be "interpreted and applied in the same spirit." The manufacturing group of states, led by the United States and Great Britain, proposed much weaker language, including an attempt to place the phrase "and other" between the words "scientific" and "purposes" in the fifth paragraph. This maneuver failed, but the important clause—"should not be unduly restricted"—was retained. When it became clear that the manufacturing group and its allies would compromise no further, the states in favor of tougher language acquiesced and accepted a preamble that was much weaker than both the 1961 preamble and the wording of the 1971 draft text.

Another difference between the two documents concerns the estimates system, long a cornerstone of the international control regime. The 1961 convention adopted the relevant sections of earlier treaties that dealt with the gathering of estimates of drug needs. Under the treaty, each signatory is responsible for determining how much of each of the substances under control is needed for the upcoming year. The government then reports this information to the International Narcotics Control Board (INCB), a newly created body incorporating the control supervision functions of several predecessors. Under other sections of the treaty, parties are required to furnish the INCB with statistical returns on imports, exports, production, manufacture, conversion, and consumption. By utilizing all this information, the INCB can determine if a state has accumulated a surplus. If the surplus cannot be accounted for, the offending state must explain the discrepancy or apply the surplus to the next year's estimated need. Though never invoked, there are even provisions for the declaration of an embargo against offenders who show no inclination or capacity to meet their treaty obligations. Additionally, the INCB is empowered to make estimates for states that are not signatory to the Single Convention, so that large-scale smuggling can be detected and publicized.[36]

At the 1961 conference there was almost no discussion about the desirability or efficacy of the estates system.[37] It was probably assumed by all that it would continue to operate as a vital part of the mechanism for keeping track of the flow of drugs from production to consumption. The Soviet Union tried to weaken the powers of the INCB by arguing that the organic states should do more to control the illicit traffic within their own borders and that if all states did their part, national enforcement would be sufficient. These importunings fell on deaf ears, because the system had worked to the satisfaction of all the other major groups for many years and there was little interest in trying to fix the part of the machinery that was not broken.

The estimates-of-need system is *entirely missing* from the 1971 treaty. According to the official records of the conference, no provisions for it were made in the draft text and it was not even discussed in Vienna. This omission was clearly in the interests of the manufacturing states, because without estimates of need it is impossible to calculate whether more of a substance than can legitimately be put to use is being fabricated. Not content with this concession to their interests, the manufacturing states went on the offensive during the conference in an attempt to weaken other portions of the treaty requiring statistical reports about manufacture, imports, and exports of synthetic drugs by claiming that the proliferation of reports would impose an expensive and cumbersome administrative burden of only marginal value.[38] This move was supported by Denmark, Switzerland, Belgium, Austria, Japan, Great Britain, Spain, and others. India's delegate advocated retaining more stringent regulations about statistical reporting. Referring to the provisions of the 1961 treaty, he asked why the provisions of the new treaty should be any less rigorous. Supported by organic states such as Iran, Iraq, Mexico, Pakistan, Thailand, Burma, and Turkey, strict control states including Sweden, Yugoslavia, and France, and the United States and Canada, India's position won in a close vote, and statistical reporting requirements approximating those in the 1961 treaty were adopted. Nevertheless, the omission of a system of estimates from the 1971 treaty was a major defeat for the forces in favor of substantive control and a victory for the interests of the manufacturing group.

The 1961 Single Convention also utilized the concept of "schedules of control," an idea pioneered in earlier drug control treaties, to delineate between drugs deemed to be of different levels of danger and usefulness.[39] During the course of the deliberations in New York, quite a bit of time was spent wrangling about what should, and should not, be included in each of the several schedules.[40] The American delegation, representing the views of the manufacturing group of states, consistently argued that organic raw materials should be placed in the most restrictive category, whereas drugs manufactured from those substances should be less rigorously controlled.[41] The Indian delegation, speaking for the organic group of states, tried to exempt various parts of the poppy and cannabis plants from controls, or at least to lower the level of controls placed on them. For the most part, the manufacturing group, working in conjunction with the strict control group, was successful. Most of the disputed substances were placed in schedules that were objectionable to the organic states. The assumption of the 1961 Single Convention was that organic drugs should be considered dangerous until proven otherwise.[42]

Delegates to the 1971 Vienna Psychotropic Convention also agreed upon several schedules of control, but their scope and substance were much different than those of the 1961 Single Convention.[43] The manufacturing group, and in particular the United States, reversed its 1961 position by arguing that unless there was substantial proof that a substance was harmful, it should remain uncontrolled. Some of the manufacturing states even attempted to eliminate schedule IV (which concerned tranquilizers) because they believed the drugs in that schedule were not dangerous enough to warrant international control. They argued that national controls were sufficient to deal with any threat these substances might pose. The organic states and the strict control states opposed this line of reasoning, but to little avail. Schedule IV was retained, but the number of drugs included in it was drastically reduced.[44]

In addition, proposals were advanced to put precursor chemicals under a special schedule of control.[45] The representatives of Turkey, India, Argentina, and the Soviet Union supported the addition of a fifth schedule for this purpose. In the course of the debate, the Turkish delegate pointed out that his nation had agreed to control organic precursors in the 1961 treaty and called upon the industrialized countries to make a similar sacrifice.[46] This proposal was opposed by the United States, Great Britain, and Canada, who complained that so many substances would have to be controlled that the job would be impossible. The Swedish delegaton attempted to negotiate a compromise; nevertheless, the manufacturing states would have none of it, and the proposal for a special schedule concerning precursors was defeated.

The framers of both the 1961 and 1971 treaties realized that over the course of time drugs not listed in the original schedules of control would need to be added to the control regime. Examining the criteria established by each convention to place previously unregulated drugs under control reveals another important area of difference between the two agreements.

Under the 1961 Single Convention, an uncontrolled drug would be placed under control if it was "liable to similar abuse and productive of similar ill effects" as the drugs included in the original schedules.[47] Although not spelled out explicitly in the treaty, assessing the risk to public health and social welfare would become an important factor in determining suitability for control.[48] Yet there was essentially no discussion on this point at the conference; all parties were outwardly content with this broad criteria for amendment.

In comparison with the Single Convention, the 1971 Vienna Psychotropic Convention is much more specific about the qualities a synthetic drug must possess in order to be placed under control. In order to be considered for addition to the 1971 schedules, a drug must have the capacity to produce:

(a) (i) (1) a state of dependence, and
(2) central nervous system stimulation or depression, resulting in hallucinations or disturbances in motor function or thinking or behavior or perception or mood, or
(ii) similar abuse and similar ill effects as a substance in Schedule I, II, III, or IV, and
(b) sufficient evidence that the substance is being or is likely to be abused so as to constitute a public health and social problem warranting the placing of the substance under international control.[49]

The 1971 conference considered at length the exact wording of this paragraph, including the use of "and" versus "or" and the placement of commas.[50] American and British representatives were the most persistent of the manufacturing group in calling for highly restrictive language, arguing that only reliable evidence that substantial abuse had occurred justified international controls. India, speaking for the organic group, preferred control decisions to be based upon criteria similar to that of the Single Convention: the degree of seriousness of the danger a substance represented to public health and the social problems resulting from its abuse. Once again, the manufacturing group used the threat of nonacceptance to insert more acceptable language, language that would make it much more difficult to place new synthetic substances under international controls.

Another area of contention in both 1961 and 1971 was the manner in which amendments to the schedules would be approved and how those decisions could be appealed. The main disagreements concerned: what body or bodies would be responsible for initiating amendment procedures; what body or bodies would have the authority to rule on the merits of the case; on what their judgment would be based; and, if an appeals process were approved, what authority would be invested with the power to overrule previous decisions and on what basis the decision would be made.

Under the provisions of the 1961 Single Convention, the World Health Organization, using the broad criteria of the Single Convention, received extensive responsibility for determining whether a drug should be placed under international control. The WHO was empowered to make recommendations that would be passed on to the Commission on Narcotic Drugs (CND), a political organ of the Economic and Social Council. The CND then would decide whether to accept or reject the recommendation of the WHO. If a WHO recommendation to place a substance under controls were accepted by the CND, it would notify all parties to the convention. The notification then would become effective upon receipt by signatory governments. A party to the Single Convention would have the right to appeal a decision by the CND within ninety days to the full Economic and Social Council, whose decision would be final.[51]

This arrangement represented something of a compromise. Favoring the interests of the organic states was the expectation that the WHO could be counted on to operate without political bias, making its recommendations according to the scientific merits of the substance in question. Additionally, as the number of Third World states continued to multiply, the ECOSOC was likely to become an increasingly friendly appellate body. However, the CND remained the body of pivotal importance in amendment decisions; manufacturing states had always been careful to maintain enough representation there to promote their interests.[52] India tried at the 1961 meeting to insert language that would require a two-thirds vote of the CND to place new substances under control, but this initiative was defeated. The Iranian and Danish delegates complained that the only countries that would make use of the appeals process would be members of the manufacturing group, who would attempt for commercial reasons to overturn WHO decisions made on purely medical grounds.[53] This last observation was absolutely correct. The manufacturing states had prevailed once again.

The amendment and appeals process outlined in the 1971 treaty differed significantly.[54] The WHO was still charged with making recommendations to the CND concerning control. These recommendations were to be considered determinative with respect to medical and scientific matters: they could not be overruled. The CND, however, was specifically empowered to consider "economic, social, legal, administrative and other factors it may consider relevant" before making a decision about control. Any addition to the schedules would need approval by a two-thirds majority of the Commission. Also, any state in the process of appealing a decision of the CND could exempt the substance in question from some measures of control, a right specifically denied in the Single Convention. Finally, although appeals would be referred to the ECOSOC, decisions by that body were not necessarily final. In other words, an endless right of appeal was granted, which showed further preferential treatment for the manufacturing states.

During the Vienna meetings, the actions of the strict control and organic group states with respect to amendment procedure might best be characterized as damage control. Not only had the manufacturing states made clear their unwillingness to agree to amendment procedures as rigorous as those embodied in the Single Convention, but they also tried further to weaken the provisions of the draft document. The United States, for example, attempted to insert language into the treaty that would require a three-fourths majority of the CND to amend the schedules. West Germany, Great Britain, and Switzerland, along with other manufacturing states, worked vigorously to increase the exemptions allowed while a drug control ruling was under appeal.[55]

A comparison of the 1961 and 1971 treaties indicates that the manufacturing states largely managed to have their cake and eat it too, as it were. By threatening nonagreement, utilizing their economic power, and using political pressure, the manufacturing group inserted enough loopholes, favorable language, and bureaucratic safeguards into both documents to protect the majority of their interests. These same tactics were far less successful when employed by the organic group. In order to gain agreements that would preserve only their most vital interests, they yielded on many issues. The strict control states fared even worse, always settling for provisions that they deemed less than adequate. The weak control states, with only one item of importance on their agenda, found enough allies at both conferences, although they were different in each case, to achieve their objectives.

The successes and failures of attempts to create a system of international drug control illustrate the difficulty of conflict resolution in the international arena. Nevertheless, the history of global drug control provides an interesting window through which various aspects of the international system can be viewed. First, the way in which the present regime of drug control was established demonstrates that the international system has long worked to the advantage of powerful nations. A plentitude of material, as well as diplomatic, and human resources, has historically given the Western industrialized states and on occasion the Communist bloc a distinctive advantage over the more numerous but resource-poor states of the Third World. And yet the relative advantage of these states has declined, especially since 1960. That a convention to control synthetic drugs was signed at all is evidence of the increasing clout of Third World states.[56]

Second, cultural differences play an important part in international conflicts. The attempts to fashion a regime of international drug control illustrate how deep the rifts between cultures can be and also serve as a useful reminder that nations routinely posit an admixture of high ideals and hypocrisy that are perfectly congruent to those espousing them. A lack of respect for the mores or customs of another culture inevitably leads to misunderstanding, lack of cooperation, and conflict.

Third, the moral force of world public opinion, an often-maligned concept, has played a limited role in promoting international drug control. In both 1961 and 1971, nations resistant to controls came to the bargaining table, in part because it would have been embarrassing to do otherwise. Once at the table, though, states opposed to controls generally went about the business of obfuscation with scant regard for the opinions of others. The most striking evidence of the limited power of public opinion is the fact that as of 1 January 1990 the 1971 Vienna Convention on Psychotropic Substances still had not been ratified by Switzerland, Belgium, the Netherlands, Japan, and Austria—the country that hosted the conference.[57] These manufacturing states seem not to have suffered any serious negative consequences as a result of their inaction.

Finally, this study helps to explain why the worldwide drug problem has been so difficult to tackle. In short, the primary goal of the international drug control regime has never been to eliminate illicit drug use. The most important objective of the delegates to the 1961 and 1971 conventions was to protect sundry economic, social, cultural, religious, and/or geopolitical interests. The amount of time actually spent at the conferences discussing the problems of addicted individuals, how to help them, and how to prevent more people from joining their ranks was minimal. Until these priorities change, problems with widespread drug abuse, and the attendant cost in human and material capital, will continue.

University of Virginia

Notes

1. There are, in addition, dozens of bilateral and regional agreements that deal with drug control. (See Peter H. Rohn, *World Treaty Index* (Santa Barbara, 1984), for listings through 1975. A composite overview is supplied on pages 356–57 of volume 1. The present endeavor will limit its scope to the major treaties designed to deal with the issue on a worldwide basis. Also, the 1961 Single Convention was amended in 1972, but the revisions were of a relatively minor nature. See *Single Convention on Narcotic Drugs, 1961 as Amended by the 1972 Protocol Amending the Single Convention on Narcotic Drugs, 1961* (New York, 1977) and *Commentary on the Protocol Amending the Single Convention on Narcotic Drugs, 1961 done at Geneva on 25 March, 1971* [U.N. document E/CN/.7/588] (New York, 1976). There is, in my opinion, no single adequate general work on this issue. Arnold Taylor's *American Diplomacy and the Narcotics Traffic 1900–1939: A Study in International Humanitarian Reform* (Durham, N.C., 1969) is the most thorough account of the 1898–1939 period, but U.S. motivations and actions are viewed in an extremely favorable light. In addition, by relying almost entirely on American sources, this account describes inadequately what the other major players were doing and how they viewed the role of the United States. A necessary counterbalance is provided by S. D. Stein's British-oriented view in *International Diplomacy, State Administrators, and Narcotics Control* (Brookfield, Vt., 1985), but after 1920 he detours into the story of the implementation of domestic drug legislation in England and Wales. Stein's doctoral dissertation, "The Origins of the Hague Opium Convention 1912, and its Implementation in England and Wales" (University of London, June 1978), at almost 700 pages, is an expanded version of the book, the extra space being taken up with an extensive discussion of political theory. William O. Walker III, *Drug Control in the Americas,* revised edition (Albuquerque, 1989), gives an excellent account of events in the Western Hemisphere up to about 1950 and a brief description of events since that date. This work provides a good "case study" illustration of the dilemmas surrounding the implementation of effective international drug control, but because it limits its scope to the Americas, many aspects of the issue receive too little attention. Two short historical accounts of international developments are provided in Griffith Edwards and Awni Arif, eds., *Drugs Problems in the Socio Cultural Context: A Basis for Policies and Program Planning* (Geneva, 1980), and David Musto's *The American Disease,* expanded edition (New York, 1987). Kettil Bruun, Lynn Pan, and Ingemar Rexed, *The Gentlemen's Club: International Control of Drugs and Alcohol* (Chicago, 1975), provides a more thorough treatment, but the historical narrative is mixed in throughout the book, making it difficult to recover in a coherent manner. Finally, readers wanting "just the facts" might consult Hsien Chou Liu's *The Development of a Single Convention on Narcotic Drugs* (Bangkok, 1979). A strange little book, just an outline really, it lists the basic facts about drug control treaties up to 1953 in as brief a manner as possible. However, because of a large number of inaccuracies, this book should be used only in conjunction with other works.

2. See Stein, *International Diplomacy, State Administrators, and Narcotics Control,* 8–23; and David Edward Owen, *British Opium Policy in China and India* (New Haven, 1934), 259–335.

3. Nations attending were: France, Britain, Russia, China, the United States, Germany, Italy, Portugal, Siam, the Netherlands, Japan, and Persia.

4. For an excellent discussion of the type and extent of American missionary interests in China, see James Reed, *The Missionary Mind and American East Asian Policy, 1911–1915* (Cambridge, Mass., 1983).

5. See Stein, *International Diplomacy, State Administrators, and Narcotics Control,* 73–78; Taylor, *American Diplomacy and the Narcotics Traffic,* chaps. 4–5; W. W. Willoughby, *Opium as an International Problem: The Geneva Conferences* (Baltimore, 1925), 25–43; and John Palmer Gavit, *Opium* (New York, 1927), 13–19.

6. Taylor, *American Diplomacy and the Narcotics Traffic,* chap. 5; Stein, *International*

Diplomacy, State Administrators, and Narcotics Control, chap. 7; Walker, *Drug Control in the Americas,* chap. 2; and Willoughby, *Opium as an International Problem,* 43–49.

7. The reason why two meetings were convened is disputed. One hypothesis holds that this arrangement was necessary to facilitate agreement on issues that were truly separate. Another maintains that the governmental and League officials charged with responsibility for drug control were incompetent and created an unnecessary division of effort. A third interpretation is that the industrialized states of Western Europe engineered the split in order to avoid substantive controls on themselves while creating tighter restrictions for East Asian countries. This last explanation is the most convincing, for reasons that will become clear later in this article. See Raymond Leslie Buell, "The International Opium Conferences with Relevant Documents," *World Peace Foundation Pamphlts* 8:2–3 (1925): 39–330; Gavit, *Opium;* Taylor, *American Diplomacy and the Narcotics Traffic;* and Willoughby, *Opium as an International Problem,* for varying views on this question.

8. Under Article 280 of the treaty of Sèvres (10 August 1920), Turkey was required to ratify the Hague Opium Convention (see *Treaties of Peace 1919–1923, Volume II* [New York, 1924], 886), but the Turkish government never did so and refused to carry out the obligations of the Hague treaty.

9. Taylor, *American Diplomacy and the Narcotics Traffic,* chaps. 8–11; and Walker, *Drug Control in the Americas,* chaps, 3–4.

10. See Terry M. Parssinen and Kathryn B. Meyer, "International Narcotics Trafficking in the Early Twentieth Century: Development of an Illicit Industry," *Past and Present* (forthcoming November 1991), for an excellent description of this phenomenon.

11. Illicit drugs were defined as contraband and confiscation of smugglers' assets was approved. A list of known and suspected traffickers was to be drawn up and disseminated to national police authorities, but language calling for a listing of offending companies was eliminated from the final document. Once again, colonial possessions, precisely where the majority of the problems existed, could be exempted if a signatory so chose.

12. For an overview of the system as it functioned (at least on paper) as of 1943–44, see Bertil A. Renborg, "Principles of International Control of Narcotic Drugs," *American Journal of International Law* 37 (1943): 436–59; and Herbert L. May, "Dangerous Drugs," in Harriet Eager Davis, ed., *Pioneers in World Order: An American Appraisal of the League of Nations* (New York, 1944), 183–92.

13. See Liu, *The Development of a Single Convention on Narcotic Drugs;* Bruun et al., *The Gentlemen's Club,* 20, 39; and Taylor, *American Diplomacy and the Narcotics Traffic,* epilogue.

14. The seven countries were the Soviet Union, Bulgaria, Greece, Turkey, India, Iran, and Yugoslavia.

15. This treaty entered into force on 8 March 1963, but its provisions were superseded by the Single Convention less than two years later, on 13 November 1964.

16. For the sake of clarity I have deleted some of the less important agreements from this overview.

17. See ECOSOC resolutions: 159 II D (VII) of 3 August 1948 and 246 D (IX) of 6 July 1949.

18. A good sense of the goals of individual states can be ascertained by reading the general statements that delegates were invited to make at the beginning of the conference. See *United Nations Conference for the Adoption of a Single Convention on Narcotic Drugs, Official Records, Volume I* (hereafter referred to as *1961 Official Records, Vol. I*), 4–16.

19. This law was repealed in 1969 when it became apparent that it was not effective in eliminating or even decreasing the problem. See Bruun et al., *The Gentlemen's Club,* 207–8.

20. For example, see Bruun et al., *The Gentlemen's Club,* chaps. 13, 16.

21. The categories described below are my own invention. They are derived from a careful reading of the positions taken by the national delegations to the 1961 and 1971 conferences.

22. In order to avoid cumbersome explanations within the body of the text, and in order

to be as accurate as possible, certain words have been given very specific meanings for the purposes of this article. In addition to this note, see notes 25 and 26. *Manufacture, manufacturing, manufacturer, & etc.* refers to the fabrication of organic and/or synthetic drugs. *Production, producing, producers, & etc.* refers to the process of growing organic raw materials.

23. Although France would normally be expected to fall into the manufacturing states category, the French government has traditionally felt little compunction to protect pharmaceutical interests. This is because the French pharmaceutical industry is largely foreign-owned. That portion which is not is decentralized, thus weakening its influence on the government. See Bruun et al., *The Gentlemen's Club,* 129–30.

24. The Nationalist Chinese government does not really fit the normal profile of a strict control state, but it could usually be counted on to endorse a very stringent control regime. This was primarily because a strict control position afforded Chiang's government a platform for embarassing the Communist Chinese. Throughout the 1950s accusations had been made that the mainland Chinese had been producing opium for export in a deliberate campaign to poison the West through drug addiction. The Nationalist Chinese took advantage of every opportunity to bring attention to this alleged activity. The Communist Chinese government was hampered in responding to these allegations by not being represented at the conference, a fact that the Soviet Union complained about at every possible opportunity.

25. *Organic raw materials* refers to the agricultural products opium, coca, and cannabis. *Organic drugs or organic substances* refers to drugs that can be obtained from organic raw materials. Opium is the organic raw material necessary for the manufacture of heroin, morphine, codeine, and other narcotics. In addition, raw opium can, with a minimum of preparation, be smoked, eaten, or drunk. Coca is the organic raw material necessary for the manufacture of cocaine. Cannabis refers to marijuana, hashish, and their resins.

26. *Synthetic drugs of synthetic substances* refers to drugs fabricated from nonorganic raw materials. Examples include amphetamines, barbiturates, and hallucinogens.

27. For example, see the declarations and reservations made to the 1961 Single Convention in Bruun et al., *The Gentlemen's Club,* appendix A.

28. Walker, *Drug Control in the Americas,* epilogue; see chap. 4 for pre-1945 examples.

29. Narasimhan was Under-Secretary for Special Political Affairs, representing the Secretary-General. For his opening statement, see *1961 Official Records, Vol. I,* 1–2.

30. For example, see *1961 Official Records, Vol. I,* 64, 200–201.

31. For information pertinent to this section, see the general statements of delegations to the Vienna conference: *United Nations Conference for the adoption of a Protocol on Psychotropic Substances, Vienna, 11 January–19 February 1971, Official Records, Volume II* [U.N. document E/CONF/ .58/7] (New York, 1973), 6–19 (hereafter referred to as *1971 Official Records, Vol. II*). See also Bruun et al., *The Gentlemen's Club,* chap. 16.

32. The quotation is taken from the first four paragraphs of the preamble to the 1961 Single Convention. For full text, see United Nations, *Treaties Series,* vol. 520, 151ff.

33. The quotation is taken from the first five paragraphs of the preamble to the 1971 Psychotropic Convention. For full text, see United Nations, *Treaty Series,* vol. 1019, 175ff.

34. *United Nations Conference for the adoption of a Single Convention on Narcotic Drugs, New York, 24 January–25 March 1961 Official Records, Volume II* [U.N. document E/ CONF/ 34/24/Add. 1] (New York, 1964), 297 (hereafter referred to as *1961 Official Records, Vol. II*).

35. See *United Nations Conference for the adoption of a Protocol on Psychotropic Substances, Vienna, 11 January–19 February 1971, Official Records, Volume I* [U.N. document E/CONF/ .58/7] (New York, 1973), 51–52 (hereafter referred to as *1971 Official Records, Vol. I*). See also *1971 Official Records, Vol. II,* 86–89.

36. See 1961 Single Convention, Articles 12–14, 18–21.

37. See *1961 Official Records, Volumes I and II,* discussions of Articles 27 and 28.

38. *1971 Official Records, Vol. II,* 51–54.

39. The schedules determined what kind of licensing, manufacturing, accumulation, dispensation, import, and export restrictions would be imposed on the drugs covered by the treaty. For example, in the 1961 Single Convention, the drugs considered the most dangerous (cocaine, cannabis, opium, heroine, and morphine) were put under stricter controls than those believed to be less harmful (codeine and its derivatives).

40. See *1961 Official Records, Vol. II,* 95–123, 263–67, and *1961 Official Records, Vol. I,* 190–201.

41. The manufacturing group did not wish to hinder the legitimate manufacture of substances such as codeine, much of which was made in industrialized countries.

42. The manufacturing states also prevailed on the important issue of derivatives. Included in the schedules were footnotes which indicated that the salts, esters, ethers, and isomers of all the substances listed were also controlled unless specifically exempted. The inclusion of derivatives in the schedules meant that it would not be necessary to list every possible chemical combination in the treaty itself, and that adding substances to the schedules at a later date would be a much easier matter. In fact, most new substances concocted from organic raw materials would automatically come under control. This was a victory for the manufacturing states because they had already set up the schedules to favor their own commercial interests. Any new substances they might invent that used organic raw materials would be subject to controls less stringent than those placed on the raw materials themselves.

43. See *1971 Official Records, Vol. I,* 106–12, and *1971 Official Records, Vol. II,* 110–14.

44. The salts, isomers, ethers, and esters of synthetic drugs were not included in the schedules of the 1971 treaty unless specifically noted. The committee in charge of the schedules claimed that it did not have the time to consider the issue fully, but this contention has a hollow ring to it. It is evident from the lack of objection in the plenary session to this rather lame excuse that the manufacturing states had made it clear (no doubt "off the record") that if derivatives were included in the schedules there would be no agreement.

45. Precursors are the synthetic equivalent to "raw materials." For example, lysergic acid is a precursor necessary to the manufacture of LSD. See *1971 Official Records, Vol. II,* 75, 181.

46. *1971 Official Records, Vol. II,* 181.

47. See 1961 Single Convention, Article 3.

48. See *Official Records, Vol. II,* 263–67. This was the criteria used by the technical committee. See also *Commentary on the Single Convention on Narcotic Drugs* (New York, 1973), 74–107.

49. From Article 2, paragraph 4, of the 1971 Psychotropic Convention.

50. See *1971 Official Records, Vol. II,* 128–30, 176–83.

51. See 1961 Single Convention, Article 3.

52. See *1961 Official Records, Vol. I,* 19–25, 63–68, 188–90, and *1961 Official Records, Vol. II,* 3–4, 33–37, 86–94.

53. *1961 Official Records, Vol. I,* 65, 67.

54. See 1971 Psychotropic Convention, Article 2.

55. See discussions concerning Articles 2 and 2 *bis* in *1971 Official Records, Volumes I and II.*

56. It must be noted, however, that because of the domestic drug abuse problems, there was substantial support in manufacturing group states as well for controls on synthetic drugs.

57. *Multilateral Treaties Deposited with the Secretary General: Status as at December 31, 1989* [U.N. document ST/LEG/SER.E/8] (New York, 1990), 268–74, and *Treaties in Force: A List of Treaties and Other International Agreements of the United States in Force on January 1, 1990* (Washington, D.C., 1990).

WILLIAM O. WALKER III

Bibliographic Essay

This bibliographic essay is a selective compilation and annotation of existing literature on drug-control policy. It includes both historical and relevant contemporary literature. With the exception of two Ph.D. dissertations and a number of articles, the emphasis is upon books written largely by scholars and journalists that elucidate the history of drug policy in the United States and other countries. Readers who are interested in pursuing further any particular topic or theme are directed to the notes in the works cited here and in the six articles in this volume. I have chosen not to include pertinent government documents, but researchers should be aware of the harvest of information on drug policy that is provided by the U.S. government in the form of congressional hearings and reports, Department of State publications, and reports by the General Accounting Office.

A modern history of international drug control remains to be written. Thematically suggestive, however, is Arnold H. Taylor, *American Diplomacy and the Narcotics Traffic, 1900–1939: A Study in International Humanitarian Reform* (Durham, N.C., 1969). Taylor demonstrates that, despite the worthy objective of international control, political and economic considerations often prevented interested powers from adopting effective antinarcotics accords. No author has addressed domestic constraints on drug policy more authoritatively than David F. Musto, M.D., in *The American Disease: Origins of Narcotic Control* (New Haven, 1973; expanded ed., New York, 1987). Musto's books remains the starting place for all who write about U.S. drug policy.

Nearly as influential as Musto is David T. Courtwright, *Dark Paradise: Opiate Addiction in America before 1940* (Cambridge, Mass., 1982);

Courtwright successfully shows how and why the addict population of the United States came to be seen as something of a pariah in American society. Useful, too, in this regard is H. Wayne Morgan, *Drugs in America: A Social History, 1800–1980* (Syracuse, 1981). A fuller appreciation of the effect of drug use on society can be gained from two books: H. Wayne Morgan, ed., *Yesterday's Addicts: American Society and Drug Abuse, 1865–1920* (Norman, Okla., 1974); and David T. Courtwright, Herman Joseph, and Don Des Jarlais, *Addicts Who Survived: An Oral History of Narcotic Use in America, 1923–1965* (Knoxville, Tenn., 1989).

Less useful analytically than the work of Courtwright and Morgan, but a quasi-memoir that still must be consulted, is Harry J. Anslinger and Will Oursler, *The Murderers: The Shocking Story of the Narcotic Gangs* (New York, 1961). The power of Anslinger's pen and his position as commissioner of the Federal Bureau of Narcotics (FBN) from 1930 to 1962 make it impossible to ignore his writings. Offering a highly critical account of Anslinger's tenure as commissioner and of American drug policy in general is Rufus King, *The Drug Hang-Up: America's Fifty-Year Folly* (New York, 1972). King should be read in conjunction with Alfred R. Lindesmith, *The Addict and the Law* (Bloomington, 1965), an insightful study of American and, to an extent, international drug-law enforcement. Similarly profitable is Edwin M. Schur, *Narcotic Addiction in Britain and America: The Impact of Public Policy* (Bloomington, 1962).

Studies are beginning to appear that focus extensively on Commissioner Anslinger, his policies, and their legacy. John C. McWilliams, *The Protectors: Harry J. Anslinger and the Federal Bureau of Narcotics, 1930–1962* (Newark, Del., 1990), is a useful place to begin after consulting Musto. McWilliams conclusively shows that Anslinger and his bureau were involved in far more than merely domestic drug-control activities. Indications of the catholic nature of Anslinger's interests can be found in Douglas Clark Kinder, "Foreign Fear and the Drug Specter: Harry J. Anslinger and the Illicit Narcotics Traffic" (Ph.D. diss., Ohio University, 1991). More accessible are Douglas Clark Kinder, "Bureaucratic Cold Warrior: Harry J. Anslinger and Illicit Narcotics Traffic," *Pacific Historial Review* 50 (May 1981): 169–91; Douglas Clark Kinder and William O. Walker III, "Stable Force in a Storm: Harry J. Anslinger and United States Narcotic Foreign Policy, 1930–1962," *Journal of American History* 72 (March 1986): 908–27; and John C. McWilliams and Alan A. Block, "All the Commissioner's Men: The Federal Bureau of Narcotics and the Dewey-Luciano Affair, 1947–54," *Intelligence and National Security* 5 (January 1990): 171–92. Of related interest concerning the links between the FBN and intelligence operations is John Marks, *The Search for the "Manchurian Candidate": The CIA and Mind Control* (New York, 1979).

The literature about the control of particular drugs in America (and elsewhere) has often been polemical in nature, but nevertheless it offers a number of useful insights and information for scholarly research. An appropriate starting place is Edward M. Brecher and the editors of *Consumer Reports, Licit and Illicit Drugs: The Consumers Union Report on Narcotics, Stimulants, Depressants, Inhalants, Hallucinogens, and Marijuana—including Caffeine, Nicotine, and Alcohol* (Boston, 1972). Depending on individual attitudes, the following books provide greater or lesser assistance for policy studies about marijuana: Lester Grinspoon, M.D., *Marihuana Reconsidered,* 2d ed. (Cambridge, Mass., 1977); John Kaplan, *Marijuana—The New Prohibition* (New York, 1970); David Solomon, ed., *The Marihuana Papers* (Indianapolis, 1966); and Larry Sloman, *Reefer Madness: The History of Marijuana in America* (Indianapolis, 1979). The best historical work about marijuana and public policy is Richard J. Bonnie and Charles H. Whitebread II, *The Marihuana Conviction: A History of Marihuana Prohibition in the United States* (Charlottesville, Va., 1974). It is as authoritative for marijuana as Courtwright's *Dark Paradise* is for opiate addiction. An updated edition would be a most welcome addition to the literature. Of fundamental importance for an informed discussion of marijuana policy in contemporary America is Mark A. R. Kleiman, *Marijuana: Costs of Abuse, Costs of Control* (Westport, Conn., 1989).

Research on heroin policy in America must begin of course with Courtwright and Musto, but other studies also deserve the close attention of scholars. Foremost among them is Arnold S. Trebach, *The Heroin Solution* (New Haven, 1982). Trebach's book is both history, detailing the story of heroin use and control in Great Britain and the United States, and advocacy, calling for a revamped and less punitive approach to the drug. Critical, too, of U.S. heroin policy, particularly in the 1970s, is David J. Bellis, *Heroin and Politicians: The Failure of Public Policy to Control Addiction in America* (Westport, Conn., 1981). Bellis argues that neither repression nor rehabilitation, as then constituted, were notably effective responses to extensive heroin usage. More recently, Jara Krivanek, *Heroin: Myths and Reality* (Sydney and Boston, 1988), has attempted a thorough reconsideration of the social, political, and economic context in which users have turned to heroin and in which, internationally, public policy on heroin has been formulated. Likewise important for any ongoing debate about heroin is Nicholas Dorn and Nigel South, eds., *A Land Fit for Heroin?: Drug Policies, Prevention, and Practice* (New York, 1987).

As these latter two books suggest, awareness of the British experience with drugs can prove useful in providing an analytical framework as scholars ask new questions about the history of drug use and policy in the United States. Two studies that ought to command the attention of scholars are Virginia Berridge and Griffith Edwards, *Opium and the People: Opiate Use in Nineteenth-Century England* (London and New York, 1981), and Terry M. Parssinen, *Secret Passions, Secret Remedies: Narcotic Drugs in British Society, 1820–1930* (Philadelphia, 1983). The Berridge and Edwards book shows how class functioned to create a "deviant" addict population, whereas Parssinen carries the story into the twentieth century and emphasizes the evolution of the "British" response to drug use and addiction.

The relative scarcity or inaccessibility of source materials along with conceptual complexity has made problematic the writing of a modern history of international drug control. Even were that not the case, Taylor's *American Diplomacy and the Narcotics Traffic* would still remain a starting point. Less satisfactory as a broad, comprehensive study but of considerable value as an interpretive administrative history is Kettil Bruun, Lynn Pan, and Ingemar Rexed, *The Gentlemen's Club: International Control of Drugs and Alcohol* (Chicago, 1975), which deftly analyzes the international movement in the era of the United Nations and calls for significant structural and functional changes in the movement. William O. Walker III has written two books that place regional attempts to control drugs into a wider policymaking perspective. *Drug Control in the Americas* (Albuquerque, 1981; rev. ed. 1989) examines drug control as an aspect of inter-American relations and highlights the importance of culture to an understanding of the success and failure of control. *Opium and Foreign Policy: The Anglo-American Search for Order in Asia, 1912–1954* (Chapel Hill, 1991) demonstrates that the history of international relations in East Asia and Southeast Asia in the first half of the twentieth century is more comprehensible when the role of opium and opiates is accounted for.

Walker's book on opium is the latest in a long line of works about political, social, and economic importance of opium in Asia. More than a few studies deserve high praise; the earliest of these can be found in Walker's bibliography. The more modern studies are especially instructive for the study of drug policy. A general overview is C. P. Spencer and V. Navaratnam, *Drug Abuse in East Asia* (Kuala Lampur and New York, 1981). For China: John K. Fairbank, *Trade and Diplomacy on the China Coast, 1842–1854*, 2 vols. (Cambridge, Mass., 1953); Hsin-pao Chang, *Commissioner Lin and the Opium War* (Cambridge, Mass., 1964); Peter Ward Fay, *The Opium War, 1940–1842* (Chapel Hill, 1975); Jonathan Spence, "Opium Smoking in Ch'ing China," in Frederic Wakeman, Jr., and Carolyn Grant, eds. *Conflict and Control in Late Imperial China* (Berkeley and Los Angeles, 1975); Jonathan Marshall, "Opium and the Politics of Gangsterism in Nationalist China, 1927–1945," *Bulletin of Concerned Asian Scholars* 8 (July–September 1976): 19–48. For colonial Asia: James R. Rush, *Opium to Java: Revenue Farming and Chinese Enterprise in Colonial Indonesia, 1860–1910* (Ithaca, 1990); Carl A. Trocki, *Opium and Empire: Chinese Society in Colonial Singapore, 1800–1910* (Ithaca, 1990). For Southeast Asia: Joseph Westermeyer, *Poppies, Pipes, and People: Opium and Its Uses in Laos* (Berkeley and Los Angeles, 1982); Alfred W. McCoy with Cathleen B. Read and Leonard P. Adams II, *The Politics of Heroin in Southeast Asia* (New York, 1972, 1973); and, concerning more recent events, Jonathan Kwitny, *The Crimes of Patriots: A True Tale of Dope, Dirty Money, and the CIA* (New York, 1987).

To include Kwitny's fine book is to raise the question of whether scholars can benefit from the writing of journalists about contemporary events. On the matter of drug policy, the answer is decidedly affirmative. While not all journalistic or participant accounts have the same ring of authenticity as that of Kwitny, the likely difficulty of future access to reliable sources renders them indispensable for the research scholar. At the same time, scholars have written about the structure of drug-law enforcement. James Q. Wilson, *The Investigators: Managing FBI and Narcotics Agents* (New York, 1978), and Ethan A. Nadelmann, "Cops Across Borders: Transnational Crime and International Law Enforcement" (Ph.D. diss., Harvard University, 1987), are the most authoritative. Also useful is James A. Inciardi, *The War on Drugs: Heroin, Cocaine, Crime, and Public Policy* (Palo Alto, 1986).

Several accounts of relatively contemporary events by participants or journalists merit consultation. See Andrew Tully, *The Secret War Against Dope* (New York, 1973); Edward Jay Epstein, *Agency of Fear: Opiates and Political Power in America* (New York, 1977); portions of Victor Marchetti and John Marks, *The CIA and the Cult of Intelligence*, 2d ed. (New York, 1980); James Mills, *The Underground Empire: Where Crime and Governments Embrace* (New York, 1986), which is more about global smuggling than drug policymaking per se; Henrik Krüger, *The Great Heroin Coup: Drugs, Intelligence, and International Fascism* (Boston, 1980), which also discusses smuggling but from an entirely different perspective; and Mathea Falco, *Winning the Drug War: A National Strategy* (New York, 1989). Falco served under President Jimmy Carter as the first assistant secretary of state for international narcotics matters.

The works by Epstein, Mills, and Krüger suggest, albeit in sharply contrasting ways, how politicized drug policy can be. In this regard, see also McCoy, *The Politics of Heroin in Southeast Asia;* Walker, *Opium and Foreign Policy;* Jonathan Marshall, *Drug Wars: Corruption, Counterinsurgency, and Covert Operations in the Third World* (Forestville, Calif., 1991); portions of Panny Lernoux, *In Banks We Trust* (New York, 1984, 1986); Leslie Cockburn, *Out of Control: The Story of the Reagan Administration's Secret War in Nicaragua, the Illegal Arms Pipeline, and the Contra Drug Connection* (New York, 1987); Jonathan Marshall, Peter Dale Scott, and Jane Hunter, *The Iran-Contra Connection: Secret Teams and Covert Operations in the Reagan Era* (Boston, 1987); John Dinges, *Our Man in Panama: How General Noriega Used the U.S.—and Made Millions in Drugs and Arms* (New York, 1990); Peter Dale Scott and Jonathan Marshall, *Cocaine Politics: Drugs, Armies, and the CIA in Central America* (Berkeley and Los Angeles, 1991); and Rachel Ehrenfeld, *Narco-terrorism* (New York, 1990), which asserts that a number of governments have fostered the global drug trade in order to underwrite terrorist activities.

Inevitably, the conjunction of drug-control policy and other political interests leads to a consideration of cocaine and crack usage in the late 1970s and 1980s. A useful starting point is Gabriel G. Nahas, *Cocaine: The Great White Plague* (Middlebury, Vt., 1989). Of interest, too, for context more than for policy purposes and George Andrews and David Solomon, eds., *The Coca Leaf and Cocaine Papers* (New York, 1975), and Terry Williams, *The Cocaine Kids: The Inside Story of a Teenage Drug Ring* (Reading, Mass., 1989). Providing an essential framework for policy research are Deborah Pacini and Christine Franquemont, eds., *Coca and Cocaine: Effects and Policy in Latin America* (Cambridge, Mass., 1986), and Edmundo Morales, *Cocaine: White Gold Rush in Peru* (Tucson, 1989).

Studies by the RAND Corporation are as incisive as any regarding contemporary U.S. policy. See Peter Reuter, Gordon Crawford, and Jonathan Cave, *Sealing the Borders: The Effects of Increased Military Participation in Drug Interdiction,* RAND/R-3594-USDP (Santa Monica, Calif., January 1988). See also the fine study by Rensselaer W. Lee III, *The White Labyrinth: Cocaine and Political Power* (New Brunswick, 1989); along with Scott B. MacDonald, *Mountain High, White Avalanche: Cocaine and Power in the Andean States and Panama* (New York and Westport, Conn., 1989), Lee analyzes recent U.S. policy and the obstacles to more effective control of cocaine in the Western Hemisphere. The political economy of the cocaine trade is dealt with in a more anecdotal fashion in Gregorio Selser, *Bolivia: El cuartelazo de los cocadolares* [Bolivia: The Cocadollar Coup] (Coyoacán, Mexico, 1982); Paul Eddy with Hugo Sabogal and Sara Walden, *The Cocaine Wars* (New York, 1988); Guy Gugliotta and Jeff Leen, *Kings of Cocaine: Inside the Medellín Cartel—an Astonishing True Story of*

Murder, Money, and International Corruption (New York, 1989), an excellent journalistic account; and partially in Elaine Shannon, *Desperados: Latin Drug Lords, U.S. Lawmen, and the War America Can't Win* (New York, 1988).

Insiders, too, have a story to tell about the traffic in drugs out of Latin America. For an account of the inner workings of the Medellín cartel by someone later sheltered by the Federal Witness Protection Program, see Max Mermelstein, as told to Robin Moore and Richard Smitten, *The Man Who Made It Snow* (New York, 1990). From the other side, see Michael Levine, *Deep Cover: The Inside Story of How DEA Infighting, Incompetence, and Subterfuge Lost Us the Biggest Battle of the Drug War* (New York, 1990). Readers and scholars will have to judge for themselves the reliability of these two revealing and impassioned books.

For a more general overview of drug policies in the United States and Latin America, see Walker, *Drug Control in the Americas;* Bruce Michael Bagley, ed., "Assessing the Americas' War on Drugs," *Journal of Interamerican Studies and World Affairs* 30 (Summer/Fall 1988), which is a special issue of the journal that surveys hemispheric drug-control efforts in the 1980s; Scott B. MacDonald, *Dancing on a Volcano: The Latin American Drug Trade* (New York and Westport, Conn., 1988); and Donald J. Mabry, ed., *The Latin American Narcotics Trade and U.S. National Security* (Westport, Conn., 1989). On Colombia, see Juan G. Tokatlian and Bruce M. Bagley, ed., *Economia y politica del narcotrafico* [The Political Economy of the Drug Traffic] (Bogotá, 1990). On Mexico, see relevant portions of Walker, *Drug Control in the Americas;* Guadalupe González and Marta Tienda, eds., *The Drug Connection in U.S.-Mexican Relations,* vol. 4 in *Dimensions of United States-Mexican Relations,* ed. Rosario Green and Peter H. Smith, 4 vols. (San Diego, 1989), which includes papers prepared for the Bilateral Commission on the Future of United States–Mexican Relations; Shannon, *Desperados,* which is largely a case study of the assassination of Drug Enforcement Administration agent Enrique Camarena Salazar and is highly critical of the Mexican government.

Finally, for three informative ways of understanding the historical complexity of the public-policy problem that is drug control, see Arnold S. Trebach, *The Great Drug War: And Radical Proposals That Could Make America Safe Again* (New York, 1987); Steven Wisotsky, *Beyond the War on Drugs: Overcoming a Failed Public Policy* (Buffalo, 1990); and Ethan A. Nadelmann, "Global Prohibition Regimes: The Evolution of Norms in International Society," *International Organization* 44 (Autumn 1990): 479–526. These scholars, it should be noted, are three of the leading critics of current drug-control strategies in the United States.

Contributors

WILLIAM O. WALKER III (editor) is the James S. Britton Professor of History at Ohio Wesleyan University. He is the author of *Drug Control in the Americas* (Albuquerque, 1981; rev. ed., 1989), and *Opium and Foreign Policy: The Anglo-American Search for Order in Asia, 1912–1954* (Chapel Hill, 1991). During 1988–90 he held a Social Science Research Council–John D. and Catherine T. MacArthur Foundation Fellowship in International Peace and Security for the study of U.S. drug control strategy since 1980.

JOHN C. McWILLIAMS is Assistant Professor of History at The Pennsylvania State University, DuBois Campus. He is the author of *The Protectors: Harry J. Anslinger and the Federal Bureau of Narcotics, 1930–1962* (Newark, Del., 1990) and numerous articles and scholarly papers on U.S. drug policy. He is currently working on a book about drug law enforcement, organized crime, and the intelligence community.

DAVID T. COURTWRIGHT is Professor of History at the University of North Florida. He is the author of *Dark Paradise: Opiate Addiction in America before 1940* (Cambridge, Mass., 1982) and, with Herman Joseph and Don Des Jarlais, *Addicts Who Survived: An Oral History of Narcotic Use in America, 1932–1965* (Knoxville, 1989). He has written on social, legal, and medical history, and has been researching the history of drug and alcohol use since 1975. At present he is working on the history and social consequences of large numbers of single men.

KATHRYN MEYER is Assistant Professor of History at Lafayette College. With Terry M. Parssinen of the University of Maryland, she is writing a book about international drug trafficking networks in the first half of the twentieth century. She is the author of several scholarly papers on drug control policy and was the recipient of a 1990 fellowship from the National Endowment for the Humanities, enabling her to conduct research in Japan.

JONATHAN MARSHALL is the economics editor for the *San Francisco Chronicle*. He is the author of *Drug Wars: Corruption, Counterinsurgency, and Covert Operations in the Third World* (Forestville, Calif., 1991), and with Peter Dale Scott and Jane Hunter, *The Iran-Contra Connection: Secret Teams and Covert Operations in the Reagan Era* (Boston, 1987), and with Peter Dale Scott, *Cocaine Politics: Drugs, Armies, and the CIA in Central America* (Berkeley and Los Angeles, 1991).

DOUGLAS CLARK KINDER received his Ph.D. from Ohio University in June 1991. His dissertation is a political biography of Harry J. Anslinger: "Foreign Fear and the Drug Specter: Harry J. Anslinger and the Illicit Narcotics Traffic." He has taught at Colgate University, Hillsdale College, Washburn University, and Iowa State University. He is the author of several articles and numerous scholarly papers on U.S. drug policy.

WILLIAM B. McALLISTER is a Ph.D. student studying modern European history at the University of Virginia. His research interests include international aspects of drug history, the history of military medicine, and the history of the Red Cross. Previously, he taught in a juvenile crime and deliquency prevention program that focused largely on drug- and alcohol-related issues.